Solar Architecture in Europe

These studies were produced under the guidance of **Theo C Steemers, CEC DGXII**

by **The ECD Partnership**, 11-15 Emerald Street, London WC1N 3QL, UK.
Series editors:- Mike Buckley, Simon Burton, Alison Crompton and John Doggart

and researched by:

Belgium
André de Herde & Anne Minne
Centre de Recherches en
Architecture
Université Catholique de Louvain
Place de Levant 1
1348 Louvain-La-Neuve

Denmark
Poul Kristensen
Esbensen
Havnegade 41
1058 Copenhagen K

France
Eric Durand
Service Habitat et Tertiaire
Agence Française pour la
Maîtrise de l'Energie
Avenue Emile Hugues
06565 Valbonne Cedex

Germany
Ulrich Luboschik
IST Energietechnik GmbH
Ritterweg 1
7842 Kandern-Wollbach

Italy
Gianni de Giorgio e Paola
Fragnito
Progettazione e Ricerca
C so Como 9

20154 Milan

Netherlands
Ton Trijssenaar
Provinciaal Bureau
Energiebespaaring Noord-
Holland
Postbus 633
2003 RP Haarlem

Portugal
Eduardo Maldonado
INEGI
Faculdade de Engenharia
Rua dos Bragas
4099 Porto Codex

Spain
Albert Mitja i Sarvisé
Direcció General d'Energia
Departament d'Industria i Energia
Generalitat de Catalunya
Av Diagonal 449-7e
08036 Barcelona

UK
John Doggart and Simon Burton
The ECD Partnership
11-15 Emerald Street
London WC1N 3QL

Solar Architecture in Europe

PRISM
PRESS

Published in 1991 by Prism Press, 2 South Street, Bridport, Dorset DT6 3NQ
in collaboration with The ECD Partnership and The Commission of the
European Communities

ISBN 1 85327 073 3

Published simultaneously in The Netherlands by Uitgeverij Jan van Arkel,
A. Numankade 17, 3572 K P Utrecht. Tel: (0)30-731 840

ISBN 90 6224 998 1

PUBLICATION Nº EUR 12738 EN
Commission of the European Communities,
Directorate-General Telecommunications,
 Information, Industries and Innovation,
Luxembourg.

Printed in Singapore by Kyodo.

Contents

Preface

A recent study of the potential of passive solar energy as a fuel* reveals that the equivalent of 13% of the primary energy used in houses and non-domestic buildings in the European Community is already provided by solar energy. Positive action to increase the adoption of solar design principles in the building sector could increase this amount by more than 50%, by 2010. The publication of this book should be seen as a small contribution to such positive action.

The energy consumed in buildings in Europe for heating, cooling, lighting and appliances, constitutes 40% of Europe's primary energy consumption. Thus the potential for energy saving and the consequent reduction of the environmental impact of energy use, is significant for Europe.

It has been the policy of the Commission of the European Communities over a period of 15 years, to reduce Europe's consumption of primary energy. The reasons behind this policy are three-fold:

- a political reason: to reduce Europe's dependence on imported oil;
- an economic reason: to lighten the financial burden on the Member States particularly in view of rising oil prices;
- an environmental reason: to reduce the pollution of our environment.

One of the instruments the Commission uses to pursue this policy is financial support for research and development on energy within the European R & D programme.

Project Monitor, one of the many projects within the Commission's R & D programme on non-nuclear energy, formed the basis for the current publication. Information on the performance of passive solar buildings in Europe was collected and published in carefully designed, full-colour brochures, together with architectural and constructional details as well as occupant response. A selection of thirty schemes from Project Monitor are presented in this book.

Let us hope that a study of the examples of energy-conscious design given in this book will encourage the European building designer to join the growing group who are keen to take advantage of the progress being made in bio-climatic architecture.

Theo C Steemers
Commission of the
European Communities

* 'Passive Solar Energy as a Fuel 1990 - 2010' is a report from the Commission of the European Communities available from DG XIII, Luxembourg under nr EUR-13094.

Passive solar buildings in Europe

PASSIVE SOLAR ARCHITECTURE

Passive solar buildings are designed to collect energy from the sun to provide heating and lighting within the buildings, and to reject solar energy when it can lead to overheating. All buildings collect some solar energy, unless they are completely shaded, and the task of the solar designer is to increase the useful heating and lighting whilst minimising the risks of overheating.

Direct solar heating is increased by large south-facing windows with unobstructed access to the sun, particularly to the low spring and autumn sun. By locating the main living rooms on the south side, maximum use will be made of the solar gains. The mass in the walls and floors of a building will absorb a certain amount of solar heat both reducing overheating when the sun is shining and providing a store of heat when the sun goes down.

By increasing the solar gain in a building the use of fossil fuel for heating and lighting is reduced, and by reducing overheating the use of active cooling systems is reduced and may even be eliminated. Comfort may also be increased, particularly where full heating is not supplied and where air conditioning is not available.

Thus passive solar design is part of the climate respecting, or bioclimatic movement in architecture, sharing the goals of reducing the consumption of fossil fuels and consequent pollution and producing buildings that act in conjunction with natural forces and not in opposition to them.

The 30 case studies in this book come from The Project Monitor series of studies of passive solar buildings and groups of buildings. The significance of this series is that all the buildings have been occupied for the appropriate function, the reactions of the users are recorded and the energy performance has been monitored.

This introduction presents an analysis of the case studies and is intended to give an overview of passive solar architecture in practice in Europe. It provides designers with some guidelines for the successful incorporation of passive solar systems and details into building design. However, designers must bear in mind that the passive solar details apply to particular buildings in a prevailing climate, and may not be applicable to other climates.

Successful passive solar architecture has not only to combine solar heating, daylighting and passive cooling but has also to create good external layouts and appearances, together with pleasant internal arrangements. This is the challenge for the designer.

SOLAR DESIGN IN BUILDINGS

A passive solar building works as an integrated system which includes solar energy collection, distribution and storage, together with ventilation and auxiliary heating. Different elements and systems have been included in the various solar designs, with varying degrees of success.

Most solar schemes adopt the basic direct gain principles of providing large south-facing windows, so that the sun shines directly into occupied rooms. This is achieved by orienting buildings to face within 45° of the north/south axis, planning internal layouts to put 'service' areas such as halls, stairs and bathrooms on the north sides and redistributing window areas to put most glazing on the south elevation, consistent with adequate lighting. Overall window areas should not be increased as heat losses can easily cancel out additional solar gains. Shading from adjacent buildings and trees is avoided by careful site planning, to allow the low winter sun to enter the building.

Many schemes within the Project Monitor series incorporated no other solar measures and yet gave good solar performances, a particular example is the housing at Overbos 8 in the Netherlands. There is little doubt that these measures provide good solar gains at low cost, with few ill effects.

Conservatories or Sunspaces

Sunspaces are defined as south-facing conservatories designed to collect solar energy. They are commonly used in passive solar design and nearly three-quarters of the houses or housing schemes in Project Monitor included them. Energy savings from sunspaces are threefold: the 'buffer' or insulation effect, the supply of pre-heated ventilation air throughout the year and the supply of sun warmed air to the house when the sun is shining, via open windows, doors or ventilators. Their actual energy contribution cannot easily be separated out from the overall savings. Those Project Monitor schemes achieving the highest solar contributions almost invariably used sunspaces; however, some of the schemes with poor solar contributions also incorporated sunspaces. It should be remembered that sunspaces are not simply solar features, in practice frequently their function of energy saving is secondary to that of amenity and additional space. As retrofit measures, sunspaces, produced by glazing in balconies or as new build extensions, can be one of the most useful measures and were used in both the refurbishment projects described.

Other Solar Collection Systems

Solar air heating panels on walls or roofs which provide warmed air to the inside of buildings, and unvented 'Trombe' walls, which provide heat storage and conduction to inside, are also used in passive solar designs. Poor use of systems frequently results in disappointing performance, particularly where control is other than very simple and obvious. One particular use of air heating panels is to provide solar heating ducted to northern spaces where direct solar heating is not possible. Solar reflectors can also be used and are included in two non-domestic case studies (Los Molinos School and Polysportive Esterri d'Aneu sports hall, both in Spain) where in combination with other measures they are deemed successful. Passive solar water heaters are also available and proved successful at the housing scheme at Smakkebo in Denmark.

Distribution of Solar Gains Around Buildings

Careful design can enable solar heated air from the south side of buildings to convect around the building to areas not receiving direct solar gains. A clearly defined loop with large openings is needed for effective heat transfer, as demonstrated in the houses at La Salut in Spain. Using fans to move warmed air around a building can be effective (though not strictly fully 'passive'), but the energy used by the fans can easily outweigh that gained from the solar heating. The school in Belgium, Ecole Primaire de Tournai, suffered from this problem despite generally good design.

Thermal Storage

Heavyweight construction in floors (particularly of sunspaces), walls and stairs enhances solar performance by providing 'thermal mass' to store solar energy. This both extends the use of solar heating and mitigates overheating from excess solar gain. The provision of additional thermal mass over normal brick or concrete construction in houses, as in the sunspaces at Les Basses Fouassieres in France, has not been shown to improve thermal performance significantly. Some schemes which specifically required thermal storage used in-situ mass and were more successful, particularly at the two schools Los Molinos and Scuola Massa Finalese.

Five Project Monitor schemes made use of 'active' rock or brick stores to spread the use of solar gains over longer periods, but not one was particularly successful. This was due to heat losses from the store and to the low temperatures of both the incoming and outgoing air. The use of water storage at Case Termicamente Optimizada in Portugal was not seen as effective, but at Los Molinos as part of the 'Blanco Wall' system, it provided good results

Auxiliary Heating and Controls

With some notable exceptions, for example Los Molinos School and Polysportive Esterri d'Aneu sports hall, solar design does not eliminate the need for auxiliary heating. Many schemes, particularly in southern latitudes, use only electric room heaters to supply auxiliary heating but in all solar buildings careful control of auxiliary heating is required to take advantage of the solar potential by providing only top-up heating when necessary.

'Behavioural' means can also be used to maximise the use of solar heating. Just as conservatories can be used in summer but should not be occupied in winter when heating is required, different parts of buildings themselves can be occupied when sufficiently heated by the sun and closed off when too cold. This principle has been used in Maison Quinet (a private house) and Ecole Primaire de Tournai, both in Belgium.

Avoiding Overheating

In southern latitudes, passive solar design is as much about the avoidance of summer overheating as about the provision of winter heating. Sun that gives rise to overheating must be restricted from entering the building and high ventilation rates must be achievable in the building to remove excess heat.

Fixed external shading devices can be used which allow low spring and autumn sun to enter the building but stop the high summer (and midday) sun from producing overheating. Movable internal and external blinds can also be used but these have to be manually or automatically operated as required.

Ventilation openings must be provided on both sides of the building to provide through ventilation and preferably at both high and low levels to encourage 'stalk effect' ventilation. Thermal mass within the building is an essential part of any strategy to control overheating.

Sunspaces need internal blinds or external awnings and ventilation openings at high level to stop heat being passed into the dwelling. A common feature of the sunspaces in the apartment blocks in Italy, are solid roofs which cut out high summer sun.

Even in northern climates, overheating can be a problem and sunspaces particularly need shading devices and adequate ventilation. At Christopher Taylor Court, the sheltered housing scheme in the UK, overheating even without sunspaces was the cause of minor complaints, and high temperatures were recorded in several sunspaces on other projects where blinds and ventilation were inadequate or not operated to best advantage. Overheating in non-domestic buildings is common, and at the JEL factory considerable effort was made to overcome this problem without resorting to air conditioning.

HOW MUCH SOLAR GAIN

The amount of useful solar energy varies not only with the passive design and particular solar features included, but also with the type and use of the building, and the climate in which it is located.

Individual houses, blocks of flats or apartments, refurbishment schemes and a sheltered housing scheme were included in the Project Monitor series, together with schools and some other non-domestic buildings. Typical solar contributions to heating have been calculated for the different building types as far as possible, but these figures can only be seen as achievable targets rather than as fixed quantities, as in all cases the building occupiers have a great effect on the level of solar heating contributions achieved in practice.

As well as geographical location, another factor affecting the amount of usable solar energy for heating is the overall heating demand of the dwelling. This is falling over time as insulation standards increase. Whilst high percentage energy savings from solar design are still achievable in low energy dwellings, the actual amount of fuel saved will obviously be smaller the lower the total heat demand.

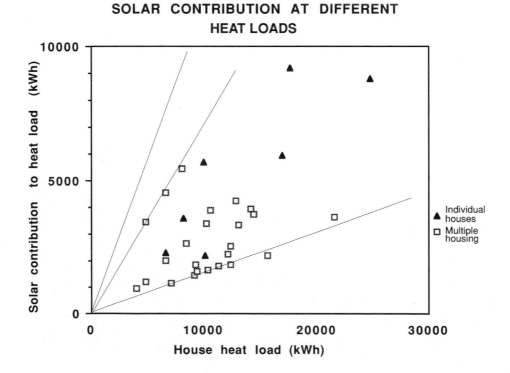

SOLAR CONTRIBUTION AT DIFFERENT HEAT LOADS

xii

One further point to be borne in mind is that all buildings benefit from solar gain to some extent even if not specifically designed to do so. On average the solar gain for the existing housing stock is estimated to vary from around 10% to 15.5% for northern climates.

Unfortunately no quantified assessment of the contribution of passive design to reducing cooling loads has been made on the basis of the Project Monitor series, nor any assessment of daylighting contribution to auxiliary lighting loads. More examples, more analysis tools and more experience are needed to make reasonable estimates for passive savings in cooling and lighting.

Multiple Housing

Blocks of flats are by their nature occupied by a range of people who do not necessarily understand 'solar energy' and may well not be interested in maximising the use of it, particularly if they do not pay their own fuel bills directly. Nevertheless with good design and good operation at least a 30% solar contribution (around 3,300 kWh per year) to the space heating load is obtainable, as indicated by more than a third of the schemes analyzed. Higher percentage contributions can be gained in southern latitudes (up to 70% was recorded), but even in northern latitudes 40% contributions were achieved in some examples.

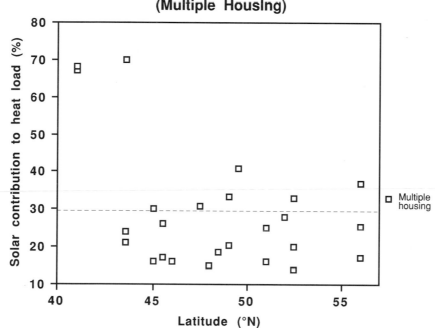

% SOLAR CONTRIBUTION AT DIFFERENT LATITUDES (Multiple Housing)

Individual Houses

Larger solar contributions to heating can generally be achieved by passive design in individual houses compared with blocks of flats. Fewer financial constraints in construction and a higher level of interest from the occupiers, both in the solar systems themselves and in the potential for reducing fuel bills, can result in solar contributions above 35%. Such percentage savings were achieved in the majority of the examples giving energy savings of above 8500 kWh per year.

Even where the heating demand per unit area is small due to high levels of insulation, high percentage and absolute solar contributions can be achieved. It is interesting that latitude has less influence on these figures than size and heat loss.

% SOLAR CONTRIBUTION AT DIFFERENT LATITUDES
(Individual Houses)

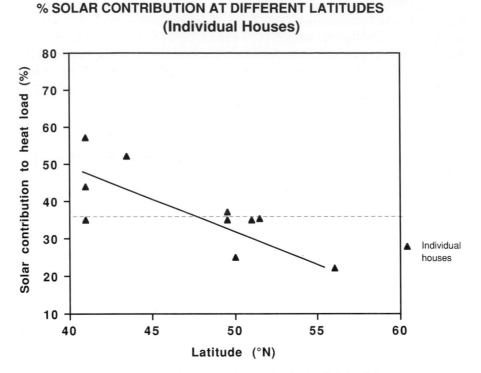

Thus designing to maximise solar gain in individual houses can save significant amounts of fossil fuel energy, and this applies at all latitudes. However, the effect of the occupants in controlling their houses is frequently thought to have been one of the most important influences on the amount of solar gain achieved in practice.

Housing Refurbishment

Adding passive solar features to an existing building or incorporating solar features during refurbishment, has great potential for the wider use of solar energy, due both to the large numbers of existing houses and the high heating demand of the older housing stock. The two examples included, flats at Lievre d'Or in France and at Baggesensgade in Denmark, between them use increased areas of south-facing glazing, Trombe walls and sunspaces. Solar contributions of 20% and 27% respectively were achieved.

Sheltered Housing

Due to the twenty-four hour occupation of housing designed for old people and the higher temperatures generally expected, the energy savings due to solar heating in this type of housing can be large. One example is included, Christopher Taylor Court in the UK, where an annual solar contribution of nearly 50,000 kWh is recorded.

Non-domestic Buildings

Non-housing buildings designed on passive solar lines are much less common than passive solar dwellings, but included in this series are schools, a sports hall, a combined factory office and a hospital. Large, valuable solar heating gains are possible in such buildings but due to the variety of designs and uses, it is not possible to assign general values to the solar heating potential. Equally, passive solar design can contribute great savings to lighting and active cooling use. These are likely to be greater than the solar contribution to the heating load in many cases, notably offices due to the extensive use of artificial lighting and the growing use of air conditioning. Unfortunately no quantitative assessment of these savings can be made here.

Some building types are particularly well suited to passive solar design. Schools, for example, are only occupied in daytime when solar gains are directly available for heating and daylighting and they tend not to be occupied in the hottest summer months, reducing the chances of overheating. At Los Molinos College in Spain, no auxiliary heating was required, as solar gains supplied 80% of the heating, with internal gains supplying the remainder. In more northern latitudes, the JEL factory/office building in the UK achieved a 29% solar contribution to the heating demand.

There is great potential for the use of passive solar design in non-domestic buildings of most types. Passive design techniques and methods of assessment are developing for heating, cooling and lighting and these should be of great assistance to designers.

How People React To Passive Solar Buildings

Using solar energy to provide heating in buildings, and designing to reduce overheating by passive means, is a strategy that will only work if users are happy with the design. Occupant surveys show that users generally feel positive about the buildings from the point of view of comfort and appearance. Passive solar buildings are seen as being light and airy, though lack of privacy in houses due to large south-facing windows can be a problem, as can low lighting levels in northern rooms with small windows. Sunspaces are universally liked by users and are generally well used as additional living space.

External Appearances

Passive solar buildings offer an opportunity of using glass and light to achieve a distinctive appearance and this can be used to advantage. At the JEL factory/office building in the UK, the owner, an energy controls manufacturer, wanted a distinctive building where its controls could be demonstrated in practice. In two school projects, Los Molinos in Spain and Ecole Tournai in Belgium, the building design was intended to be used as part of the teaching, to make the children aware of their interaction with nature.

Planning to achieve a south aspect for a complete housing estate can lead to regimented parallel rows, but the estates at Les Basses Fouassieres at Angers in France and at Smakkebo in Denmark, are good examples of more imaginative layouts. Am Lindenwaeldle in Germany demonstrates an imaginative terrace layout to achieve correct orientation. Smaller sites sometimes present difficulties in achieving south aspects and unconventional layouts may meet with initial local opposition from planning authorities, as was the case at Am Lindenwaeldle.

User Awareness

It is important that users of solar buildings understand something about the designs if the potential solar gains are to be realised. The monitoring of the projects shows that frequently house occupants fail to understand the solar systems and so waste available solar gains, or simply do not control the solar and heating systems to best advantage. The more complex systems understandably suffer particularly in this way.

Whether this is failure on behalf of the designers to accommodate the users adequately, or a failure of the users to adapt to the designs, is open to argument. In two schemes 'education' of the occupants greatly improved the solar performance, demonstrating the advantages of bringing the two sides together. At the housing refurbishment project at Baggesensgade in Denmark, energy savings in the first year after refurbishment were very small, while in the second year, after education of the tenants had achieved changed behaviour, energy savings of 27% were realised.

A considerable difference in attitude towards energy efficiency arises between occupants who directly pay their fuel bills and those who pay a fixed amount unrelated to the individual use. Designers need to bear in mind the capabilities and interests of their clients, and design systems appropriate to these, as well as to likely maintenance facilities

THE COSTS AND BENEFITS OF SOLAR DESIGN

The assessment of the capital costs and benefits of passive solar design in practice is even more difficult than the evaluation of the direct energy savings. Additional costs for passive design vary from zero additional costs over normal design or cost yardsticks (for example, housing at Overbos 8 in the Netherlands), up to a 20% increase in extreme cases. Zero or minimal costs are associated with planning and relocation of glazing, whereas sunspaces, Trombe walls, etc. can be expensive. Frequently some solar features, particularly sunspaces and larger areas of glazing, are included for reasons of amenity and thus the full costs should not be attributed simply to the desire for energy saving.

Benefits

The benefits of passive solar design should not be measured simply in payback times on direct energy savings. In some projects a major objective will be to provide housing for lower income families and the reduced heating costs resulting from the passive solar design can be an important part of this strategy.

Passive solar measures also provide occupants and users with pleasant living conditions and reduced heating energy costs lasting throughout the life of the building, since the measures generally require little or no additional maintenance. This is reflected in the higher value that occupiers frequently put on their 'solar' houses. In the case studies, there was a below average turnover of tenants recorded at three estates, Lievre d'Or outside Paris, Lou Souleu in Southern France and Carrigeen Park in Ireland. At Les Basses Fouassieres, a private estate in France, three-quarters of the owners expressed the desire to live in another 'solar house' if they ever moved, and at Les Cochevis (also in France) the solar features were considered to increase the resale value of the houses.

The inclusion of a sunspace, where a house is to be privately sold, is frequently seen as a selling point, though it is likely that it is more the nature of the space provided than the additional solar gain, that is the attraction. Similarly at Lievre d'Or, newly attached sunspaces were one of the features used to improve the overall appearance of the estate, helping to reverse the serious deterioration of physical and social conditions on the estate.

Simple payback times based on the energy savings resulting from the introduction of passive solar measures vary, but in half the housing schemes a payback period of less than 10 years was achieved where figures were available. These figures were based on fuel costs fixed at the time of monitoring and are thus likely to improve in time as fuel prices increase.

Finally, passive solar design as part of a low energy construction or refurbishment strategy to reduce consumption of fossil fuel will result in long-term beneficial environmental effects in terms of reduction in pollution and emissions of carbon dioxide over the whole lifetime of the building.

SOLAR BUILDINGS

The wide success of the projects described demonstrates that passive solar design in buildings is here to stay. Passive solar buildings can be designed with confidence to give increased solar heating, reduced auxiliary heating, control of summer overheating, attractive and distinctive buildings and satisfied users. Solar design can be applied to most buildings, new and old, well insulated and poorly insulated, housing and non-domestic buildings, big and small, and will give benefits at all latitudes within Europe. In design terms the rule is 'keep it simple', and this will ensure a building with minimal costs, that is understood and used correctly and that performs without problems.

The Projects

GIFFARD PARK CREDITS

Client
Society for Co-operative Dwellings Ltd
209 Clapham Road
London SW9

Architects and Energy Consultants
The ECD Partnership
11-15 Emerald Street
London WC1N 3QL

Structural Engineers
Price & Myers
2 Morwell Street
London WC1B 3AR

Quantity Surveyors
Davis Belfield & Everest
84 High Street
Stony Stratford
Milton Keynes MK11 1AH

Contractor
Bushby Construction Ltd
54 High Street
Kempston
Bedford MK42 7AP

Monitoring Organisation
The Open University
Energy Research Group
The Open University
Walton Hall
Milton Keynes MK7 6AA

Funding Organisations
The Housing Corporation
149 Tottenham Court Road
London W1P 0BW

BRECSU
Building Research Establishment
Garston
Watford WD2 7JR

Commission of the European Communities

● High levels of insulation and passive solar design features reduce space heating requirements by 61 per cent.

GIFFARD PARK
MILTON KEYNES
UNITED KINGDOM

● Space heating costs significantly reduced so that a four person home can be heated for less than £1 per week.

● Capital cost of energy saving measures is modest, with a simple payback in 8.5 years.

● Demonstrates the importance of careful site planning and orientation to allow maximum solar gains.

Project Background

Traditional materials are used throughout and the flats blend sympathetically with the surrounding properties in Milton Keynes.

The Giffard Park Housing Co-operative project consists of 36 flats and houses, all purpose designed for occupation by single people or childless couples. The flats are arranged in four identical two storey terraces on a rectangular site alongside the Grand Union Canal in Milton Keynes.

OBJECTIVES

The client required accommo-dation for a total of 92 people arranged in a mixture of flats and houses for either one, two or four people. Buildings of this type, including 'starter homes', are forming an increasing proportion of the new-build housing sector in the UK.

The aim of the project was to cut the space heating requirement by 60% (compared to 'standard' UK housing) and to demonstrate the cost effectiveness of the package of thermal insulation and passive solar measures that were incorporated.

Very little additional money was available to incorporate these energy saving features. Typically the cost of the new features was limited to about £500 per dwelling.

ENERGY SAVING FEATURES

The main energy saving features adopted included a significant increase in the thermal insulation levels and in the design and

orientation of the flats so that they made the most of passive solar gains. For example the dwellings are all arranged so that habitable rooms face due south, and the terraces are spaced so as to minimise winter over-shadowing. The living space in the larger homes also has a

conservatory type extension to increase the total area of south facing glazing. Extra insulation is provided under the floor slab, in the loft area and in the wall cavities. All windows are double glazed and good draughtstripping systems are provided throughout.

CONCLUSIONS

As no 'control' house was available with which to compare fuel bills, computer modelling techniques were used to assess the effectiveness of the energy saving measures. These simula-tions confirmed that space heating requirements in the flats are 61% lower than the equivalent 'standard' UK dwellings. Fuel bills for space heating have been very low; less than £1 per week for the four person house. The pay back period is estimated at

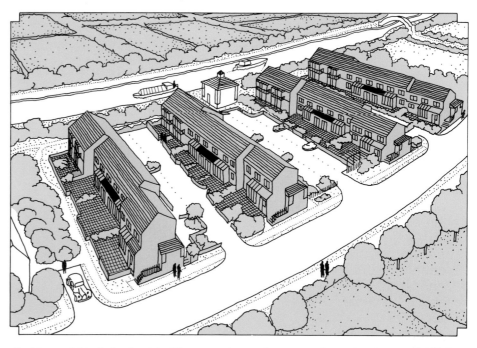

Each terrace is identical and contains 3 four-person houses, 5 two-person flats and 1 one-person flat. To the south of each terrace there is a patio or sitting out area. The remaining space between the terraces is used for car parking. The four-person houses have solar panels for a gravity fed hot water system.

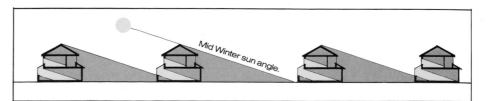

Mid Winter sun angle.

The terraces all face due south and are carefully spaced so as to avoid winter overshadowing. 75% of the glazing is on the south side and the section permits penetration of sunlight into the interior.

8.5 years. Passive solar design boosted the solar contribution to the heating load to 25% compared with about 10% for the equivalent standard UK dwelling.

The most noticeable "solar" features are the conservatory type extension to the main living space in the four person houses.

SITE AND CLIMATE

The site is on the northern edge of Milton Keynes, which is a rapidly expanding new city about 60 miles to the north of London. The City's Development Corporation has had a policy of encouraging innovative buildings, especially energy efficient ones. The area is fairly flat, although the site is adjacent to a canal which is raised about 2m above the surrounding level. On three sides of the site are other modern two storey houses and on the west side is the canal with open fields beyond. The site has good solar access, but there is a small amount of overshadowing from neighbouring houses and vegetation along the southern boundary. The elevated canal also causes some loss of sunlight in late winter afternoons.

There are no exceptional geographical features influencing the micro-climate which is similar to the mild temperate weather of middle England. The minimum average daily temperature in January is 1.6°C and the maximum 21.8°C in July. During the heating season from October to April, the average amount of sunshine is 2.7 hours per day and average solar radiation 1.47 kWh/m² per day. For the whole year the average for sunshine is 4.0 hrs per day and for radiation it is 2.59 kWh/m² per day. There are 2308 degree days (at 15.5°C base).

CLIMATE (Kew)
External temperature and global solar radiation on horizontal plane

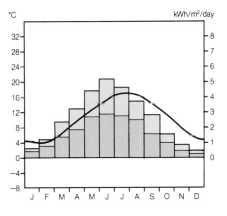

—— average external temperature
◻ direct radiation
◻ diffuse radiation

There is more diffuse than direct radiation even in the summer.

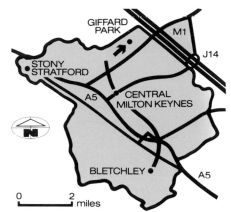

The easiest way to approach the site is by car off Hainault Avenue. The nearest railway station is Milton Keynes Central, 4km away, and the nearest motorway junction is Junction 14, about 5km away.

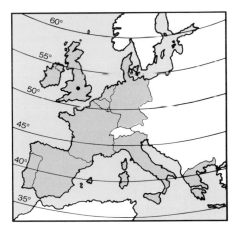

Milton Keynes is located 60 miles to the North of London right in the centre of England and is approximately 85m above sea level. Its climate is broadly similar to large swathes of Northern Europe.

The flats occupy an attractive site alongside a canal.

Design Details

The dwellings are constructed on conventional concrete strip foundations with external walls up to first floor level consisting of a 105mm brickwork outer leaf and a 100mm lightweight concrete block inner leaf. At first floor level the outer skin is replaced with a 75mm lightweight concrete block with timber cladding. This solution was chosen for both aesthetic and cost reasons. The 75mm cavity is fully filled with glass fibre batts.

All internal walls are constructed of load bearing dense concrete blocks and the floor between the ground and first floor level is of 150mm thick pre-cast concrete construction. This solution provides good internal thermal mass and helps improve the sound insulation and fire compartmentation between the flats. The ground floor slab is of 100mm concrete, with 25mm expanded polystyrene slabs between the concrete and the damp proof membrane.

The roof is finished with concrete tiles supported on timber trussed rafters, and is insulated with 140mm of glass fibre. In order to reduce the likelihood of condensation Glidevale eaves ventilators and Redland eyebrow roof ventilators were fitted.

The ceilings below employ foil backed plasterboard as a vapour barrier.

Double glazed sashless windows were used and all doors and windows were draught proofed with a 'Totalseal' silicon sealant.

PASSIVE SOLAR DESIGN

The basic stepped cross section through the building resulted from the requirement to provide, as economically as possible, single storey porches on the north side and a single storey extension, with a glazed sloping roof, on the south side.

This arrangement enabled the area of glazing to be increased on the south side, resulting in

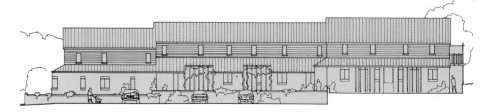

NORTH ELEVATION

The terraces are all designed so that living rooms and bedrooms face south, with staircases, bathrooms and other service areas on the north side. Kitchens are also arranged on the north side in order to minimise the risk of overheating. Some 75% of the total window area is on the south elevation. The northern side has minimal windows.

SOUTH ELEVATION

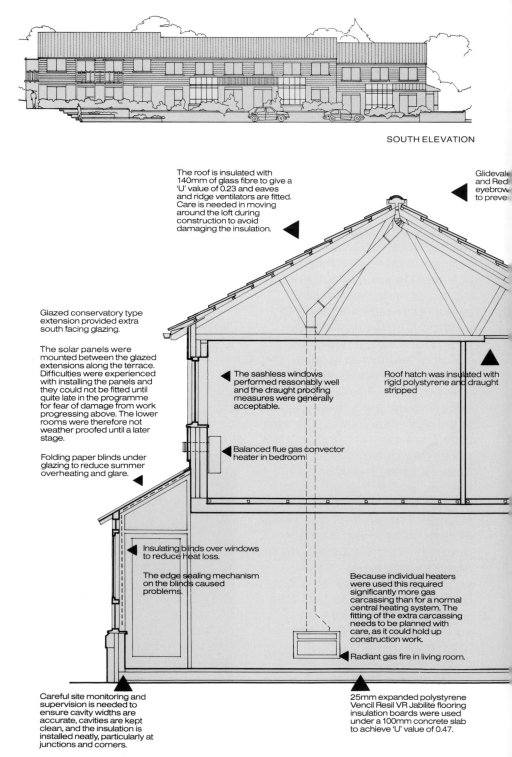

The roof is insulated with 140mm of glass fibre to give a 'U' value of 0.23 and eaves and ridge ventilators are fitted. Care is needed in moving around the loft during construction to avoid damaging the insulation.

Glidevale and Redland eyebrow to preve...

Glazed conservatory type extension provided extra south facing glazing.

The solar panels were mounted between the glazed extensions along the terrace. Difficulties were experienced with installing the panels and they could not be fitted until quite late in the programme for fear of damage from work progressing above. The lower rooms were therefore not weather proofed until a later stage.

Folding paper blinds under glazing to reduce summer overheating and glare.

The sashless windows performed reasonably well and the draught proofing measures were generally acceptable.

Roof hatch was insulated with rigid polystyrene and draught stripped

Balanced flue gas convector heater in bedroom

Insulating blinds over windows to reduce heat loss.

The edge sealing mechanism on the blinds caused problems.

Because individual heaters were used this required significantly more gas carcassing than for a normal central heating system. The fitting of the extra carcassing needs to be planned with care, as it could hold up construction work.

Radiant gas fire in living room.

Careful site monitoring and supervision is needed to ensure cavity widths are accurate, cavities are kept clean, and the insulation is installed neatly, particularly at junctions and corners.

25mm expanded polystyrene Vencil Resil VR Jabilite flooring insulation boards were used under a 100mm concrete slab to achieve 'U' value of 0.47.

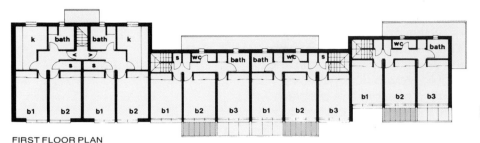

FIRST FLOOR PLAN

0 1 2 3 4 5 m

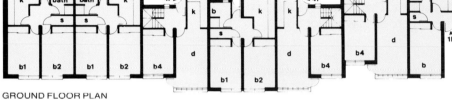

GROUND FLOOR PLAN

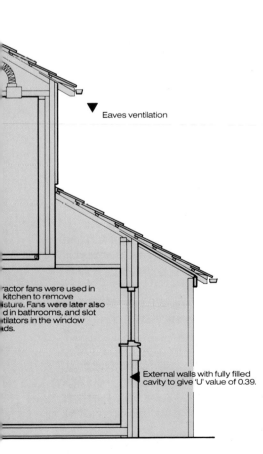

ntilators
and
s were used
idensation.

▼ Eaves ventilation

ractor fans were used in
kitchen to remove
isture. Fans were later also
d in bathrooms, and slot
itilators in the window
ids.

▼ External walls with fully filled
cavity to give 'U' value of 0.39.

considerable extra direct solar gain to the habitable parts of the flats. The total glazing area is about 20 per cent more than it would have been if constructed to 'standard' UK Building Regulations. The sloping roof alongside the glazed extension was used on the four person houses to mount an experimental gravity fed solar water heating system, and insulating blinds were installed to all the south facing windows in one of the terraces. The blinds were of novel construction and contained a metallic film to reflect infra red radiation. An extruded plastic edge sealing strip was supplied to clip them into place. The roof of the glazed extension in one terrace was also fitted with folding paper blinds in order to avoid glare and summer overheating. The gravity fed solar hot water panels were fitted to the four person homes because it was felt these would provide a greater demand for hot water, making the system more cost effective. Each house had nine pre-glazed and pre-insulated modular stainless steel panels installed, all measuring 1m × 0.5m. Each panel acts as a combined collector and intermediate storage unit between the cold

water feed in the loft and the hot water cylinder. The system therefore acts as a simple pre-heat for the domestic hot water.

OPERATING MODES

In summer the blinds are positioned so as to exclude the sun, and the gravity fed water heating system operates. In winter the water heating system is drained to avoid freezing problems, and the blinds are folded back so that solar gains can be absorbed and stored in the dense internal walls and floors. All control of the passive features is manual.

AUXILIARY HEATING SYSTEMS

A full central heating system was thought to be unneccesary because of the type of occupancy, the high insulation standards and the expected solar gains. Space heating is therefore provided by balanced flue gas convectors in the bedrooms and bedsitting rooms, and by radiant gas fires in the living rooms. Gas multi-point water heaters were installed in the smaller flats and small gas fired water circulators and conventional storage cylinders in the four person houses. These installations were considerably cheaper than full central heating, and the savings made were used partly to offset the extra cost of the other energy saving measures.

CONTROLS

Thermostatic controls were fitted to the convector heaters in the bedrooms and a humidistat controlled mechanical extract fans installed in the kitchens. A similar system was later installed in the bathrooms to prevent condensation.

Performance Evaluation

This electronic recorder stored ½ hourly temperature and humidity readings in its memory.

MONITORING

Monitoring was carried out from September 1983 to February 1986, to assess energy savings and the 'buildability' of the energy aspects of the design. Fuel consumption, temperatures and a survey of the occupiers' opinions of the houses was also undertaken.

Temperature and relative humidity were measured using Freeman Enercon Temperature Memory Readers, set to record every 30 minutes. At weekly intervals the data on these memory readers was transferred to a Husky Hunter portable micro computer and subsequently transferred to a VAX11-750 mini computer.

Special machine code software was required to extract data from the memory recorders and this was incorporated into a customised data collection program, which included readings for gas and electricity. The 144K RAM was sufficient to store data from all recorders and meters during each site visit.

USER RESPONSE

The passive solar features were popular. Some residents thought that the larger south facing windows reduced privacy; this could have been due to a long delay in fitting the blinds. The blinds and sashless windows also proved difficult to use in a number of cases.

There was dissatisfaction with the levels of condensation and mould growth during the first heating season. This problem was thought to be connected with the building drying out and disappeared with the installation of mechanical ventilators in the bathrooms.

The gas fires and convectors were popular as they were easy to control and gave a quick response. The lack of heating in the bathrooms was not liked.

COMPARISON WITH CONVENTIONAL DESIGN

50220 kWh (86 kWh/m²) would be required to heat whole terrace designed to Building Regulations standard.

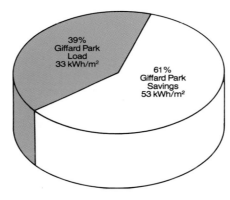

The design reduced the space heating load by nearly two thirds of that for the standard building regulations design giving a net requirement of 33 kWh/m² for the whole terrace.

PERFORMANCE OF THE PASSIVE SOLAR FEATURES

● The energy required for space heating has been reduced to just 39% of that required for a 'standard' house built to UK Building Regulations.

● Solar gains contributed 25% to the total space heating require-ments, incidental gains another 31%, and auxiliary heating only 44%.

CONTRIBUTIONS TO ANNUAL SPACE HEATING DEMAND

43900 kWh (75 kWh/m²) gross load for a Giffard Park terrace.

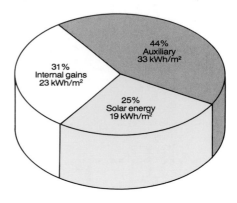

Solar gains provided a quarter of the total space heating requirements.

● The buildings were very airtight with pressure tests inferring an infiltration rate of 0.2 ac/hr under typical winter conditions.

● Average total annual fuel bills were low: approximately £300 for four person houses, under £200 for two person and one person flats.

● In all dwellings, space heating costs were very low: between 61p and 96p per week per dwelling, averaged over the year (excluding standing charges).

● Space heating costs were comparable with those for hot water. They were significantly less than those for lights and appliances and formed less than 20% of the total fuel bill. Standing charges were the largest cost component in the two person and one person flats, at nearly 40% of the total bill.

However, two aspects of the design were not so successful.

● The hot water systems that used gas fired water circulators proved to be relatively inefficient. The reasons for this are not clear.

● The hot water solar panels did not perform well, providing only about 12% of the hot water requirement.

COST EFFECTIVENESS

It is difficult to separate the passive solar features from the other energy conservation measures as the project involved a package of measures to reduce energy consumption.

COSTS OF FUEL USED

The cost of delivered energy for a 2 person flat was £198/yr.

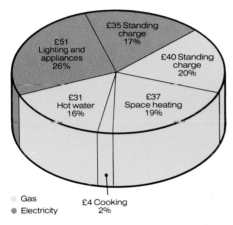

- Gas
- Electricity

£4 Cooking 2%

The cost for heating the flat was less than the cost for lighting and appliances and not much more than the hot water cost.

FUEL USED

The delivered energy consumption for a 2 person flat was 7523 kWh/yr.

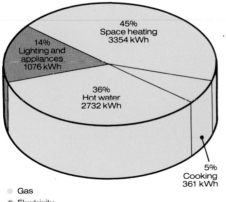

- Gas
- Electricity

5% Cooking 361 kWh

Although almost half the fuel was used for space heating and just over one third used for hot water, the cost of electricity and the standing charges reduced the cost of space heating to 19% and the cost of hot water to 16% of the total fuel costs. This demonstrates the increasing relative importance of other energy conserving factors in low energy design.

● The annual average saving in delivered gas per dwelling was 5222 kWh (18.8GJ), worth £58.4 at 1984 prices (this excludes the contribution of the solar water heaters).

NET MONTHLY SPACE HEATING DEMAND AND SUPPLY

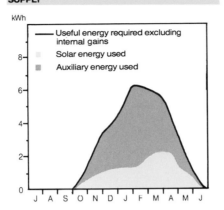

Passive solar gains during the winter months make a valuable contribution to the space heating load.

● The net cost of the package of measures (excluding solar water heater and insulating blinds) was £17895 for the whole development, or £497 per dwelling.

● The simple payback time is 8.5 years, which is considered cost-effective for this type of housing.

MONTHLY AVERAGE TEMPERATURES

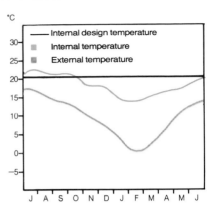

There was no real problem with overheating in the summmer.

● The solar water heater did not prove to be cost-effective, with a payback time greatly exceeding the expected lifetime of the system. Significant improvements in system performance and large cost reductions would be required to approach cost-effectiveness.

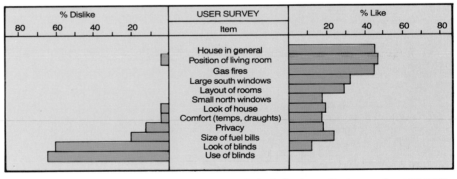

Although fuel costs were low, many residents were in their own flat for the first time and had no experience of fuel bills. The delay in supplying blinds to one terrace may be responsible for some feeling of lack of privacy. The blinds were difficult to operate due to poor edge sealing which led to fouling or jamming.

PROJECT DATA

Building (2 Person flat mid-terrace)	
Heated floor area	46 m²
Heated volume	110 m³
Ext. wall area (incl. windows)	36 m²
Window area: total (19% of wall)	6.9 m²
south 85%	5.95 m²
north 15%	0.95 m²
Building (4 Person house mid-terrace)	
Heated floor area	87 m²
Heated volume	209 m³
Ext. wall area (incl. windows)	78 m²
Windows area: total (30% of wall)	23 m²
south 67%	15.5 m²
north 25%	5.7 m²
Glazed roof area	4.2 m²
Terrace	
Heated floor area	580 m²
Climate	
Altitude	85 m
Latitude	51°N
Average ambient temp. Jan.	4.2°C
July	17.5°C

Thermal	
U value roof	0.23 W/m²K
floor	0.36 W/m²K
ext. walls	0.39 W/m²K
windows	2.60 W/m²K
glazed roof	3.00 W/m²K
Global heat loss coefficient	846 W/K
Design infiltration rate	0.5 ach
External/Internal design temp.	0°C/20 °C
Net heat load	33 kWh/m²
Costs for one terrace (1984/85)	
Whole terrace	£190 000
Solar collectors	£1397
Additional insulation & draught proofing	£8281
Savings on aux. systems due to additional insulation & draught proofing	£3808
Fuel: Electricity	£0.053 kWh
Gas	£0.012 kWh
Degree days (15.5°C base)	2308
Ann. global irradiation	945 kWh/m²
Sunshine hours	1460 hrs.

MAISON QUINET CREDITS

Client
Mr and Mrs Quinet
Fond du Tombeu 9
4150 Nandrin

Architect
E Moureau
Avenue de l'Observatoire 12
4000 Liège

Monitoring organisations
Université Catholique de Louvain
Centre de Recherches en Architecture
Place du Levant 1
1348 Louvain-la-Neuve

Université de l'Etat à Liège
Laboratoire de Physique du Bâtiment
Avenue des Tilleuls 15
4000 Liège

Faculté Polytechnique de Mons
Centre de Recherches en Energie Solaire
Boulevard Dolez 31
7000 Mons

Faculté Universitaire Luxembourgeoise
Cellule Energie
Avenue des Déportés 140
6700 Arlon

Commission of the European Communities

MAISON QUINET

NANDRIN

BELGIUM

● Good use of site and orientation to maximise solar gains and provide shelter helps to reduce the space heating load by 33%.

● Design demonstrates a seasonal zoning approach to spaces whereby the living space is expanded in the summer and contracted in the winter.

● A centrally placed 'courtyard' conservatory provides living space and a place to cultivate exotic plants.

● Heated volume reduced by dividing plan into separate 'day' and 'night' wings.

Project Background

Maison Quinet is a detached private house built in 1978 to suit the requirements of one family. It has an unusual plan form with a conservatory in the middle, which expresses both the client's interest in the culture of exotic plants and his ideas about the relationship between living patterns and energy saving.

DESIGN OBJECTIVES

The client is a teacher of industrial design and works at home for most of the week whilst his wife has a part time job. The house is therefore almost continuously occupied. The client believes that the issue of energy saving is more a question of rational occupancy of the different rooms and of efficient temperature management than to do with the use of a sophisticated heating system. The design had therefore to take into account the clients' keen interest in both outdoor and indoor gardening, and their willingness to adapt their living patterns to suit this interest and fulfill their ideas about energy saving.

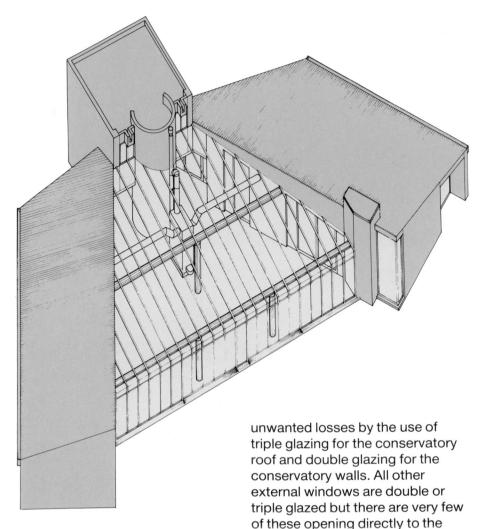

The conservatory is surrounded by the house and as it serves also as a circulation space the heated area is reduced.

ENERGY SAVING FEATURES

The main feature of the house is the large centrally placed conservatory the volume of which at $211m^3$ is one third that of the volume of the whole building. All the rooms are planned to open off the conservatory so that they can benefit from any small increase in temperature in the conservatory. Conversely, when it is cold, the heat losses from the rooms prevent the temperature in the conservatory from dropping too far and damaging the plants. Losses from the boiler, which is placed in the conservatory, also maintain the temperature.

The design accepts heat transfers between the conservatory and the rooms, but attempts to limit unwanted losses by the use of triple glazing for the conservatory roof and double glazing for the conservatory walls. All other external windows are double or triple glazed but there are very few of these opening directly to the outside, since the sleeping area

The conservatory is steel framed with a double glazed front and effectively triple glazed roof.

has a blind external wall and the living area has the laundry as a buffer against the outside. The floor of the conservatory, and the earth, act as a heat store for solar gains.

CONCLUSIONS

Maison Quinet is an unusual project in the sense that the conservatory is not just attached to the house as a buffer but is surrounded by the house so that each may benefit from heat gains from the other. In its central position, it is a circulation route to all parts of the house, and therefore reduces the amount of conventional heated space.

The north facade has only a small window area for habitable rooms and is well sheltered.

The strong hierarchical relationship from the interior living spaces to the conservatory and from the conservatory to the garden reflects the clients' passion for gardening, and their willingness to adopt a seasonal and nomadic lifestyle in pursuit of their belief in rational occupancy of spaces as a means of saving energy. The family therefore lives in the garden and conservatory in the summer, in the conservatory and interior spaces in the spring and autumn and retreats into the interior in the winter.

SITE

The house is at Nandrin, a village in the eastern part of Belgium. The site is at the bottom of a lane outside the village. The house is

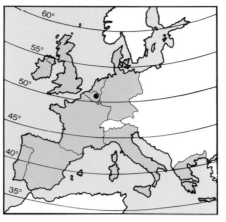

The house is in Eastern Belgium

built on the south facing slope of a low wooded hill with a stream running along the southern boundary at the bottom of the hill. The house has been placed on the north side of the site at the top of the garden and looks down the slope towards an artificial pond. The north side of the house is partially below ground as it is built into the hillside.

There are trees surrounding the

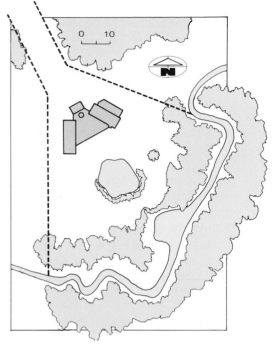

The house is at the top of the site. There is an artificial pond in the middle and a river at the bottom.

site, but those on the south side are not large enough to shade the house.

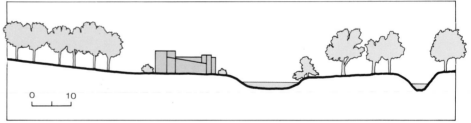

The house is sited on a south facing slope to catch maximum sunshine and is sheltered from cold NE winds by trees.

CLIMATE (Spa)

Average global solar radiation on horizontal surface and external temperature.

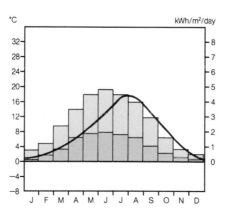

- diffuse radiation
- direct radiation
- —— daily external temperature.

CLIMATE

The Belgian climate is a temperate, sub-oceanic one with humid south westerly, and cold, dry, north easterly prevailing winds. The annual insolation is on average 1443 hours and the mean annual global irradiation is **1016 kWh/m²** The mean monthly maximum daytime temperature is 1.5°C in January and 18.9°C in July. There are 2100 degree days (base temperature 15.5°C)

The micro climate of the site is good because of the building's situation on the southern slope of a hill, which, with the wood behind the house, provides protection from the cold north east winds.

Design Details

The conservatory is the hub of the house and its fan-shaped plan expresses the opening up of the house to the south. As well as being the place where nature is brought right into built space, it is the main circulation space with all rooms leading off it. Sheltering the north side of the conservatory is a cloakroom and store. Above these is the owner's office reached by a spiral staircase. On the west side of the conservatory is the 'night' wing containing the bedrooms and on the east side is the 'day' wing containing the kitchen and living room, and behind this the utility room.

CONSTRUCTION

The walls are built with an external leaf of 80mm, and an internal leaf of 190mm expanded clay blocks with a 20mm cavity. The inside walls are of 190mm clay blocks. The floor is 150mm concrete with expanded clay on 20mm cork. The flat roofs are insulated with 150mm mineral fibre.

With the conservatory in the middle of the house it doubles as a circulation space and any solar heat gains are transferred to the rooms by opening windows or doors. In cold dull weather the conservatory benefits from any heat losses from the rooms.

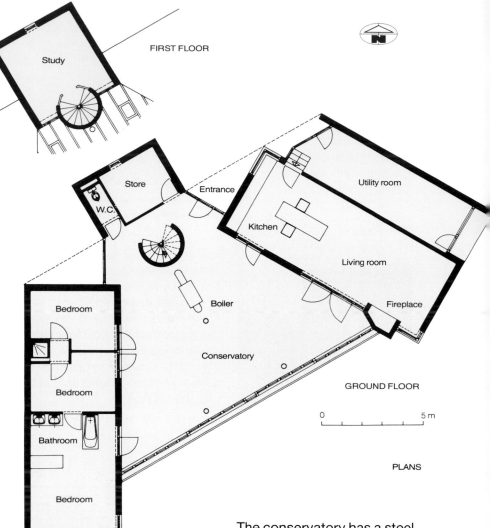

FIRST FLOOR

GROUND FLOOR

PLANS

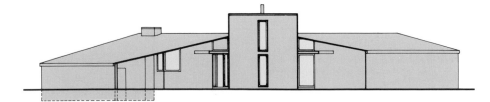

NORTH ELEVATION

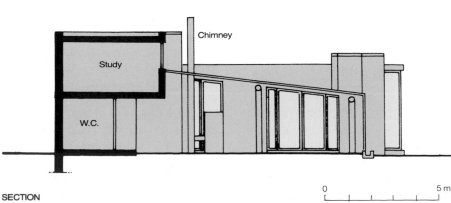

SECTION

The conservatory has a steel structure.
The windows opening onto the conservatory are single glazed in wood frames. All other glazing is double, except for the con-servatory roof which is in effect triple glazed. It has double glazing placed under single glazing.
The wall 'U' value is 1.0 W/m²K but the mean 'U' value for the building envelope, excluding the conservatory, is 0.6 W/m²K due to the roof and floor insulation. The house is not a 'super insulated' house. Instead, the energy savings come from solar gains, building shape and occupancy pattern.

PASSIVE SOLAR DESIGN

The external windows have been positioned to admit daylight and to provide views of the garden rather than provide direct solar gain. It is through the conservatory that solar gains are made and distributed to the inner rooms by opening the doors. The block walls, the tiled floor and the earth around the plants all store solar heat.

There is no shading device for the conservatory, although the plants provide shade within it, and

During cool spring and autumn evenings, it is usually only necessary to use the woodburning stove to heat the living room, in which the thermostat for the warm air system is positioned. In terms of energy content, more wood is used than oil to provide the heating.

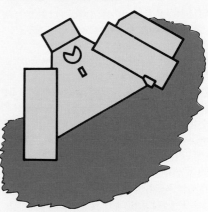

DAYTIME – HOT WEATHER

MODERATE WEATHER

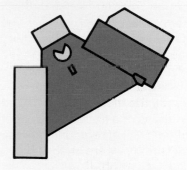

COLD WEATHER

In hot weather the garden is mostly used. When it gets cooler the family use the conservatory and only retreat into the living room, where the wood fire is, in the winter.

NIGHT-TIME

ventilation is therefore necessary. This is achieved by opening the doors onto the garden and by opening the high level windows. In summer a through-draught is created by also opening the front door. It is not possible to directly ventilate to the outside, the 'day' and 'night' wings either side of the conservatory.

AUXILIARY HEATING SYSTEM

Auxiliary heating is provided by two means. The living area (day wing) is chiefly heated by a wood burning stove. Additional heat to this room and the rest of the house is provided by warm air distributed via ducts at high level from an oil fired boiler in the conservatory. The air is partially recycled . The placing of the boiler in the conservatory is deliberate in order to protect the exotic plants from frost damage. Domestic hot water is produced by an electric boiler. The heating system is controlled by a room thermostat.

OPERATING MODES

In order to get the most out of the design of the house, the clients' living habits are varied to suit the weather and different spaces are occupied according to the temperature within the conservatory. On hot sunny days the family lives outside in the garden. They open the doors of the conservatory in order to ventilate it and they come back into it in the evenings. In the mid-season they live in the conservatory and in the winter retire into the living room.

This seasonal nomadism is coupled with a diurnal one, in which living is divided between the east wing in the day and the west wing at night. Such a utilisation of spaces in relation to the activities and the temperature reduces the heated volume, since the 'night' wing does not need to be heated during the day. The rational management of internal temperature is, in this house, one of the main ways of saving energy.

Performance Evaluation

MONITORING

The house was monitored for one year between September 1982 and September 1983 within the framework of the competition "Concours pour un Habitat Thermique" organised by the Walloon Region. The aim was to find the best examples of innovative design to reduce fuel consumption.

The infiltration rate was evaluated by a pressurization/depressurization test and a tracer gas test. The first test estimated the air flow through small apertures under a differential pressure of 4 Pa (yearly natural average value) in order to evaluate the air infiltration apertures. The tracer gas test estimated the airchange per hour by the measurement of the variations of a tracer gas concentration (SF6) at regular intervals. The samples were analysed by a chromatograph.

The space heating requirement was evaluated by a coheating system test. This test substitutes the existing heating system for an integral electric one in order to determine the net heating demand on the basis of a chosen heating programme. This system allows, for example, the calculation of the net heating demand without solar contribution.

Data for horizontal solar radiation, ambient dry bulb temperature and mean radiant temperature were recorded on mini-cassettes. Total energy input for auxiliary space heating, water heating, and lighting and appliances were recorded by hand.

USER RESPONSE

The clients are generally happy with their house – which was designed to suit their own particular requirements – with the exception of three problems which have occured. These are firstly the appearance of condensation on the conservatory glazing, to which the plants contribute in large measure. Secondly, the level of

Exotic plants are grown in the conservatory and the temperature must not fall below freezing. The temperature is maintained by losses from the boiler and warm air distribution ducts.

daylighting in the interior rooms is low, as they rely mostly upon light from the conservatory. Again, the plants reduce the light available. Thirdly, overheating can occur in the interior rooms in the summer and they are difficult to ventilate since they have few or no external windows to open.

PERFORMANCE OF PASSIVE SOLAR DESIGN

● The energy required for space heating has been reduced to 67% of that of a standard house

COMPARISON WITH CONVENTIONAL DESIGN

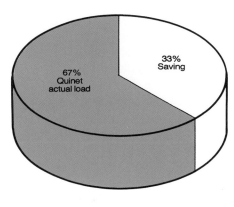

Compared with a new house designed to Walloon standards the design saves 33% of the space heating need.

designed to the Walloon region new building regulation (K70) thus making a saving of 33%.

CONTRIBUTIONS TO GROSS ANNUAL SPACE HEATING DEMAND

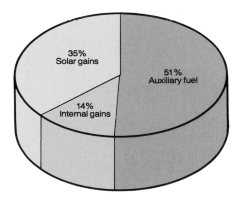

Passive solar gains supplied 35% of the demand but in four of the eight months heating season they contributed more heat than the auxiliary fuel.

● Solar gains contributed 35% to the gross annual space heating requirement, incidental gains 14% and auxiliary heating 51%.

● In four out of the eight months of the heating season, the heat provided by passive solar gains was greater than the heat provided by the auxiliary heating system.

ANNUAL FUEL CONSUMPTION
38 000 kWh

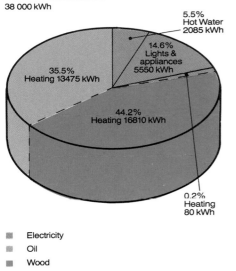

5.5%
Hot Water
2085 kWh

14.6%
Lights &
appliances
5550 kWh

35.5%
Heating 13475 kWh

44.2%
Heating 16810 kWh

0.2%
Heating
80 kWh

- ▨ Electricity
- ▨ Oil
- ▨ Wood

The wood-burning stove used the most fuel.

● The net space heating requirement after the deduction of solar and internal gains, was 0.28 GJ/m^2.

● The house was reasonably airtight having an air change rate of 0.38 per hour.

COST OF FUEL USED
59504 BF (December 1984 prices)

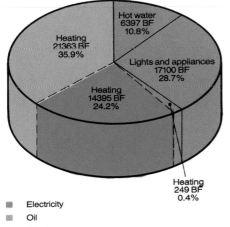

Hot water
6397 BF
10.8%

Heating
21363 BF
35.9%

Lights and appliances
17100 BF
28.7%

Heating
14395 BF
24.2%

Heating
249 BF
0.4%

- ▨ Electricity
- ▨ Oil
- ▨ Wood

Wood supplied the most energy and cost the least whereas electricity supplied the least but cost the most.

● The amount of fuel oil required was 35.5% of the annual energy consumption compared with 44.2% for wood. However the cost of the oil was 35.9% of the total energy costs compared with only 24.2% for wood.

MONTHLY SPACE HEATING DEMAND AND SUPPLY

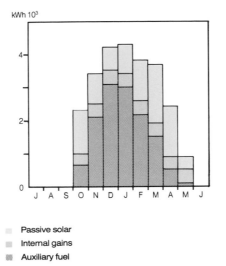

kWh 10^3

J A S O N D J F M A M J

- ▨ Passive solar
- ▨ Internal gains
- ▨ Auxiliary fuel

● On a typical winter day, the conservatory temperature was higher than the inside temperature for approximately 3 of the 5 daylight hours, when there was an even input of solar radiation reaching a peak of about 450 W/m^2 at 1pm.

TEMPERATURE AND RADIATION ON TYPICAL WINTER DAY

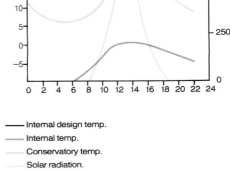

°C | W/m^2

0 2 4 6 8 10 12 14 16 18 20 22 24

- —— Internal design temp.
- —— Internal temp.
- ⋯⋯ Conservatory temp.
- ⋯⋯ Solar radiation.
- —— External temp.

On a typical winter day the conservatory temperature was always above the outside temperature by between 5° and 25°C.

● When the outside temperature fell to −10°C the conservatory temperature was +6°C, amounting to a 16°C differential between inside and outside, at 6.00 am.

PROJECT DATA			
Thermal		**Building**	
U value roof	0.25 W/m^{2}K	House	
floor	0.52 W/m^{2}K	Volume	435 m^3
external walls	1.00 W/m^{2}K	Floor area	165 m^2
Mean U value	0.60 W/m^2	Roof area	147 m^2
Global heat loss coefficient	339 W/K	External wall area	137 m^2
Infiltration rate	0.38 ach	Glazing: double	67 m^2
Design temp. Internal	20°C	triple	78 m^2
External	−10°C		
Heated floor area	165 m^2	Conservatory	
Heated volume	435 m^3	Volume	211 m^3
Net heat load	0.28 GJ/m^2	Floor area	70 m^2
	(78 kWh/m^2)	Glazed area	113 m^2
		Solid wall area	53 m^2

POLYSPORTIVE ESTERRI CREDITS

Client
Ajuntament d'Esterri d'Aneu
Major, s/n
25580 Esterri d'Aneu, LLeida

Architect
Francesc Sotomayor i Rðdriguez
Gran Via Carles III, 15, entr, 2a
08028 Barcelona

Services Consultant
Jocelyne de Botton/Francisco Penella Ros
Rocafort, 244, 7è
08029 Barcelona

Contractor
Juan Lapedra Pifarrer
Historiador P. Sanahuja, 10
25600 Balaguer — LLeida

Monitoring Organisation
Departament d'Industria i Energia
Direcció General d'Energia
Catalunya

Commission of the European Communities

● Low cost and low maintenance building relying on passive solar for 70% of its space heating demand.

● Passive solar gain increased 20% by use of automatically operated reflecting shutters which also provide insulation to the sunspace at night and in the summer.

● Natural daylighting and natural ventilation reduce capital and maintenance costs.

● The passive solar design is estimated to add 14% to the cost of the building for a saving of 41,571 kWh per year.

POLYSPORTIVE ESTERRI
ESTERRI D'ANEU
CATALUNYA — SPAIN

Project Background

The Polysportive is a general purpose sports hall, mainly for school children, in a small Catalan village of 550 inhabitants in the Pyrenees. By careful design along passive solar principles, no heating is required in the sports hall.

DESIGN OBJECTIVES

The client, the community of Esterri d'Aneu, wanted an indoor sports and social centre because the winter climate is too harsh for outdoor sports. The design had to obtain maximum benefit from the clear sunny winter days and to reduce construction and maintenance costs. For this reason it was decided to rely on solar and internal gains and avoid the need to install any auxiliary heating system. In order to explore the cost effectiveness of low energy design, the Department of Industry and Energy of Catalunya funded monitoring of the building.

ENERGY SAVING FEATURES

● The building has a low surface/volume ratio and is planned to have service rooms and small windows on the north side and large areas of glazing on the south side.

● There is a sunspace along the south elevation with a massive wall at the rear for heat storage.

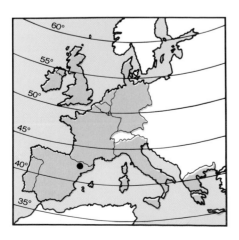

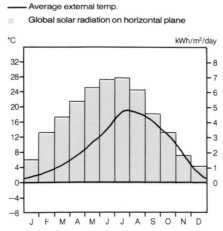

CLIMATE (Lleida)

—— Average external temp.

▨ Global solar radiation on horizontal plane

● To the front of the sunspace are fitted bottom hinged shutters which reflect additional solar radiation into the sunspace when open, and act as insulation when closed.

● Direct heat gain, daylighting and natural ventilation is introduced by carefully positioned windows.

● The construction is well insulated.

SITE AND CLIMATE

Esterri d'Aneu is a small town of 550 inhabitants located at the centre of an agricultural district in the Pallars Sobirà region in the Catalan Pyrenees. It is 950m above sea level and has sunny but cold winters and mild, cool summers. The average temperature during the winter period is 7°C and there are 2870 degree days (18°C base). The site has good solar access being on a south facing slope and sheltered on the north side by an apartment block and some mountains. The east side of the site is partially shaded in the morning by the mountain range and the Polysportive was therefore placed on the north west corner of the site.

Design Details

PLANNING

The building, which has a heated area of 818m² and volume of 3750m³, has been planned on two levels to suit the slope of the site. The lower level contains the sunspace and sports hall and the upper level on the northern side contains the seats and locker rooms. This upper level has been extended all the way to the east side so as to emphasise the entrance and provide a place for storage.

The section demonstrates the compact layout designed to enclose the necessary volume with the minimum building envelope area at a low cost.

The 60° pitch of the roof shell is designed to provide daylighting and solar gain into the building.

CONSTRUCTION

The basic construction of the building comprises a 380mm wide cavity wall and a pitched roof covered with metal composite panels. The outer leaf of the wall is 200mm concrete block rendered with sand-cement and the inner leaf is 80mm hollow concrete blocks with 100mm of fibreglass filling the cavity. The holes in the

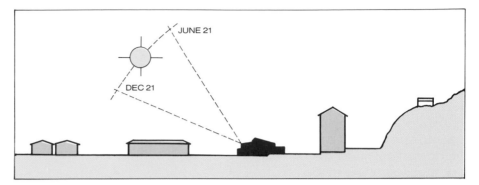

The building is well sited on a south facing slope, is sheltered on the north side and is not overshadowed by any other building.

This mountainous region is ideal for solar design having cold but clear sunny days. The north side has small windows and contains the changing and service rooms.

blocks of the inner leaf have been filled with sand in order to improve thermal inertia. The U value of the wall is 0.25 W/m²K. The roof panels have 100mm of expanded polystyrene as insulation and there are 70mm expanded polystyrene slabs under the floor. The roof U value is 0.26 W/m²K. The windows have galvanised iron frames and those facing north, having an area of 28m², are double glazed.

The main design problems were to maintain internal thermal inertia and provide a well insulated envelope avoiding cold bridges and draught gaps. But there were problems with the reflector shutters closing mechanism and the desired airtightness was not achieved.

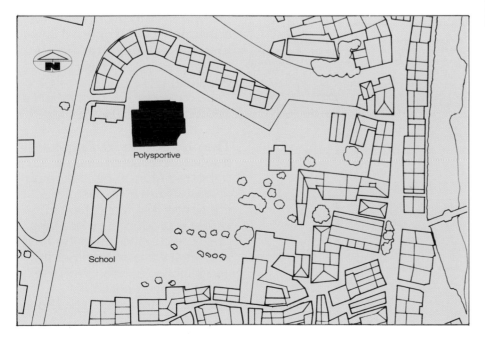

Polysportive

School

Design Details

The sunspace stretches across the length of the south elevation and is the lowest part of the building. It is 28m long and 1.5m wide. The wall and roof is of 4mm single glazing in galvanised glazing bars. In front of the vertical glazing are fixed composite panels made up of galvanised sheet steel on the outside, 100mm of rigid polystyrene foam in the middle and stainless steel sheet on the inside. The panels are hinged at the bottom and when lowered, the stainless steel surface reflects additional solar radiation into the sunspace.

At the bottom of the conservatory wall, below the glazing, there are vents which bring outside air under the floor and up through vents at the base of a 350mm concrete wall at the back of the sunspace. There are vents at the top and bottom of this wall, which stores and evenly distributes heat by radiation and convection into the sports hall. The wall also has windows insulated with 16mm

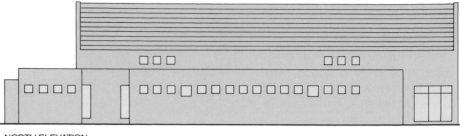

NORTH ELEVATION

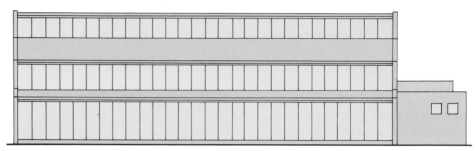

SOUTH ELEVATION

The south elevation has two upper rows of windows to provide light solar gain and ventilate the sports hall. The lower row of glazing encloses the sunspace. Cross ventilation is achieved by opening the windows on the north and south elevation.

twin walled plexiglass to allow direct sun into the sports hall and permit ventilation when needed in summer.

In order to increase solar gain, the upper part of the south facade has two rows of windows. The lower row has vertical windows with an area of

40.5m². The upper row has 47.5m² of 60° sloping glazing. Both rows are glazed with 16mm twin walled plexiglass and are fitted with internal venetian blinds to control the amount of daylight and solar penetration. When both the venetian blinds and the insulating reflector shutters are closed at night they serve to reflect heat back into the building and therefore act as additional insulation.

In order to ventilate the building the vertical windows above the sunspace can be opened together with those on the north elevation to allow cross ventilation.

AUXILIARY SYSTEMS

The only auxiliary system for heating consists of electric panel radiators in the changing rooms. There is no system in the sports hall. Ventilation in winter is produced by two fans positioned at the top of the east and west walls. In summer the ventilation is natural using the windows and ventilation openings. Hot water is provided by electricity.

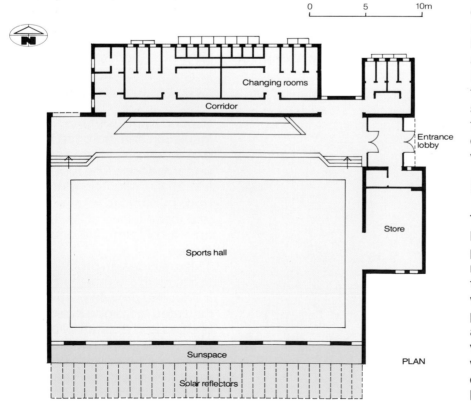

0   5   10m

PLAN

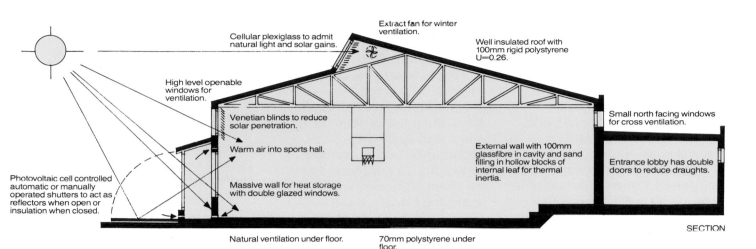

Extract fan for winter ventilation.

Cellular plexiglass to admit natural light and solar gains.

Well insulated roof with 100mm rigid polystyrene U=0.26.

High level openable windows for ventilation.

Venetian blinds to reduce solar penetration.

Warm air into sports hall.

Massive wall for heat storage with double glazed windows.

External wall with 100mm glassfibre in cavity and sand filling in hollow blocks of internal leaf for thermal inertia.

Small north facing windows for cross ventilation.

Entrance lobby has double doors to reduce draughts.

Photovoltaic cell controlled automatic or manually operated shutters to act as reflectors when open or insulation when closed.

Natural ventilation under floor.

70mm polystyrene under floor.

SECTION

Shutters and blinds closed in summer to prevent overheating.

Sports hall with shutters and blinds open in winter to admit sunlight and heat.

CONTROLS

The only controls for the passive and auxiliary system are very simple in accordance with the brief for a low cost and low maintenance building. The reflector shutters are controlled by a photovoltaic cell which lowers or raises the shutters according to the intensity of the light. The cell can be over-ridden manually by a button. The venetian blinds to the upper windows are controlled manually, as are the ventilation openings. The fans are switched on and off manually. The electric radiator panels in the changing rooms are fitted with individual thermostats.

PASSIVE OPERATING MODES

During the winter, when days are generally sunny but cold,
the reflector shutters are automatically lowered in order to admit both direct and reflected radiation. At night these shutters are automatically closed up to act as insulation to the windows in order to retain the solar gains stored in the concrete wall at the rear of the sunspace. Winter ventilation is by fan.

During the summer, the shutters are lowered halfway in order to let in light but to exclude direct solar radiation, and prevent the sunspace from overheating. At night they are lowered completely for radiative cooling of the building. Summer ventilation is natural and achieved by opening the ventilators and windows.

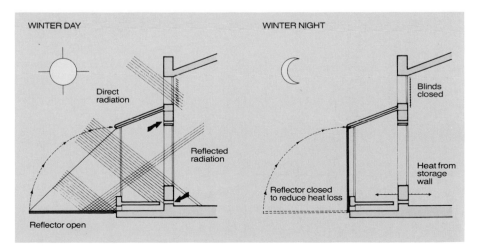

WINTER DAY

Direct radiation

Reflected radiation

Reflector open

WINTER NIGHT

Blinds closed

Heat from storage wall

Reflector closed to reduce heat loss

Performance Evaluation

MONITORING

Monitoring took place from October 1984 to May 1985 with hourly readings of internal and external temperature, solar radiation on an horizontal plane, electric lighting and electric heating consumption. In September 1986, monitoring was completed. Diffuse solar radiation, external humidity, temperature of stratification in sunspace and sports hall, and of the inertia wall were measured. The number of people using the Polysportive was also monitored. The equipment used for the monitoring included a Hewlett-Packard HP-3421A data logger with capacity for measuring up to 20 analogue channels, controlled by a HP-41CX programmable pocket calculator. All the data channels were scanned every minute, and the hourly mean values recorded on floppy disks every hour, except for the radiation data, which was recorded every 5 minutes. Every other month the floppy disk was replaced, and the data recorded on it transferred to a Hewlett-Packard HP-310 mini computer. The treatment and analysis of monitored data was made by specially designed software.

USER RESPONSE

Both the client, Esterri d'Aneu Municipality, and the school children, who are the main users of the building, are enthusiastic about the passive solar design in terms of its novelty, appearance and its comfort conditions. At the same time the client is pleased with achieving the proposed objective of having a building with low maintenance costs and acceptable comfort levels.

COMPARISON WITH CONVENTIONAL DESIGN

The estimated load of a conventional design is 9130 kWh compared with the Polysportive load of 2487 kWh.

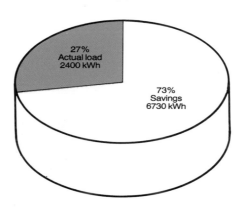

27% Actual load 2400 kWh

73% Savings 6730 kWh

The figures for net heating load are considerably lower than the gross load, because even a conventional design has high internal and solar gains. It also has a low design temperature

PERFORMANCE OF PASSIVE SOLAR DESIGN

The passive design has been shown to operate properly.

● During the heating season the solar contribution to the space heating load was 94.4%.

● The energy required for the auxiliary heating electric radiators was minimal — the internal gains from lights and people contributed 6 times more to the heating requirement than these electric radiators.

● In normal weather conditions the temperatures inside

CONTRIBUTIONS TO GROSS ANNUAL SPACE HEATING DEMAND

The gross heating demand for the polysportive is 59250 kWh. A large proportion is supplied by internal gains

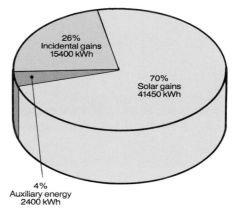

26% Incidental gains 15400 kWh

70% Solar gains 41450 kWh

4% Auxiliary energy 2400 kWh

The solar design produced large savings so that the auxiliary energy requirement was only 4%.

the sports hall during sports sessions ranged from about 14°C in December and March to 21.5°C in October, which were considered tolerable for sports activity. However in January with abnormal weather when temperatures fell to —8.5°C, the inside diurnal temperature was maintained over 11°C.

● The thermal inertia of the wall moderated the temperature fluctuations so that whilst the outside daily temperature fluctuated on average by 15°C (even 20-25°C on clear days), the internal temperature fluctuation maintained an average below 6°C.

● The use of the reflectors increased the total incident solar radiation by 19.6% in the heating season.

But there were two aspects which were not as anticipated.

● Ventilation problems arose sometimes in summer. The problem was that ventilation by fans was not enough in some summer periods to avoid overheating and windows were not openable. The solution was to modify the south facing windows so that they can be opened.

● Useful solar energy was 149.6 GJ, not the 253.5 GJ predicted. With the reflectors boosting received radiation by 19.6%, it was anticipated that 55% of the radiation from direct gain, sunspace and reflectors would be useful. But this figure was 33.6%, mainly because the measured radiation was less than predicted and because the reflectors were often shut during the autumn and spring when the building was not in use.

● The infiltration rate was higher and the winter much colder than predicted.

COST EFFECTIVENESS

Assessment of cost effectiveness is difficult because some of the passive features are an integral part of the building.

MONTHLY NET SPACE HEATING DEMAND AND SUPPLY

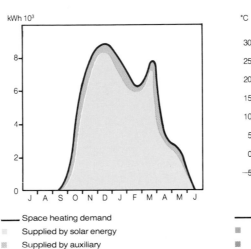

kWh 10³

— Space heating demand
▫ Supplied by solar energy
▪ Supplied by auxiliary

MONTHLY AVERAGE TEMPERATURES

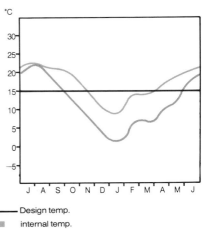

°C

— Design temp.
▪ internal temp.
▪ external temp.

The design temperature for this type of building is relatively low. Therefore the passive solar design was able to provide most of the heat. The internal toperature fell below the design temperature mainly due to exceptionally cold weather during January and February.

However the Polysportive has been compared with another one of similar size designed by the same architect in a nearby district and it was established that the cost difference is about 4 100 000 Pts (31 060 ECU) which represents an additional cost of 14% for the passive design. The cost of the sunspace has been calculated at 1 420 000 Pts (10 760 ECU) and of the reflector shutters at 2 680 000 Pts (20 300 ECU). For this expenditure, the annual solar contribution to space heating was 41 571 kWh (150 GJ) which represents a cost saving of 420 000 Pts/yr (3182 ECU/yr).

The sunspace has a massive rear wall and floor to store heat. The windows are to provide daylight and additional direct gain for the sports hall. The reflector shutters can be automatically or manually controlled.

FUEL USED

Total consumption which was all electricity was 8860 kWh.

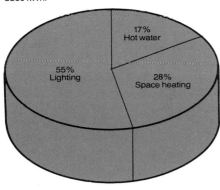

17% Hot water
55% Lighting
28% Space heating

The fuel used for space heating was less than half that used for lighting and not even double that used for hot water.

PROJECT DATA

Building		
Volume		3750m³
Floor area		818m²
Roof area		564m²
External wall area		545m²
Windows: total area	100%	188m²
south	80%	150m²
north	20%	38m²

Sunspace	
Volume	136m³
Floor area	40m²
Wall area: glass	63m²
Wall area: solid	65m²
Effective aperture	42m²
Direct heat storage area	105m²

Costs		
Whole building	33 600 000 Pts	ECU 254 545
Solar features	4 100 000 Pts	ECU 31 061
Cost of electricity	10 Pts/kWh 0·076 ECU/kWh	
	(without standing charge)	

Thermal	
U value roof	0.26 W/m²K
floor	0.28 W/m²K
external walls	0.25 W/m²K
windows	3.2 W/m²K
conservatory glazing	3.2 W/m²K
Mean U value	0.5 W/m²K
Global heat loss coefficient	1617 W/K
Infiltration rate	0.5 ach
External design temperature	−5 °C
Heated floor area	818m²
Heated volume	3750m³
Net heat load	0.194 GJ/m² (53.8 kWh/m²)

Site and Climate	
Altitude	950m
Latitude	42°35'
Longitude	1°07'
Average ambient temp: Jan	1.9°C
July	18.8°C
Degree days (base 18°)	2870 deg. days
Global irradiation on horiz.	1557 kWh/m²
Sunshine hours	2589 hr/yr

BOEGEHUSENE CREDITS

Client
Greve Almennyttige Boligselskab
and
KAB
Vester Voldgade 17
Copenhagen K

Architects
Bente Aude Lundgaard, Boje Lundgaard
Georg Rotne, Peter Soerensen
Skindergade 23
1159 Copenhagen K

Services and Energy Consultant
Thomas Petersen and Max Kjellerup
DOMINIA
Studiestraede 38
1455 Copenhagen K

Building and Services Contractor
Rasmussen & Schioetz
Datavej 26
3460 Birkeroed

Monitoring Organisation
Erwin Petersen
Technological Institute
Gregersvej
2630 Taastrup

Commission of the European Communities

● Low cost competition winning housing association scheme with a flexible plan of three 'climate zones' for the different seasons.

● Attached sunspace with system of insulating shutters and blinds, reduces energy consumption by an average of 40%

● Solar warmed air redistributed to cooler parts of house by simple system.

BOEGEHUSENE
GREVE
DENMARK

Project Background

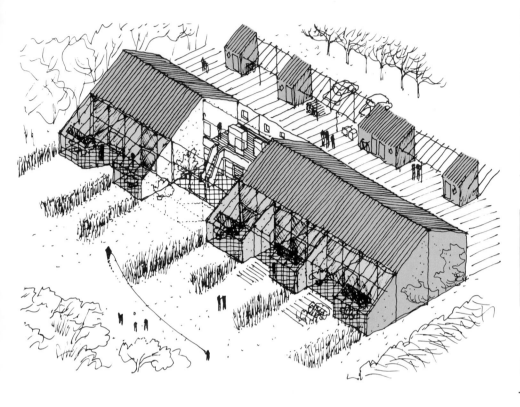

The project is a short terrace of two storey houses in a suburb near Copenhagen. There are six houses in the terrace; two are 3 bed, two 2 bed and two 1 bed houses. The houses are designed on the principle of 'climate zoning' whereby different parts of the house are used during the different seasons and the parts are therefore provided with different heating arrangements.

DESIGN OBJECTIVES

This design was the winner of a competition organised by the client, the KAB Housing Society for housing for the future. Competitors were asked to take into account many factors influencing the next 20 to 30 years, including environmental considerations and the possibility of limitations on the the availability of energy and other resources. The primary objective of the design was therefore to reduce consumption of non-renewable fuel for heating.

ENERGY SAVING FEATURES

The main features are the orientation and internal planning of the houses and the use of a sunspace.
The plan is climate zoned with a south, middle and north zone. The south zone is a single glazed sunspace heated by the sun alone and surplus heat from here is distributed to the middle zone, which is separated from the sunspace by a wall of double glazed doors. Insulating shutters are fitted to these doors

CLIMATE

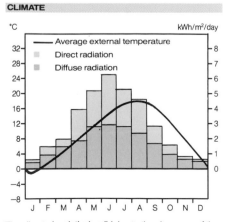

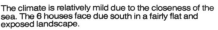

The climate is relatively mild due to the closeness of the sea. The 6 houses face due south in a fairly flat and exposed landscape.

and can be closed at night to prevent heat loss.
The northern zone is well insulated and has small windows. The front entrance is sheltered in a porch.
In order to maximise solar gains, most of the materials used for the south facing parts of the house are chosen for their ability to store heat.

The bank is designed to provide shelter from traffic noise rather than wind.

CONCLUSIONS

The Danish building code has strict energy regulations, but the aim of the project was to improve upon these and provide a flexible house for the present and future.
The houses are popular but the energy consumption, although lower than a conventional house by 15%-65%, is higher than the designers intended. This is because the middle zone, which was intended to be unused in the winter, is in fact used all year round by the tenants for additional living space.
It has been demonstrated that energy savings in these houses are highly dependent upon the

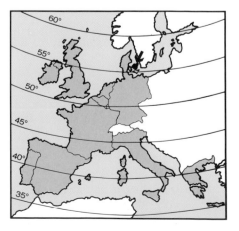

use of the space and the use of the insulating blinds and shutters.

SITE AND CLIMATE

The six terrace houses are built in a suburb of Copenhagen which is very flat and contains mostly one or two storey houses. It is fairly exposed with

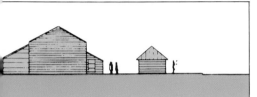

months of November to February. There are 2909 degree days in the year, and 1889 from November to February.

CONSTRUCTION

The load bearing walls of the houses are made out of prefabricated concrete elements and the internal walls are plasterboard partitions. The north and middle zones are covered with a 25° pitched timber roof with corrugated fibre-cement sheeting. Over the sunspace the pitch continues at the same angle in single glazing.

An inexpensive solution to the provision of insulating shutters was required. Sliding or rolling shutters would have been preferable.

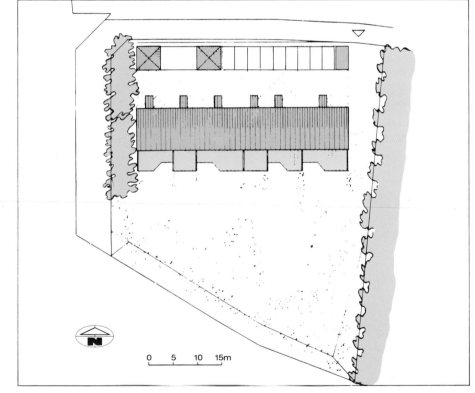

SITE PLAN
In the terrace there are 6 two storey houses. The main passive solar features are the south orientation, internal planning and sunspace.

The north elevation and the end gables of the terrace are insulated with 195mm of mineral wool and covered with dark stained horizontal boarding. Windows are white painted timber. The south elevation is the single glazed wall of the sunspace.

The ground floor is a concrete slab with the finish varying according to the zone. The north (living) zone has a beechwood parquet floor except for the bathroom which is tiled. The middle zone has a concrete finish and the sunspace has concrete flags bedded on sand.

little shelter from trees. The climate, which varies little throughout Denmark, is a coastal one with mild winters and relatively cool summers. The mean temperatures are —1°C in January and +16°C in July. The average annual sunshine total is 1500 hours, but only 10% of these are in the four

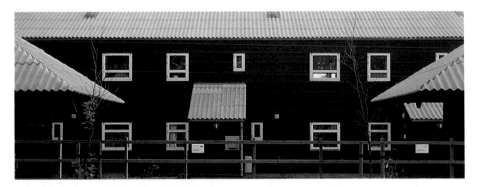

The north elevation is well insulated and protected from cold winds by porches and some storage sheds. The porches on the north side shelter the entrances. Behind the stained boarding is 195mm of mineral wool.

Design Details

PASSIVE SOLAR DESIGN

The section of the house is designed to admit as much sunlight as possible into the middle of the house. The wall separating the middle zone from the sunspace is in effect a large transparent wall with sealed double glazing units. The glazed doors open inwards, whilst the insulating shutters that cover them open outwards. Above these doors is a narrow band of ventilation windows, which are not fitted with shutters.

Finding an inexpensive and satisfactory solution for the insulating shutters proved to be difficult. Sliding or rolling shutters would have been preferred in order to prevent them projecting in the space but the budget did not allow it.

● The south facing sunspace captures available solar gain and when it's temperature is above that of the middle zone, the glazed doors can be opened to admit the warmer air.

● As the highest temperature will be at the top of the middle zone, a vertical duct is positioned from head height up to the roof. Through the duct a fan draws the warm air downwards and redistributes it to the ground level, either to the living room in the north zone or to the middle zone.

● Surplus heat in the middle zone can also be used in the first floor bedrooms by opening the windows separating the two zones.

● The concrete floors in the sunspace and in the middle zone absorb and store direct solar radiation, the sun's rays reaching into the middle zone through the roof and the glazed wall.

● Overheating is controlled by manually operated white blinds that hang internally and cover the windows and roof of the sunspace. The shutters between the middle zone and the sunspace are white painted so that they not only shade the middle zone but also reflect heat.

● Normal ventilation is achieved by opening a roof window at the top of the sunspace and cross ventilating in summer by opening the sunspace doors, the middle zone doors and the north zone windows.

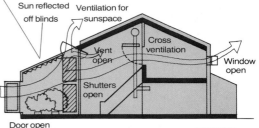

Sun reflected off blinds — Ventilation for sunspace — Vent open — Cross ventilation — Window open — Shutters open — Door open — **SUMMER**

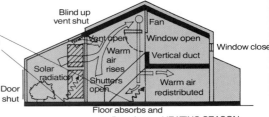

Blind up vent shut — Vent open — Fan — Window open — Window close — Warm air rises — Vertical duct — Solar radiation — Shutters open — Warm air redistributed — Door shut — Floor absorbs and radiates heat — **HEATING SEASON WITH SUN**

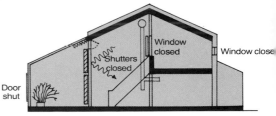

Window closed — Window close — Shutters closed — Door shut — **HEATING SEASON NO SUN**

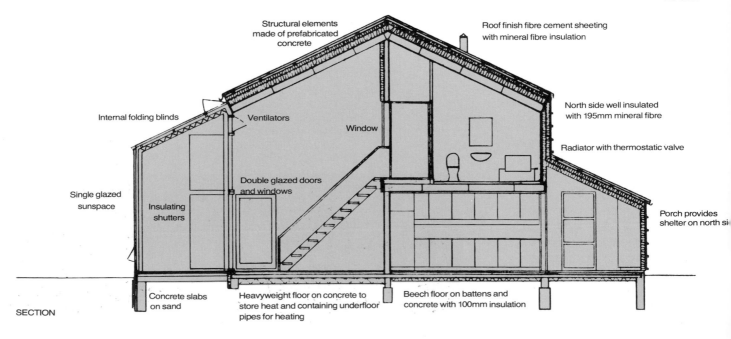

Structural elements made of prefabricated concrete

Roof finish fibre cement sheeting with mineral fibre insulation

Internal folding blinds

Ventilators

Window

North side well insulated with 195mm mineral fibre

Radiator with thermostatic valve

Single glazed sunspace

Insulating shutters

Double glazed doors and windows

Porch provides shelter on north si[de]

SECTION

Concrete slabs on sand

Heavyweight floor on concrete to store heat and containing underfloor pipes for heating

Beech floor on battens and concrete with 100mm insulation

● In winter, heat is prevented from escaping from the middle zone into the sunspace by the insulating shutters.

AUXILIARY HEATING SYSTEM

Auxiliary heating is provided by a gas-fired boiler connected to radiators in the northern zone and to hot water underfloor heating in the middle zone. There is no heating in the sunspace.

● The heating in both zones is controlled by thermostatic radiator valves and whenever solar gains result in a temperature rise in a room the heating is cut off.

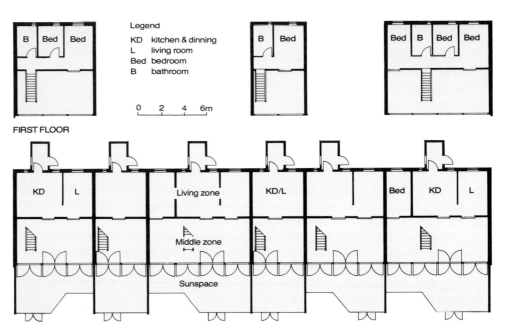

Legend
KD   kitchen & dinning
L   living room
Bed bedroom
B   bathroom

0   2   4   6m

FIRST FLOOR

GROUND FLOOR

The houses are planned in 3 zones. The north zone contains the living accommodation and is well insulated. The south zone is the single glazed sunspace for summer use and between the two is an area with well insulated roof and double glazed windows and shutters that tends to be used all year round as it has underfloor heating.

Warm air from the top of the sunspace is drawn down a vertical duct and distributed to the ground floor rooms.

NORTH ELEVATION

The north facing windows are double glazed and shelter is provided by a porch. Kitchens and bathrooms face north with living rooms facing south. The south facing sunspace is single glazed.

SOUTH ELEVATION

OPERATING MODES

It was intended that the northern zone would be used for 'living' and sleeping in the winter, whilst the middle zone would be used occasionally when the weather was fine. In the spring and autumn the living would extend out in the middle zone, with the sunspace being used only on sunny days as it is unheated. Then in summer, all zones would be in use. However, as the middle zone is provided with heating it is therefore used all year round as a general purpose room.

Solar control in the sunspace is by means of shutters and folding blinds.

Performance Evaluation

MONITORING

Monitoring commenced in 1985 and will continue into 1987. For each house the auxiliary boiler's gas consumption has been monitored, as has domestic hot water and the net contribution to space heating by monitoring the water flow and temperatures from the boiler to the radiators and under floor heating. Electricity consumption for lighting, appliances and cooking has also been monitored. Readings have been taken monthly for these, and more frequently for internal and external temperatures.

USER RESPONSE

The tenants are generally very happy with their houses and most of them use the middle zone all the year round as a living room. However they have experienced problems with the shutters in that they are difficult to use especially at first floor level, and they take up too much space.

It was intended that the middle zone would not be used much in winter, but in fact it is used all the year round as additional living space.

PERFORMANCE OF PASSIVE SYSTEMS

The monitoring programme has revealed that substantial energy savings can be achieved even compared to a house built under the strict Danish energy codes. In most cases though, the energy consumption of the houses is greater than was anticipated, primarily due to the fact that the middle zone is used as a living room all the year round and therefore requires more heating than had been anticipated.

COMPARISON WITH CONVENTIONAL DESIGN
Conventional design would need for space htg. 13970 kWh/yr (110 kWh/m² /yr)

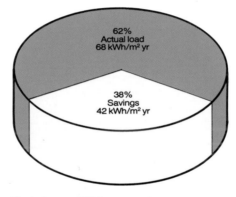

The design uses 38% less energy than a comparable house built to the Danish codes.

● The energy consumption of the houses has therefore been found to be very sensitive to the way the passive solar features and the houses in general are used.

● With the middle zone constantly heated, space heating loads increase significantly.

● The shutters and blinds need to be used as the designers planned in order to achieve high savings.

AUXILIARY FUEL USED ANUALLY
21250 kWh/yr (House A)

● The energy required for heating a well managed house compared with a house with constantly heated middle zone and with shutters and blinds not

The double glazed doors and windows of the middle zone have shutters on the sunspace side. Above them is a narrow band of ventilation windows.

operated as designed has been found to range from 39 to 94 kWh/m²/yr. The m² figure excludes the sunspace as it is not heated.

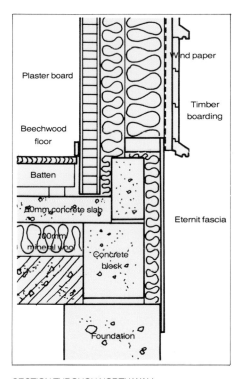

SECTION THROUGH NORTH WALL

(Labels in section: Plaster board, Beechwood floor, Batten, 50mm concrete slab, 100mm mineral wool, Concrete block, Foundation, Wind paper, Timber boarding, Eternit fascia)

COST EFFECTIVENESS

The total building costs allowed for non-profit making housing in Denmark is approximately 5,500 Kroners per m² (700 ECU). In this project it was possible to meet this

CONTRIBUTIONS TO ANNUAL SPACE HEATING DEMAND

10600 kWh/yr gross load (House C)

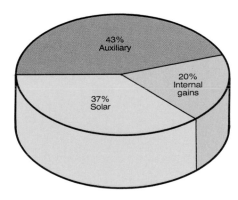

(Pie chart: 43% Auxiliary, 20% Internal gains, 37% Solar)

EFFECT OF SOLAR RADIATION ON TEMPERATURES

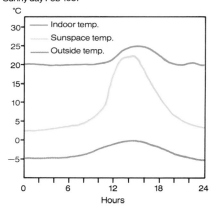

Sunny day Feb 1987

- Indoor temp.
- Sunspace temp.
- Outside temp.

Cloudy day Feb 1987

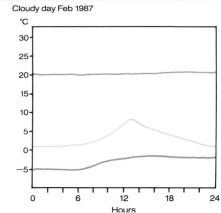

On a sunny day, auxiliary heating is not required during the whole afternoon because solar gains keep the internal temperature above 20°C.

NET MONTHLY SPACE HEATING DEMAND AND SUPPLY

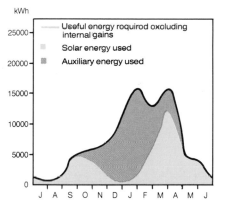

- Useful energy required excluding internal gains
- Solar energy used
- Auxiliary energy used

COMPARISON OF ENERGY USED BY DIFFERENT OWNERS FOR HEATING

94 kWh/m² was used by the household consuming the most energy. (Figures exclude the unheated sunspace).

- Highest consumer
- Lowest consumer

The well managed house used 57% less energy than the highest consumer. Consumption is sensitive to the way the owners use the middle zone and the insulating shutters.

requirement only if the sunspaces were excluded. The sunspace cost from 90,000 Kroner to 150,000 Kroner for the different sizes. The project also received additional grants for some extra design and building costs.

PROJECT DATA			Thermal	
House Type 3			U value roof	0.18 W/m²K
Volume		approx 400 m³	floor	0.26 W/m²K
Floor area		127 m²	external walls	0.2 W/m²K
Window: total area		44 m²	windows (double glazed)	3.0 W/m²K
south	86%	38 m²	conservatory glazing	7.0 W/m²K
north	14%	6 m²	Infiltration rate	0.15 ach
			External design temperature	−12 °C
			Heated floor area	127 m²
Sunspace			Heated volume	400 m³
Volume		approx 125 m³	Net heat load	68 kWh/m²/yr
Floor area		34 m²		
Glass area: roof		33 m²	**Site and Climate**	
wall		29 m²	Altitude	0 m
Wall area: solid		25 m²	Latitude	56 °N
			Longitude	12°50″E
Costs			Average ambient temp: Jan	−1 °C
Building	DK 700,000	ECU 90,000	July	+16 °C
Sunspace	DK 90-150,000	ECU 12-20,000	Degree days (base 17°C)	2909 degree days
			Global irradiation on horiz.	3.65 GJ/m²/yr
				1015 kWh/m²
			Sunshine hours	1500 hr/ann

CASALPALOCCO SCHOOL CREDITS

Client
Provincial di Roma
Ufficio Edilizia Scolastica

Designer
Ing. C Greco with V De Feo
Via Bressanone 7
00198 Roma

Services and Energy Consultant
Ing R Tito and A Fantini
ENETEC srl
Ingegneria Energetica e Realizzazione Impianti
Via Titta Scarpetta 5
00153 Roma

Contractor
ONDACLEAR SpA
Impianti Sportivi Edilizia Industrializzata
Via Archimede 112
00197 Roma

Monitoring Organisation
ENETEC slr
Ingegneria Energetica e Realizzazione Impianti
Via Titta Scarpetta 5
00153 Roma

Commission of the European Communities

LICEO SCIENTIFICO
CASALPALOCCO ROME
ITALY

● Competition winning low cost school design makes the most of solar energy and internal heat gains.

● Sunspaces attached to classrooms provide teaching space and allow passive solar gains to contribute 14% of the net heating demand.

● The school requires 76% less energy than a comparable conventionally heated design.

● Blinds and shutters insulate in winter and in summer prevent overheating and allow control over the intensity of daylighting.

● Daylight introduced into the middle of the building helps reduce electric lighting costs.

Project Background

In 1981 the Province of Rome arranged a competition to design a school which exploited solar energy. The Liceo Scientifico at Casalpalocco, a secondary school about 20km SW of Rome, is the result.

DESIGN OBJECTIVES

The brief for the project required the design to exploit solar energy and integrate any solar features into the overall design without losing an image of architectural experimentation. The client wished to find out whether the school's heating needs could be provided mainly by solar energy if solar design was incorporated along with a package of other energy saving measures.

ENERGY SAVING FEATURES

The basic principles of passive solar design have been followed by adopting a compact shape and orientating it to face south. All along the south facade on each floor, the classrooms have rows of stepped sunspaces. At the rear of the classrooms are corridors which are naturally lit from a rooflight running the length of the building. Increased levels of insulation, double glazing with external roller blinds and the elimination of cold bridges form part of the energy saving package. A large active solar hot water system with inter-seasonal store covers a major portion of the energy demand.

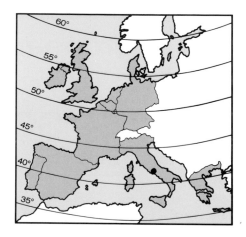

SITE AND CLIMATE

Casalpalocco is about 7km from the sea. The climate is mild and the proximity of the sea produces south westerly

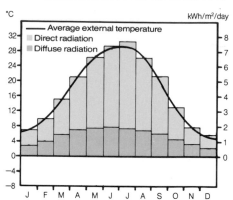

summer breezes and low atmospheric pollution. The monthly average temperature is 7.5°C for January and 9.4°C for the whole heating season. There are 1440 degree days (19°C base), and annual global solar irradiation on the horizontal is 1595 kWh/m². The site is flat and about 100m × 100m in size. A row of eucalyptus trees borders the south; there is a pine wood to the north and there is an apartment block on the east, but none of these cause any overshadowing of the building. The trees help to provide shelter from the cold north east winter winds.

Stepped rows of sunspaces immediately strike the eye as you walk up towards the school entrance.

Design Details

PLANNING

The plan is compact and rectangular, organised along a central circulation spine running from east to west. On the south side of the spine on 3 floors are all the single storey spaces of classrooms, offices and library. On the north side are the gymnasium, service rooms and a multi-purpose hall, all of which require lower temperatures. The section shows clearly the design concept, with stepped sunspaces on the south to allow maximum solar gains and daylight penetration on each floor, and a break between the north and south blocks to provide natural daylighting to the corridors.

CONSTRUCTION

The southerly block containing the classrooms has an in situ reinforced concrete frame with all the columns and beams located within the building so that the envelope of the building runs externally to the structure. The walls of the school are concrete blocks with a skin of 80mm expanded polyurethane and have a U value of 0.5 W/m²K. For the larger spans on the north side of the school, standard prestressed concrete beams from a highway viaduct catalogue were used upon which were laid 2.3m wide prefabricated concrete slab units to form the roof. On top of the concrete slabs is laid 40mm polyurethane insulation, 40mm bituminous felt and 50mm gravel. The U value of the roof is 0.8 W/m²K. The concrete ground floor has 30mm polyurethane insulation and its U value is 1.2 W/m²K.

PASSIVE SOLAR DESIGN

The design uses both direct solar gain and sunspaces to heat the building. The south elevation has 70m² of vertical

SITE PLAN
To the north of the building, a rectangular and compact form, is the seasonal storage tank as well as the new extension to the school and to the south, on either side of the entrance gate, a lawn and car park.

`0    5    10    15m`

A central corridor runs down the middle of the building with classrooms on the south side and sports hall and service rooms on the north side. Daylighting from rooflights can be seen beyond the staircase illuminating this first floor corridor.

The south facing sunspaces with some blinds drawn and the roof mounted parabolic collectors are visually prominent. The step in the roof conceals the skylight over the corridor. Pine trees shelter the north side.

The sunspace runs the length of the classroom block. It will be subdivided to reduce noise transmission between classrooms. The classrooms have sliding windows and venetian blinds. At the top of the sunspace roof is a concrete box containing a blind to provide shade in summer.

glazing and also 30 m² of 45° inclined glazing over the library. The overall direct gain is also augmented by the rooflights. The three floors of sunspaces have a combined floor area of 280m² and a volume of 660m³. The sunspaces have 120m² of opening single glazed vertical windows and 254 m² of 36° inclined roof glazing of cellular polycarbonate. The frames are anodised aluminium. An external PVC roller blind is fitted in a concrete box at the top of the sloping polycarbonate. In order to provide natural

DESIGN DETAILS

ventilation for the sunpaces, this concrete blind box has an air grille at the bottom connecting with the sunspace and another at the top connecting to the outside. Between the sunspaces and classrooms there are sliding windows, and a door which can be opened to admit warm air in winter or to help ventilate the classroom in summer. Above the doors into the classrooms there are grilles to assist cross ventilation. These were originally omitted by the builder and the natural ventilation system did not work well.

The natural daylight is uniformly good and architecturally

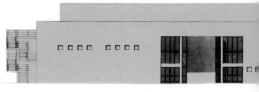

NORTH ELEVATION

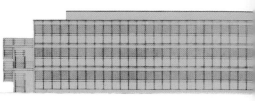

SOUTH ELEVATION

effective along the corridor where rooflights reflect the changing effects of sunlight.

AUXILIARY HEATING SYSTEM

Auxiliary heating and hot water are supplied from a 750 m³ underground inter-seasonal water storage tank which is heated by a 250 m² array of tracking parabolic solar collectors mounted on the roof. If the temperature of the water in the store is too low for use, it is upgraded by a 60 kW water to water electrical heat pump.

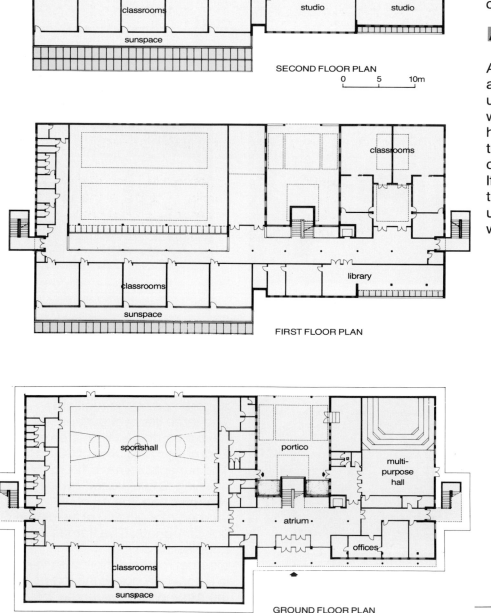

SECOND FLOOR PLAN

0   5   10m

FIRST FLOOR PLAN

GROUND FLOOR PLAN

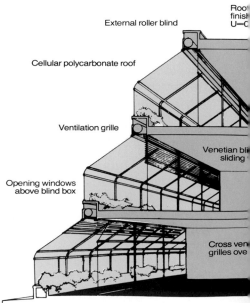

Roof finish U=0

External roller blind

Cellular polycarbonate roof

Ventilation grille

Venetian bli sliding

Opening windows above blind box

Cross ven grilles ove

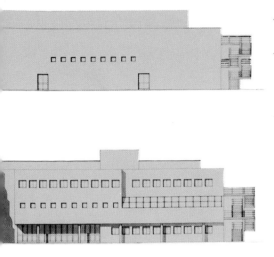

When the temperature of the storage water is between 40°C-90°C it can be used directly for space heating and hot water. When it is between 10°C-40°C it is upgraded by the heat pump. However when it is below 10°C, the heat pump uses ground water at approximately 12°C as its heat source instead of the water in the heat store. The net coefficient of performance of the heat pump, which upgrades the water to 50°C, has been recorded as 4.5 as a peak value, with a seasonal value slightly above 3.

The storage water for space heating is distributed through fan coil units, and for domestic hot water through a heat exchanger in the hot water tank. Fan coil units were selected as they can transfer heat even where the water temperatures are low, as is generally the case with solar systems.

OPERATING MODES

During the winter the air outlet grille under the blind box is closed to allow the sunspace to warm up. Direct gain into the classrooms is controlled by the venetian blinds. During the night, roller blinds are lowered to prevent heat loss from the sunspace.
During the summer, the roller blinds are lowered in the day to provide shade. The grilles at the top and bottom of the blind box are opened to ventilate the sunspace and the windows can also be opened to create ventilation across the classrooms through the grilles over the doors into the corridors.

CONTROLS

The sunspace and classroom window, the roller shutter and venetian blind, and the ventilation grilles at the top and bottom of the blind are all operated manually.

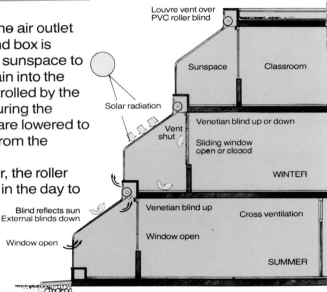

SEASONAL OPERATING MODES

Louvre vent over PVC roller blind
Sunspace Classroom
Solar radiation
Vent shut
Venetian blind up or down
Sliding window open or closed
WINTER
Blind reflects sun
External blinds down
Window open
Venetian blind up
Cross ventilation
Window open
SUMMER

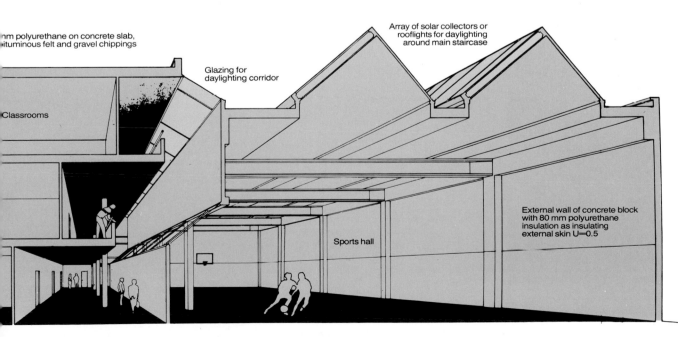

nm polyurethane on concrete slab, bituminous felt and gravel chippings

Glazing for daylighting corridor

Array of solar collectors or rooflights for daylighting around main staircase

Classrooms

Sports hall

External wall of concrete block with 80 mm polyurethane insulation as insulating external skin U=0.5

Ground floor slab with 30 mm polyurethane U=1.2

Performance Evaluation

MONITORING

Monitoring was carried out in 1984/85. Due to the importance of the active system, with its seasonal storage and heat pump, the main purpose of the monitoring programme was to measure the energy flows between the various components of the system. Other measurements were very standard and included the internal and external ambient conditions. No experimental quantification of the rate of air changes was carried out and a value of 0.75 ac/hr was tentatively assumed over 24 hrs.

USER RESPONSE

Teachers and students enjoy the brightness and lively articulation of these school spaces. But the external shutters of the sunspaces are closed every evening and this manual operation is inconvienient.

PERFORMANCE OF PASSIVE SOLAR DESIGN

The passive and active systems have worked well in that there is hardly any auxiliary energy consumed, but there have been

The sunspace has blinds to provide shade, and opening windows for ventilation across the building. The blind rolls up into the concrete box above which is a grille through which hot air in the sunspace escapes.

problems of overheating and of poor ventilation

The north entrance is the full height of the building. Daylight from a rooflight illuminates the main staircase. The solar collectors can also be seen against the light.

● The total solar contribution to the gross space heating load of 546 GJ was 43%, of which 11.5% was from passive gain and 31.5% from the seasonal water store and its collectors.

CONTRIBUTIONS TO TOTAL SPACE HEATING REQUIREMENT

151800 kWh/ann (546 GJ/ann)

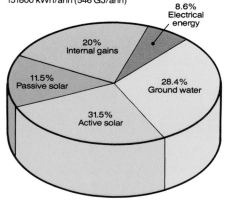

- 8.6% Electrical energy
- 20% Internal gains
- 11.5% Passive solar
- 28.4% Ground water
- 31.5% Active solar

The active system accounts for a large proportion of the energy savings, and passive solar saves a further 11.5%

● Ground water, which served as a low temperature heat source for the heat pump when its temperature was higher than the storage water temperature,

contributed 28.4%

● Internal gains provided another 20% leaving only 8.6% for auxiliary energy (electricity) to run the heat pump and the water circulators.

COMPARISON WITH CONVENTIONAL DESIGN

Primary energy for conventional building space heating 173285 kWh/ann (624 GJ/ann)

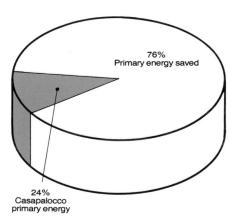

- 76% Primary energy saved
- 24% Casapalocco primary energy

It is estimated that the Liceo Casalpalocco saves 76% of the energy that would be used by a conventional design with a gas boiler. This assumes boiler efficiency of 70% and 33% efficiency for electrical conversion.

However there were problems.

● The working drawings were done by the building contractor and there were many ventilation problems due to defective construction details.

● The air gratings over the classroom entrance doors were

HEAT FLOWS GJ/ann

Aux energy for HW 7GJ

Aux energy for Sp Htg 47GJ

Ground water for Sp.Htg 155GJ, for HW 16GJ

Solar activity for Sp.Htg 172GJ, for HW 31GJ

Solar passive 63GJ

Internal gains 109GJ

left out thereby inhibiting cross ventilation. A mechanical ventilation system will be installed to provide the legal minimum of 5 airchanges per hour.

● Fixed windows in the library caused overheating.

● The continuous sunspace along the balconies outside the classrooms created acoustic problems when it was used and it will be subdivided into separate sunspaces for each classroom.

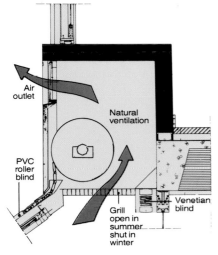

DETAIL OF BLIND BOX

MONTHLY NET SPACE HEATING DEMAND AND SUPPLY

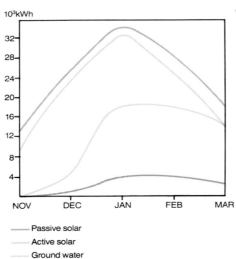

10³kWh

— Passive solar
— Active solar
— Ground water
--- Auxiliary

MONTHLY AVERAGE TEMPERATURE (24 hrs)

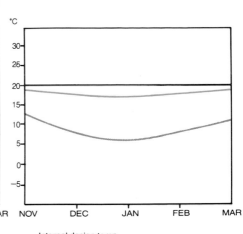

°C

— Internal design temp.
— Internal temp.
— External temp.

AUXILIARY FUEL USED

27500 kWh/ann (99 GJ/ann)

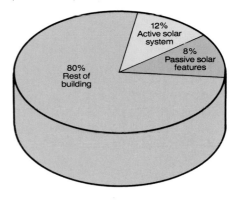

45.5% Lighting appliances

47.5% Heat pump for space heating

7% Heat pump for hot water

All the auxiliary energy is electricity. The consumption of the heat pump is a little larger than that for lights and appliances.

COST OF BUILDING AND SOLAR ON-COST

Total project cost approx. L.3000 million (2.5 million ECU)

12% Active solar system

8% Passive solar features

80% Rest of building

The on-cost for passive solar features, mainly sunspaces, was 8%

COST EFFECTIVENESS

Compared with a school of the same volume built to satisfy Italian building codes, Liceo Casalpalocco uses 76% less fuel. The cost of the school at 3,000 million Lire was low because it was the result of a design and build competition.

This cost worked out at some 700,000 L/m² in 1983 prices (approx 600 ECU/m²).

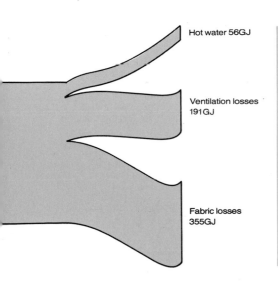

Hot water 56GJ

Ventilation losses 191GJ

Fabric losses 355GJ

PROJECT DATA			Thermal	
Building excluding sunspace			U value roof	0.8
Volume		18,300 m³	floor	1.2 W/m²K
Floor area		4,700 m²	external walls	0.5 W/m²K
Roof area		2,400 m²	windows	1.8 W/m²K
External wall area		6,300 m²	sunspace	5.0 W/m²K
Windows: total area*	7.1%	447 m²	Mean U value	0.9 W/m²K
south	4.3%	273 m²	Global heat loss coefficient	6.9 W/K
north	1.2%	79 m²	Infiltration rate	0.75 ac/h
*includes classroom windows overlooking sunspace			External design temperature	0°C
			Heated floor area	4,100 m²
Sunspace			Heated volume	14,500 m³
Volume		660 m³	Net heat load (heated area)	8.3 kWh/m²
Floor area		280 m²		
Glass area: roof (36°)		254 m²	**Site and climate**	
wall		122 m²	Altitude	5 m
Effective aperture		80 m²	Latitude	41°45′
			Average ambient temp: Jan	6.9°C
Costs (1983 prices)			July	28.9°C
Building	L 3000 million (2,500,000 ECU)		Degree days (base 19°)	1440 degree days
Active solar	L 600 million (500,000 ECU)		Global irradiation on horiz.	1595 kWh/m²
Passive solar	L 40 million (33,000 ECU)		Sunshine hours	2518 hr/ann

AM LINDENWÄLDLE PROJECT CREDITS

Client
Siedlungsgesellschaft Freiburg
Hermannstrasse 1
D 7800 Freiburg i Br

Architect
Rolf Disch
Wiesentalstrasse 19
D7800 Freiburg i Br

Energy Consultant
IST Energietechnik GmbH
Ritterweg 1
D 7842 Kandern — Wollbach

DFVLR Stuttgart
Pfaffenwaldring 38-40
D 7000 Stuttgart 80

Services Engineer
Planungsgemeinschaft Breisgau
W Broman & Partner
Blumenstrasse 39
D 7800 Freiburg i Br

Monitoring Organisation
IST Energietechnik GmbH
Ritterweg 1
D 7842 Kandern — Wollbach

Commission of the European Communities

Curved terrace of houses designed so that the south facade is wider than the north facade, with a 'sunspace' attached to the south side.

AM LINDENWÄLDLE

FREIBURG
GERMANY

● Split level floors and open plan increase daylight and sunlight penetration and promote circulation of solar heated air through the house.

● Despite solar additions, houses cost less than average house of similar size due to design and construction savings.

● Optimised boiler efficiency and control system and installation of water store contribute to fuel savings from passive design and energy insulation measures.

Project Background

The Lindenwäldle project in Freiburg consists of 18 terrace houses built in three rows of six houses. They were built on council owned land leased for 99 years to the City's Building Society for sale to young families with several children.

DESIGN OBJECTIVES

The Building Society already had some experience with solar technology, and wanted to demonstrate further the possibilities of using passive solar energy in low cost housing. The future owners were selected after they had replied to an advertisement and were involved in the design. They could also participate in the construction work in order to reduce the cost.

ENERGY SAVING FEATURES

The terraces are fan shaped and orientated to the south so that the south elevation is wider than the north. The houses have their entrances on the north elevation onto which is also added unheated storage sheds which act as a north buffer zone. The section of the houses allows daylight and sunlight penetration in winter. The houses have increased insulation levels higher than the German standard, north facing windows are triple glazed; all others, including the sunspace are double glazed. Two storey

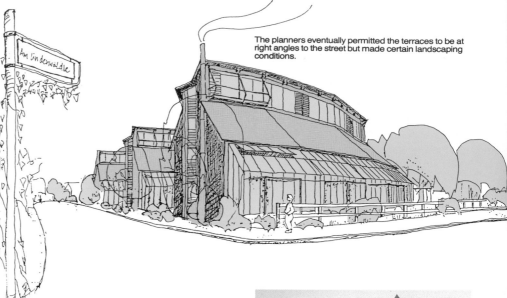

The planners eventually permitted the terraces to be at right angles to the street but made certain landscaping conditions.

high sunspaces attached to the south elevation offer extra living area as well as additional passive solar space heating.

SITE AND CLIMATE

The project is situated on the southern outskirts of Freiburg, a city lying on the plain of the Rhine and on the edge of the Black Forest. Both of these influence the climate, with the Rhine producing fogs in winter and the Black Forest thunderstorms in the summer. The climate is relatively mild although the minimum design temperature for buildings is −12°C and in summer it can be hot with temperatures rising to 35-38°C. There are on average 3469 degree days (15°C base) and 1808 sunshine hours per annum. The average daily

Unheated storage sheds attached to the north side of the houses provide shelter and the windows are triple glazed, but the front doors have no external porch nor internal lobby, which could have reduced any draughts.

temperature in January is 0.7°C and in July the average is 18.5°C. The site is in a mixed area containing small industrial estates and detached houses built in the 1940-60's surrounded by gardens and trees. The project is sheltered from the prevailing west winds by these surrounding buildings and they do not overshadow the site. However, the solar houses themselves are quite tall (12m) and the two northerly terraces are partially shaded from the beginning of December to mid January by the terrace to the south.

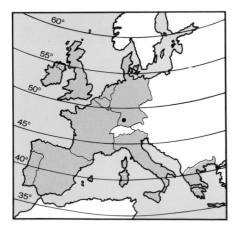

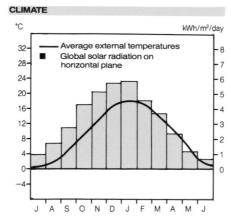

CLIMATE

°C   kWh/m²/day

— Average external temperatures
■ Global solar radiation on horizontal plane

J A S O N D J F M A M J

Design Details

PLANNING

The planning authority intended the terraces to be parallel to the street, but eventually agreed to allow them to be turned to be at right angles to the street so they could face south, providing the spaces between the houses were kept as gravel instead of paving, and all fences were identical.

The sunspace provides additional living area and is useful as a children's play area. Warm air rises into the house over the balcony.

The houses have a deep plan, 11.56m plus 3m sunspace. One of the party walls is at right angles to the front wall, but the other party wall is at an angle of 97° in order to produce the fanshape of the terrace. This is done to increase the width of the south facing elevation, which is 1.87m wider than the front elevation. The unheated storage sheds are built (or can

The terraces are curved so that the south facing elevation has a greater area than the north. This maximises solar gains and minimises exposure to the colder north side.

in future be built by owners) on the north side of the house. The section is unusual with each floor split into two levels to enhance the effect of open planning.

The children's bedroom can be

arranged as a two storey room with the bed in the upper gallery, and the top room can be separated into a 'granny' flat. There is a cellar below the north half of the house.

The size of the site means that there is some overshadowing in mid-winter, but this is kept to a minimum by reducing the height of the north elevation.

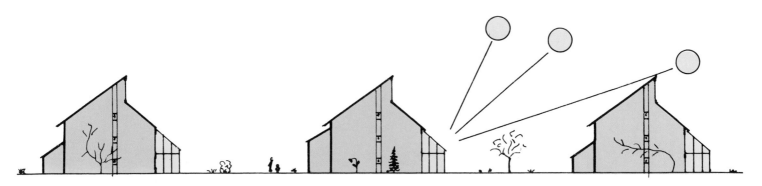

Design Details

CONSTRUCTION

The houses have 200mm thick fairfaced concrete party walls which are unplastered but painted. The rest of the house is of lightweight construction. The floor joists, which are of untreated timber and are left exposed underneath, are supported on wall plates fixed to the party walls. The external walls are clad with timber and insulated with 100mm rockwool between batterns to give an average U of 0.38 W/m^2K. The roof structure is timber. It is insulated with 150mm mineral wool and covered with profiled fibre cement sheeting. The U value is 0.26 W/m^2K. All floors are timber except the ground floor, which is concrete with a tiled finish. Internal walls are plasterboarded metal stud partitions with rockwool infilling.

PASSIVE SOLAR DESIGN

The design incorporates a number of passive solar features.

● Providing best possible solar exposure by optimum spacing of terraces and design of section to reduce overshadowing.

● Curving the terrace to minimise the north facade and increase the area of the south facade.

● South orientation of living rooms with large windows.

● Location of unheated stores on the north side to reduce heat losses and provide shelter.

● Attaching a double glazed sunspace to the south elevation.

● Increasing solar penetration into interior by split floor levels and having open staircases to allow the warm air from the sunspace to rise up through the house.

● Promoting summer ventilation by use of stack effect from the north side, up the open staircase, and through widows at high level. Large areas of the sunspace roof and walls can be opened

● Provision of internal thermal mass for heat storage with tiled floor and unplastered concrete party walls.

The fan shape of the terrace and the design of the section promote maximum solar penetration. The sunspace is double glazed and is used for drying clothes as well as extra living area. The top room has views over the Black Forest.

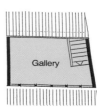
THIRD FLOOR

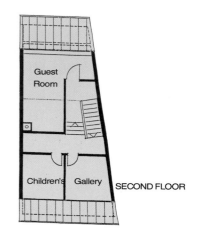
SECOND FLOOR

0 1 2m

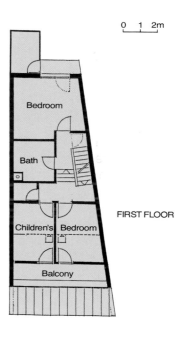
FIRST FLOOR

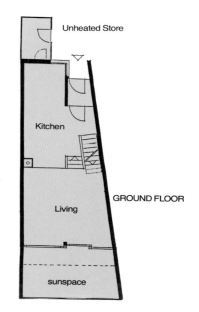
GROUND FLOOR

AUXILIARY HEATING SYSTEM AND CONTROLS

The central heating is provided by radiators with thermostatic valves and an atmospheric gas boiler fixed to an outside wall to avoid the need for a flue. Both the boiler and 150 litre hot water cylinder, which is equipped with a second heat exchanger, are sited in the top gallery in order to allow the installation of a thermosyphon solar active system if desired at a later date. The fresh air for the boiler comes in through a double walled pipe and is prewarmed by the exhaust gases.

There is also a 300 litre pressurised water storage tank, which is heated by the boiler and which feeds both the domestic hot water cylinder and the central heating radiators. The tank has two manually adjusted thermostats which turn the boiler on when the water temperature falls below the set level. When the set temperature is reached the lower thermostat turns the boiler off. In the summer, the storage tank can be bypassed and the boiler linked directly to the domestic hot water cylinder. Once the

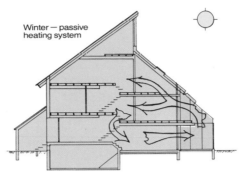

Winter — passive heating system

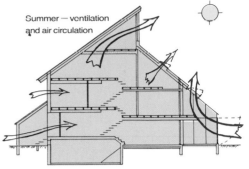

Summer — ventilation and air circulation

boiler is working it burns for at least 25 minutes, even in summer, in order to achieve optimum efficiency. The temperature of the flow to the radiators is regulated by a three-way valve according to the outside temperature. Thermostatic radiator valves cut the radiators off if internal or solar gains increase the temperature.

OPERATING MODES

The sunspace is used throughout the year as an additional living room, or as a greenhouse, or both. In winter, it is often used as a play space for children on sunny days. The air heated in the sunspace circulates up to the bedrooms above and cooler air is drawn down the stairwell and back into the sunspace. The balcony in the sunspace is used to dry washing or to air clothing or bedding.

In summer, all the openings are used to promote ventilation from the bottom of the house up the open stairs and out through the top window, with cooler air being drawn in from the north side.

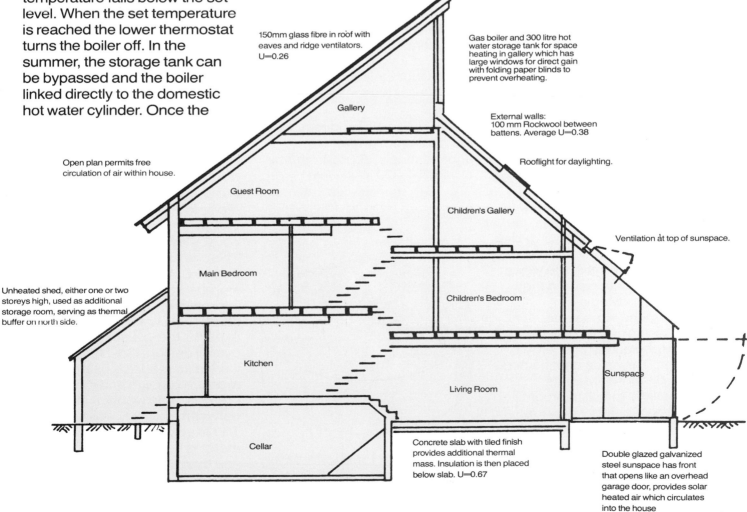

150mm glass fibre in roof with eaves and ridge ventilators. U=0.26

Gas boiler and 300 litre hot water storage tank for space heating in gallery which has large windows for direct gain with folding paper blinds to prevent overheating.

Gallery

External walls: 100 mm Rockwool between battens. Average U=0.38

Open plan permits free circulation of air within house.

Rooflight for daylighting.

Guest Room

Children's Gallery

Ventilation at top of sunspace.

Main Bedroom

Children's Bedroom

Unheated shed, either one or two storeys high, used as additional storage room, serving as thermal buffer on north side.

Kitchen

Living Room

Sunspace

Cellar

Concrete slab with tiled finish provides additional thermal mass. Insulation is then placed below slab. U=0.67

Double glazed galvanized steel sunspace has front that opens like an overhead garage door, provides solar heated air which circulates into the house

Performance Evaluation

MONITORING

Monitoring was from July 1985 to June 1986 with two of the houses being extensively monitored. In each of these houses an automatic data logger recorded 18 temperature sensors, the gas and electricity meters, a DHW volume meter, a space heating volume meter, and the position of 6 doors and windows. Ambient temperature, wind speed and direction, and solar global ventilation were also recorded. Scanning periods were every minute with averages of 15 minutes stored on cassettes which were changed once a week. Thermometers were installed in all the sunspaces to show maximum temperatures. The owners had to fill in a weekly form with these readings and also those of the gas and electricity meters.

USER RESPONSE

The owners enjoy the lightness and warmth of the houses, the house plan, which also provides a private and sunny room at the top of the house with the views over the mountains, and the benefits of having a multipurpose sunspace. However, some did have too high expectations of energy savings. They also complained regularly about draughts, especially in the sitting room. These complaints were due firstly to the shrinking of the timber construction during the first heating season, especially the outside walls of the end

houses, which was rectified by sealing the cracks: secondly, due to the open entrance into the cellar which had to be closed off and insulated: thirdly, to the open staircase, which is difficult to cure: and, lastly, due to the omission of a lobby inside the front door, which tends to become warped when the temperature is 20 °C inside and −10°C outside. There were also problems with the control strategy for the 300 litre tank, which affected the occupants' comfort, and with noise transmission. The concrete party wall is good for insulation against airborne noise, but not for impact sound.

PERFORMANCE OF PASSIVE DESIGN

The individual annual energy demand varied in 17 of the 18 houses from 13,000 kWh/yr to 22,000 kWh/yr. The remaining house had an extremely high consumption of 41,000 kWh/yr, as the inhabitants like room temperatures above 23°C which means that the actual degree days are far higher for this house.
The average of six houses with low consumption was approximately 15,000 kWh/yr of which 4,000 kWh were

COMPARISON WITH CONVENTIONAL DESIGN

Annual net sp.htg. load for a covential design would be 59 GJ (16400 kWh)

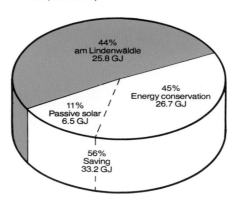

44%
am Lindenwäldle
25.8 GJ

45%
Energy conservation
26.7 GJ

11%
Passive solar
6.5 GJ

56%
Saving
33.2 GJ

A typical house conforming with the building regulations would have a specific U value of 305 W/K and an annual load of 110 kWh/m² compared with 272 W/K and 56 kWh/m² for am Lindenwäldle middle house.

electricity, 3,000 kWh for hot water and 8,000 kWh for space heating. The electricity bill was approximately the same as the total gas bill. The solar contribution was approximately 25%.
A further reduction in the overall energy load could be achieved with an active solar system for domestic hot water (1500-2000 kWh/yr) and with a forced ventilation system with heat recovery units.

CONTRIBUTIONS TO SPACE HEATING DEMAND

Annual gross load for a single am Lindenwäldle house 44.5 GJ (12371 kWh)

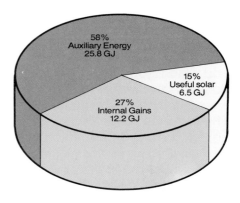

58%
Auxiliary Energy
25.8 GJ

15%
Useful solar
6.5 GJ

27%
Internal Gains
12.2 GJ

The passive solar contribution was only a part of the package of energy saving measures to reduce the total space heating energy demand. Other measures included careful planning, increased insulation and reduced ventilation.

COST EFFECTIVENESS

It is difficult to compare the total cost with a conventional design but conventional terrace houses are sold for about 1,800 to 2,200 DM/m² whereas the solar houses were sold for 1,630DM/m². The cost of the sunspace was 21,600 DM and of the heat storage 1,800 DM, but the internal finishing of the houses was simple which partly explains the low cost of the overall design. Cost reductions were also made by using a repetitive design and a partly prefabricated wooden structure between the party walls.
The fixed charge for the gas meter is high (28 DM/month) and this raises the cost of gas to 0.0696 DM/kWh. This high

charge depresses the cost benefits of energy savings, but the useful solar was 1815 kWh which is worth 95 DM, excluding the standard charge, at 1985/86 prices. Additional savings are achieved through the fact that the internal temperature of the sunspace is at least 10°C higher

AUXILIARY FUEL USED

Annual fuel consumed by single am Lindenwäldle house

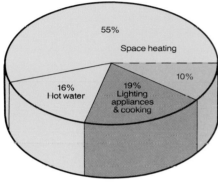

■ Wood   ■ Gas   ■ Electricity

COST OF FUEL USED

Cost of annual fuel consumed by single am Lindenwäldle house DM 2297 (1100 ECU)

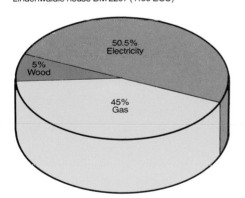

Electrical energy was 50% of the energy cost, but supplied only 19% of the energy used.

COSTS OF ENERGY SAVING

Total cost of am Lindenwäldle house DM 242000 (108500 ECU)

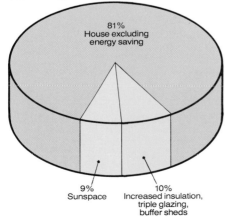

The additional cost of energy saving was 19% of which about half was for the sunspace and half for other conservation measures.

ENERGY USED FOR SPACE HEATING — MONTHLY

Single house.

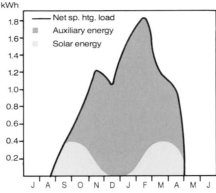

Passive solar supplied approx 15% of the total demand.

EFFECT OF SOLAR RADIATION ON HEATING LOAD AND TEMPERATURE

Data for mid-terrace house 2nd March 1986

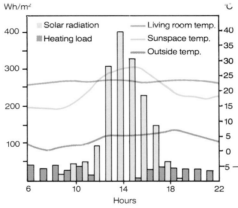

On a clear winters day solar radiation supplies all the energy required to maintain the internal temperature for 4 hours in the early afternoon and reduces the auxiliary needed in the morning and evening.

AVERAGE TEMPERATURES — MONTHLY

Single house. 24 hr temp.

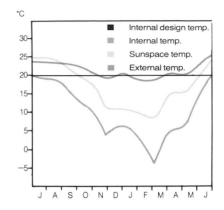

The temperature in the sunspace was such that it could be useful as a playspace when the outside temperature was well below freezing.

ANNUAL GAS CONSUMPTION FOR EACH HOUSE

Average consumption 15.72 MWh/a (14.3 MWh/a without highest consumer)

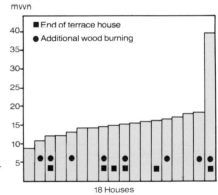

The comparison shows that most households used a similar amount of gas with the exception of one which consumed twice as much as the next highest.

than the external ambient temperature. This passive saving is estimated to be equivalent to 2300 kWh/ann (120 DM). The total financial savings are 215 DM. However, the sunspace should not be considered only as a energy saving facility since it has proved to be a very useful ammenity as an extra living room.

PROJECT DATA (Middle House)		
House without sunspace		
Volume		537 m³
Floor area		153 m²
Roof area		66 m²
External wall area		73 m²
Window area: total (41% of wall)		30m²
south 83%		25m²
north 17%		5m²
Sunspace		
Volume		77.5 m³
Floor area		17.6 m²
Glass area: roof		20.1 m²
wall		15.9 m²
Effective aperture		31.9 m²
Costs		
Building	DM 242,800	ECU 108,500
Sunspace	DM 21,600	ECU 9,700
Heat storage tank	DM 1,800	ECU 810

Thermal	
U value roof	0.26 W/m²K
floor	0.67 W/m²K
external walls	0.38 W/m²K
Windows	1.8 & 2.5 W/m²K
Conservatory glazing	3.4 W/m²K
Mean U value	1.1 W/m²K
Global heat loss coefficient	220 W/K
Infiltration rate	0.5 ach
External design temperature	−12 °C
Heated floor area	149 m²
Heated volume	513 m²
Net heat load	55.7 kWh/m² per ann
Site and Climate	
Altitude	210 m
Latitude	48 °N
Longitude	7°50'E
Average ambient temp: Jan	0.9 °C
July	18.5 °C
Degree days (base 15°C ext.)	3469 degree days
Global irradiation on horiz.	1184 kWh/m²
Sunshine hours	1808 hr/ann

J E L CREDITS

Client
JEL Energy Conservation Services Ltd
Bramhall Moor Industrial Park
Pepper Road
Stockport
Cheshire

Architects and Mechanical Engineers
Dominic Michaelis Associates
(Now Michaelis Francis Le Roith Architects Ltd)
Bay 8
16 South Wharf Road
London
W2 1PF

Structural Engineers
Anthony Hunt Associates
West End House
37 Chapel Street
London
NW1

Energy Consultants
Dominic Michaelis Associates and
JEL Energy Conservation Services Ltd

Monitoring Organisation
JEL Energy Conservation Services Ltd

Quantity Surveyor
Peter Dudley Associates
Hawthorns
Brookledge Lane
Adlington
Macclesfield
SK10 4JU

Contractor
W Snape and Sons Ltd
Clifton House
Clifton Road
Eccles
Manchester M30 9QR

Commission of the European Communities

J E L BUILDING
STOCKPORT
ENGLAND

● Low energy and passive solar design to promote client's high-tech business image and provide focal point for industrial park.

● Warm air provided to production area from glazed south facing wall and atrium.

● Overheating from solar gain controlled by blinds or louvres and by natural ventilation.

● Maximum use of natural light and low energy lighting with automatic controls reduce electricity costs.

● Good control over heating provided by zoning the building and use of environmental controls and an energy management system.

Project Background

The JEL Building is a low energy production and office building designed for a firm which manufactures control and energy monitoring systems. The building has won a number of architectural and low energy awards and has been very successful in promoting the firm's business objectives.

DESIGN OBJECTIVES

The client wanted a building that not only demonstrated the use of low energy design techniques applied to building form, fabric, lighting and heating, but would also provide a striking showcase for his own computerised control systems. For the architects, it was important to ensure that the achievement of low running costs was not done at the expense of greatly increased capital costs, and that the building's appearance enhanced the client's business objectives of efficiency, innovation and stylishness. It also had to be capable of being readily saleable in the commercial property market.

ENERGY SAVING FEATURES

● Increased proportion of south facing glazing, including rooflights.

● Control of solar gain in both summer and winter to prevent overheating by using blinds, cross ventilation and stack effect.

● High levels of insulation and effective seals and lobbies to reduce air infiltration and draughts.

● Maximum use of natural lighting, use of low energy lamps for supplementary lighting and lighting control systems.

● Use of energy management and boiler control systems.

● Recirculating air within the building to prevent heat stratification.

● Zoning of building for more specific environmental control.

SITE AND CLIMATE

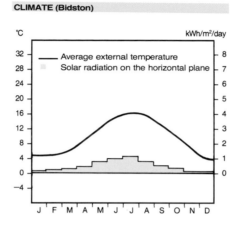

CLIMATE (Bidston)

The building is in Bramhall, a suburb of Stockport which is about 10 miles south of Manchester. The site is approximately 60m × 120m with the longer axis running north/south.

The climate is temperate, but the region is wetter than many other parts of England. The maximum daily average temperatures are 15.5°C in summer and 4.0°C in winter. There are on average, 1450 hours of sunshine a year. The site itself is flat and fairly open, except for some tall trees to the south and another building on the west, both of which provide some shelter against the prevailing south-west winds. To the east of the site is some traditional low rise housing and to the west are some industrial units.

SITE PLAN
The south elevation is not overshadowed as it faces the entrance to the industrial park and provides a focus for the park.

0   15   30m

Design Details

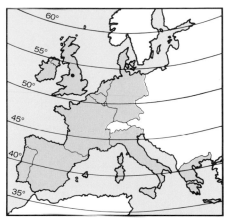

Stockport is on the southern side of Manchester and about 30 miles from Liverpool in the north west of England.

PLANNING

The glazed south elevation faces the road leading into the industrial park and creates a focal point at the entrance to the park.

The road loops around to the east to serve a public car park and this factor determined that the entrance to the building should be on the east side. The building is screened on the west side by mounding and planting. The area at the north end of the building is reserved for expansion of the production area in the future. Inside, in the middle of the building, is a double storey high production space which receives natural light from rooflights. The rest of the facilities are placed around the production space on the ground and first floor levels and receive daylighting from the windows. In the middle of the south facade is a double height atrium space which contains the boiler and control equipment; it also serves to allow more natural light into the production area.

CONSTRUCTION

The building has a steel frame which was chosen in order to reduce construction time and to allow the roof to be erected at an early stage to give shelter to the other trades. The shape of the triangular lattice beam facilitated the incorporation of sloping rooflights. The walls are cavity construction with an inner leaf of thin lightweight concrete block, a 50mm cavity fully filled with glass fibre batts and an outer leaf of 102mm brick. Brick walls were a requirement of the planners who were concerned that the walls should blend with houses around the business park. The ground floor is a concrete slab and the first floor is made of precast and prestressed concrete planks spanning between steel beams.

The south elevation makes the maximum use of solar gains by having the roof as well as the wall fully glazed. In the centre is the double height atrium which acts as a plenum for collecting solar heated air before it is ducted to the production area in winter or vented in summer.

PASSIVE SOLAR DESIGN

The building has a fully glazed south facade. In the centre of this is the two storey high atrium, which contains the boiler and control plant. The glazed wall is a sun trap to capture solar radiation and the top of the atrium serves as a collection point for the solar heated air. From this point, the air is transferred to the production area directly or, if necessary, after being heated by heater batteries. The atrium has mechanically activated louvres which let in make up fresh air for the production area in the heating season, and which allow hot air to be exhausted by stack effect in the summer.

To control glare and unwanted summer solar gains, the south wall was fitted with internal venetian blinds. The designers wanted to fit the blinds between the two panes of glass and extract heat at the top of the cavity, but this proved not to be cost effective. However, after the building had experienced its first summer, external blinds were fitted to provide better solar control at first floor level.

The blinds are opened on summer nights to allow radiative cooling and a fan is used to draw cool night air into the production area. Natural cross ventilation can be induced by opening the windows on both sides of the building. This is a manual operation.

Not only does the design attempt to exploit solar gains to the full, but it also makes the most of the warm air within the building by recirculating it to prevent stratification.

Design Details

AUXILIARY HEATING AND VENTILATING SYSTEMS

Three 50kW boiler modules provide hot water for radiators and for an air heater battery. The radiators heat all parts of the building except the production area. This area is supplied with air taken from the top of the atrium and warmed, if required, by the heater battery. The two systems operate separately, and the division of the building into zones makes greater control possible.

The fan that blows the warmed air into the production area can also be used to extract hot air from the top of the atrium and discharge it to the outside.

The plan provides as much natural lighting as possible to all areas. Rooflights illuminate internal areas. The grouping of offices etc. overlooking the production area helps to promote a feeling of togetherness.

First floor

Ground floor

Production area

0 5 10m

Atrium

Entrance

Glazed louvres from the upper corridor and offices allow visual control over the production space and provide cross ventilation.

NATURAL LIGHTING

Maximising the use of natural daylight goes well with trying to maximise solar gains. However, solar gain through the large south facing glazed facade is required to be controlled in order to avoid discomfort, glare and an uneven distribution of heat. The glazed wall was therefore fitted internally with full height reflective venetian blinds which reflect the light onto the ceiling. In the summer, they are angled at 45-60° to reflect the sunlight back through the glazing. The blinds are motorised and are controlled from the central energy management unit according to lighting levels and the internal temperature. In addition to daylight from the rooflights, natural light from the atrium also helps to light the production area and the internal offices. The effect is enhanced by light coloured walls and ceilings which ensure a good light spread and high internal reflective component.

LOW ENERGY LIGHTING

The original design intended to use task lighting beside each work station, uplighters for background lighting in offices, canteen and other areas with a false ceiling, and high bay luminaires in the production area using high pressure sodium lamps. However, this was thought not to be cost effective and the false ceilings were omitted. Fluorescent fittings with polylux tubes were used instead to maintain a low energy scheme. VDUs with non-glare screens were used to prevent problems with these overhead fittings. Using a

The glazed walls and rooflights are fitted with internal blinds. It was intended that they should be in between the double glazing with air extracted at the top. Cost limitations prevented this but external blinds were fitted on the south elevation at first floor level after the first summer to prevent excessive solar gains.

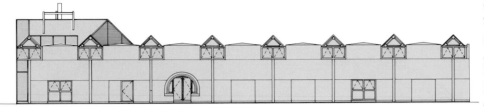

The east elevation is constructed mainly of brickwork to reflect the housing opposite.

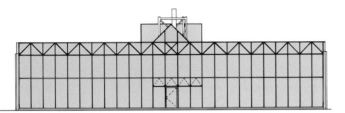

The south elevation is fully glazed.

temperature in each zone.
Winter: Blinds are set to 10° to allow maximum solar gain. Air at top of atrium is ducted to heater battery, then to production area. Anti-stratification fans in production area are on. Glass louvres between atrium and production area are open to allow air to return. Radiators operate independently.

In summer, hot air is drawn out of the office into the atrium where it is discharged to the outside. External blinds prevent excessive gains. Opening windows on the east and west elevations allow cooler air into the offices.

system developed by JEL, the levels and times of illumination are controlled according to the building's occupancy pattern.

AUTOMATIC CONTROLS

The building is divided into zones to facilitate greater control by the energy management systems located in the atrium. The system ensures a zone by zone balance and maximises plant efficiency.

OPERATING MODES

Autumn/spring: Excess heat from south wall is extracted by fan to top of atrium. Air from atrium is heated further if necessary before being distributed to production area. The blinds on the south wall are set automatically at an angle to admit or reflect solar radiation. Automatic louvres at top of atrium admit fresh air to be mixed with warm air going to production area. Fans circulate air within production area to prevent stratification. Glass louvres between offices and production area are open to allow air to return to atrium via offices. Radiators operate independently according to the

OPERATING MODES

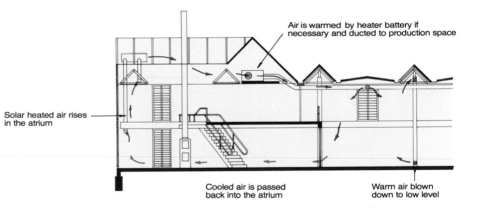

Air is warmed by heater battery if necessary and ducted to production space

Solar heated air rises in the atrium

Cooled air is passed back into the atrium

Warm air blown down to low level

AUTUMN/SPRING

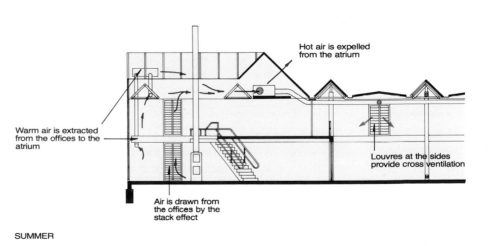

Hot air is expelled from the atrium

Warm air is extracted from the offices to the atrium

Louvres at the sides provide cross ventilation

Air is drawn from the offices by the stack effect

SUMMER

Performance Evaluation

MONITORING

The firm uses its own equipment to provide close monitoring of temperatures and of the consumption of gas, (which is used for space heating only) and electricity (which is used for all other purposes).

USER RESPONSE

The business of the client helps to ensure that energy saving measures are more readily accepted by employees. In this building, controls are all centralised leaving little that an individual can do to control his own conditions except to open a window. During the first summer, discomfort was experienced in some south facing zones which led to the decision to install external blinds at first floor level.

COMPARISON WITH CONVENTIONAL DESIGN
240,000 kWh/yr of fuel would be required to heat a comparable building.

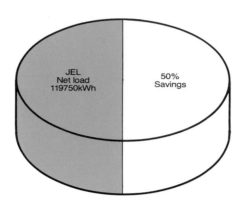

JEL design uses 50% less energy than a comparable conventional building.

CONTRIBUTIONS TO SPACE HEATING DEMAND

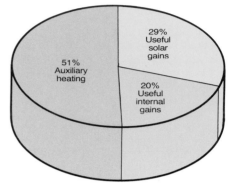

Nearly a third of the total energy needed to heat the building is supplied by useful solar gains. Auxiliary heating provides only 51% of the total.

glazing and rooflights create a light, pleasant atmosphere within the building. The automatically opening internal blinds both control the working environment and create a

and this, combined with the high thermal capacity of the production room slab, has led to longer warm-up times than would be expected normally. No lobby was fitted to the insulated loading bay doors as deliveries of large items are rare. However, when they are opened, they can cause draughts so deliveries are timed to avoid working hours. The anti-stratification fans pushing warm air downwards were found to be noisy and therefore the system has been slowed down and reversed, which has the same effect but is less disturbing.

COST EFFECTIVENESS

The building cost about 3% more than a conventional building of the same size, but achieves a 50% saving of energy worth around £3,000 a year. The cost of the services is no greater than normal and it includes an energy control computer system. The additional insulation and glazing is counted as an extra cost but the atrium, which is part of the energy saving system, is not counted as an extra cost because it is also the plant room. The payback period is estimated at 6 years.

The production area is double height and occupies the centre of the building. Offices and other facilities are arranged around it on the ground and first floor, in order to provide a strong link between all parts of the company. Rooflights provide natural lighting which is supplemented by task lighting. Fans recirculate air to prevent stratification. The louvres in the surrounding wall allow air to return to the atrium through the offices.

PERFORMANCE OF PASSIVE DESIGN

The building has functioned extremely well and has experienced very few problems.
Passive solar gains are making a significant contribution to the energy saving measures. The large area of south facing

high-tech image reflecting the nature of the company. The potential of the energy saving features designed by the architects has been fully realised by a client who is keen to promote the benefits of low energy design and is one of its leading exponents in Europe. To increase efficiency, the boilers have been kept small

Brick walls were a requirement of the planners who wanted the building to be sympathetic to the surrounding houses. The rooflights provide daylight and solar gains to offices and the internal production area.

AUXILIARY ENERGY USED

195,635 kWh was used for all purposes.

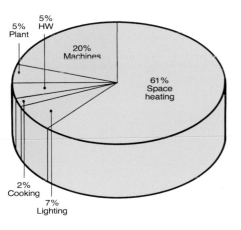

- 5% Plant
- 5% HW
- 20% Machines
- 61% Space heating
- 2% Cooking
- 7% Lighting

- Electricity
- Gas

The savings made on space heating make the use of energy for equipment more prominent.

The entrance area includes a covered porch and a draught lobby.

NET MONTHLY SPACE HEATING DEMAND AND SUPPLY

Solar gains provided 36% of the net space heating requirement.

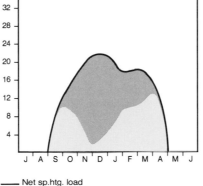

kWh 10³

- Net sp.htg. load
- Auxiliary energy
- Solar energy

COST OF ENERGY SAVING DESIGN

The whole building including energy saving measures cost £600,000 in 1983.

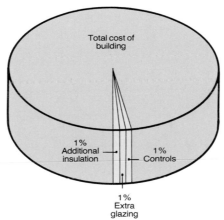

Total cost of building

- 1% Additional insulation
- 1% Controls
- 1% Extra glazing

The additional cost was 3% and the saving achieved worth about £3,000 a year.

AVERAGE TEMPERATURES

The temperature rose to unacceptable levels during the summer and external blinds have now been fitted to the south wall at first floor level.

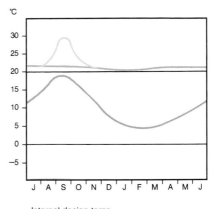

°C

- Internal design temp.
- Internal temp.
- Sunspace temp.
- External temp.

The atrium is a double height space. It contains the boiler and control equipment at ground floor level (see front cover photograph). Warm air is collected at high level and then ducted into the production space. When the warm air is not required it is ducted to the outside through the roof.

PROJECT DATA

Building

Building volume	7,100 m³
Floor area	2,087 m²
Roof area	1,316 m²
External wall area	800 m²
Window area: total	325 m²
south	235 m²

Atrium

Atrium volume	410 m³
Floor area	72 m²
Glass area: roof	10 m²
wall	36 m²

Cost	£600,000 (1983)

Thermal

U value: roof	0.36 W/m²K
floor	0.11 W/m²K
external walls	0.34 W/m²K
glazing	2.80 W/m²K
Mean U value	0.62 W/m²K
Global heat loss coefficient	2617 W/K
Infiltration rate	0.5 ac/h
External design temperature	0 °C
Heated floor area	1,899 m²
Heated volume	6,085 m³
Net heat load	57 kWh/m²

Site and climate

Altitude	75 m
Latitude	53°21 'N
Longitude	02°16 'W
Average ambient temp: Jan	4 °C
July	15.5 °C
Degree days (base 18.3°)	3158
Global irradiation	950 kWh/m²
Sunshine hours	1450 hrs

CASA TERMICAMENTE OPTIMIZADA CREDITS

Client
LNETI
National Laboratory for Engineering
and Industrial Technology
DER Department of Renewable Energies
Estrada do Paço do Lumiar
1600 LISBOA

Architects
Carlos Araujo
Santiago Boissel
Rua S.Joao Bosco 200 - 2a
4100 PORTO

Energy Engineers
Gab. Fluidos e Calor
Dep. Enga. Mechanica
Fac. Engenharia
Rua dos Bragas
4099 PORTO CODEX

Building Contractor
Engenheiros Associados
Mr. Rui Oliveira
R. Gouçalo Sampaio 379-4o
4000 PORTO

Services Contractor
Engenheiros Associados

Monitoring Organistion
LNETI and Dept. of Mechanical Engineering
Univ. of Porto

Commission of the European Communities

● Experimental design using traditional materials demonstrates that reasonable comfort conditions can be maintained with **no** fuel used for heating.

● When internal temperatures are to be maintained at constant levels, the design shows a 73% reduction in heating demand compared to a conventional house.

● Winter solar gains maximised by southern orientation of all rooms, Trombe walls, heat storage in heavy weight construction and water storage tubes.

● Overhangs, shutters, cross ventilation and large thermal mass prevent overheating in summer.

CASA TERMICAMENTE OPTIMIZADA

PORTO
PORTUGAL

Project Background

In size and in construction method, the Casa Laboratorio Termicamente Optimizada, is a typical Portuguese house. However, it has been designed to incorporate many energy saving features and has been built as an experimental house in order to assess the value of these features for new houses in Portugal.

DESIGN OBJECTIVES

The purpose of the project was to create a design for a 'typical' three-bedroom family house of 150m², which could be built either as a detached house or, with minor modifications, as a

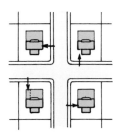

TYPICAL PLAN

TYPICAL ELEVATION

terraced house. The house was to be maintained in winter at or near comfortable temperature levels without the need for auxiliary heating or with only a minimal amount if the occupants required constant comfort levels. In common with most Portuguese houses, there was to be no central heating, and also no mechanical ventilation for summer cooling.

ENERGY SAVING FEATURES

● Orientation: the rooms face south and there are only two small windows on the north side.

● Shading: overhangs and shutters prevent excessive summer solar gains.

● Insulation: the house has exterior insulation, windows have wood frames with double glazing and draught-stripping. There is a mound of earth against the north side to provide shelter.

● Heat storage: the construction of the house is heavy weight and thermal storage is increased by vertical tubes filled with water, Trombe walls and a centrally placed masonry chimney. All of these absorb heat and re-radiate it at night.

● Natural ventilation: special ventilators in the north wall provide cross ventilation.

● Daylighting: rooflights provide natural light to stairs, corridor and dining room.

● Water heating: solar panels on the roof provide domestic hot water.

SITE AND CLIMATE

The house is within the grounds of the National Laboratory for Engineering and Industrial Technology in Porto which is the second largest city in Portugal. The climate is dry and sunny in summer, but being on the edge of the Atlantic, is cool and wet in winter.

CLIMATE

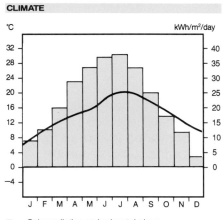

■ Solar radiation on horizontal plane
— Average external temp.

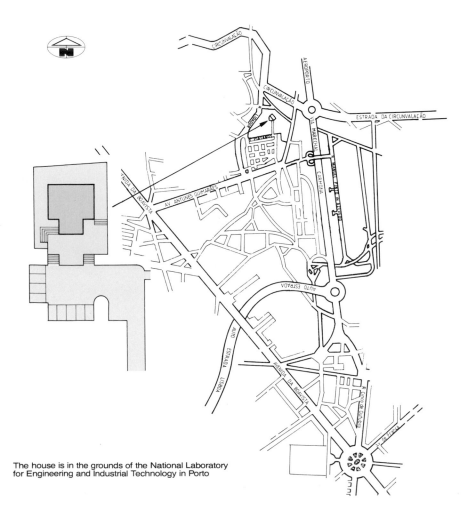

The house is in the grounds of the National Laboratory for Engineering and Industrial Technology in Porto

Design Details

The average minimum temperature in January is 4.7°C and the average maximum in July is 24.7°C. As there is a large daily swing in temperature in the summer (11°C on average),cooling by cross ventilation is available almost every day.

There are on average 1615 degree days per annum and 2667 sunshine hours (60% of the daylight hours).

The site has an unobstructed southern exposure and is protected from the north and west by other housing and large trees. There is a slight slope from east to west which required some earth moving during construction.

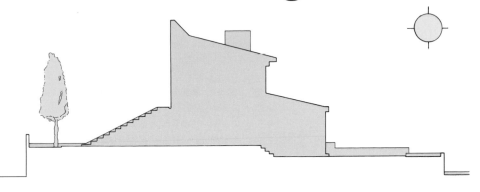

The house is orientated directly south, with excellent solar exposure.

around the main rooms. In the middle of the house where the living room, dining room and kitchen meet, is a central chimney which radiates heat to these three rooms and to two of the bedrooms above.

insulation below the slab and the first floor is precast concrete. The roof is finished with red clay tiles, the most common finish for Portugese roofs. All windows are double glazed and weather-stripped.

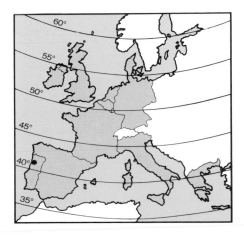

PLANNING

The house is built on an artificial mound, one metre above the surrounding area. The site section steps down from the north to the south, where there is a small car parking area. The living room is some 300mm below the rest of the ground floor on the same level as the terrace, which overlooks the parking area. The house therefore has excellent solar exposure, and its plan is wholly orientated to the south. There are only ventilation windows on the north side and small windows on the east and west. Main rooms face south and service areas are on the sides, providing a buffer zone

More than 80% of the glazing is on the south side. Solar panels on the roof provide domestic hot water.

CONSTRUCTION

The house has a precast concrete frame, with infill walls. Both exterior and interior walls are constructed of 200mm dense concrete blocks. The exterior walls, including the columns, are insulated on the outside with 50mm of expanded polystyrene beneath an exterior finish of sand/cement render. 50mm of polystyrene has also been laid above the bedroom ceilings.

The ground floor is a 150mm concrete slab with 25mm of

PASSIVE SOLAR DESIGN

Since the objective of the project was to eliminate the need for auxiliary heating, the house relies not only on direct gain to achieve this, but also on indirect gain in the form of a Trombe wall in each of the three bedrooms, and on thermal storage.

Direct gain is through the 16.2m² of south facing glazing, of which 4m² is in the bedrooms and 12.2m² is in the living room. Light coloured paving on the terrace increases solar gains by reflection.

Design Details

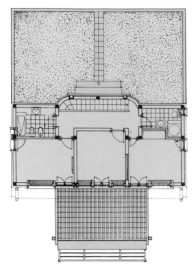

FIRST FLOOR

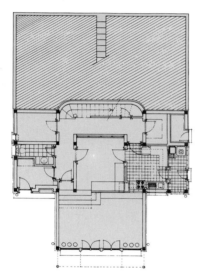

GROUND FLOOR

The living rooms and bedrooms are all located on the south side with service areas on the north.

Each bedroom has 1.3m² of window, and 2.5m² of Trombe wall in order to provide a delayed energy input and raise nightime ambient and radiant temperatures. These Trombe walls are constructed of 300mm thick concrete blocks with double glazing and a 50mm air gap. They have ventilators at the top and bottom and are fitted with roller shutters which provide shade in summer and insulation at night in winter.

Six 250mm diameter fibreglass water cylinders, each containing 180 litres of water, are located in the living room directly behind the windows, three on either side. These provide thermal mass within the room, absorbing the solar radiation falling directly on them in the daytime, for release in the evening. The thermal mass of the house is further increased by the dense concrete block walls, the massive central chimney and the concrete floor.

Summer overheating is controlled by the high thermal mass, shading and ventilation. The massive walls, chimney, floor and water filled cylinders in the living room, all moderate the temperature swings in the

Warm air from the solar wall panels circulates to the rooms and back via vents at the top and bottom.

house. Overhangs on all south facing windows, provide complete shading in summer whilst allowing full solar penetration in winter. Shutters are also provided on the windows. Cross ventilation is achieved by using the doors or windows and the ventilators in the north wall.

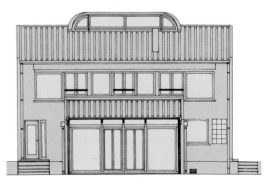

SOUTH ELEVATION

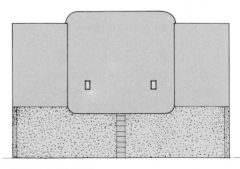

NORTH ELEVATION

There are only 0.2 sq.m of window on the north face

The inside view shows three of the six water filled heat storage cylinders to one side of the window.

OPERATING MODES

The house has had simulated occupation during two winters and has been run under two different strategies for each of them. The first was a free-floating regime without any auxiliary heating and the second a regime thermostatically controlled at 18°C. In either mode, all roller-shades were opened in the morning and closed at sunset. All the windows were kept closed most of the time.

In summer, the roller-shades over the Trombe walls and water cylinders were kept permanently closed and all others were opened enough to provide natural daylighting adequate for normal working conditions (reading, writing, etc). Cooling cross-ventilation was enhanced at night whenever the outdoor temperature fell below indoor temperature, by opening the two small windows in the north wall and a window in the south facade.

AUXILIARY HEATING SYSTEMS

The main auxiliary heating system is a fireplace located in the living room. It draws air from the outside through a duct which is normally closed except during combustion.
The fireplace is in the middle of the house, away from exterior walls, and thus its chimney acts as a radiant panel for the kitchen and the dining room, and for two of the upstairs bedrooms.

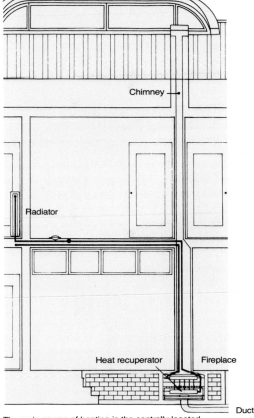

The main source of heating is the centrally located fireplace.

The third bedroom is also heated by the fireplace through a pumped water circulation system, which is thermostatically controlled by a sensor in the fireplace.
Each of the main rooms (living/dining room downstairs and bedrooms upstairs) also has a 1.5kW electric heater for use when heat is needed and the fireplace is not in operation. Water heating is provided by solar panels and by an electric heater.

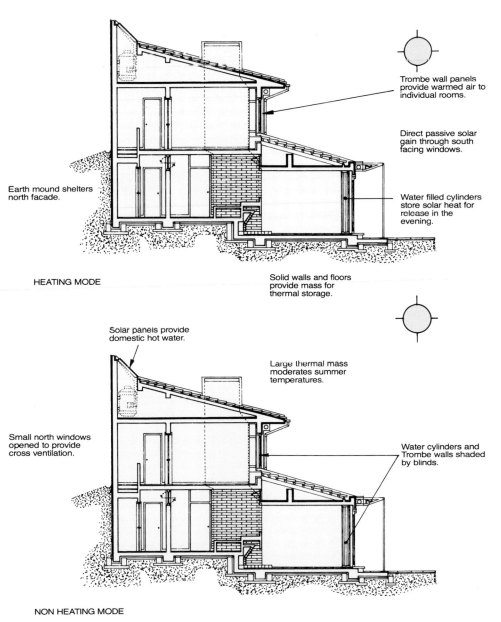

Trombe wall panels provide warmed air to individual rooms.

Direct passive solar gain through south facing windows.

Earth mound shelters north facade.

Water filled cylinders store solar heat for release in the evening.

HEATING MODE

Solid walls and floors provide mass for thermal storage.

Solar panels provide domestic hot water.

Large thermal mass moderates summer temperatures.

Small north windows opened to provide cross ventilation.

Water cylinders and Trombe walls shaded by blinds.

NON HEATING MODE

Performance Evaluation

MONITORING

The house was monitored with simulated occupation for two whole years. Measurements included indoor temperatures room by room, outdoor weather conditions (temperature, relative humidity, wind and solar radiation) and energy consumption by room and by type of use, all on an hourly basis.

Temperatures were measured with both thermocouples and Pt 100 probes.

All data were collected through an HP 3045A data acquisition system which was controlled by an HP 9816 micro computer.

USER RESPONSE

The environment inside the house was liked by users, and the house was considered easy

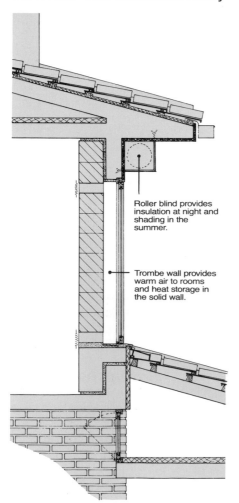

Roller blind provides insulation at night and shading in the summer.

Trombe wall provides warm air to rooms and heat storage in the solid wall.

Inside the room, two ducts allow the warmed air to circulate through the room

to run. No unusual difficulties were encountered compared to other houses, temperature control by roller-blinds and opening windows for natural ventilation is common in other Portuguese houses.

The outside appearance was considered poor by most people, but most liked the inside, especially the natural daylighting. This enters not only through the large south facing windows, but also through two skylights on the roof, illuminating the stairs and landing, and through glass tiles in the roof over the dining room.

PERFORMANCE OF PASSIVE SYSTEMS

● In the winter of 1984-85 with the house in the free-floating temperature regime, i.e. with no auxiliary heating, the average indoor temperature was 15°C in the coldest month (January), with 13°C lows during only 35 scattered hours.

● In the winter of 1985-86, with the house thermostatically controlled at 18°C, solar energy supplied 45% of the space heating, in spite of an unusually severe winter (degree days 6% higher than average, solar radiation 9% lower than average).

● Compared to a conventional house, the Casa Termicamente Optimizada used 73% less energy for heating. (Temperature controlled at 18°C).

● Space heating accounted for 36% of the total energy consumed. Appliances accounted for 49% and water heating only 6%. The equipment figure is thought to be high because the house was being monitored.

● The Trombe wall panels worked well but the water filled cylinders were not considered very effective since their thermal mass was small compared to that of the house.

COST EFFECTIVENESS

The house, being an experimental house incorporating many passive features, was relatively expensive compared with the average house. However, many of the features such as the re-distribution of glazing, shading and ventilation are all items which do not involve additional cost. No figures are available for costs.

The builder of the house claims that he could build another house to the same specification for a cost similar to that for a typical 'quality built' house.

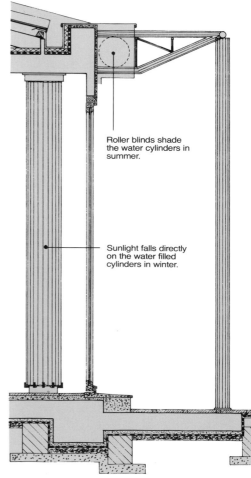

Roller blinds shade the water cylinders in summer.

Sunlight falls directly on the water filled cylinders in winter.

Section through the southern living space shows the water filled cylinders directly behind the windows.

COMPARISON WITH CONVENTIONAL DESIGN

The energy measures saved a total of 73% of the energy used by a typical Portuguese house.

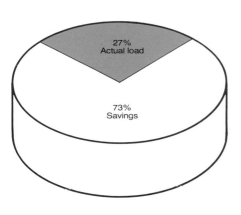

In addition, control of summer overheating was much better than in conventional housing

CONTRIBUTION TO HEATING

Despite a colder winter than normal, solar energy supplied 46% of the space heating load in 1985/86.

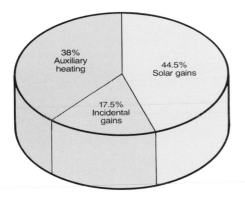

AUXILIARY FUEL USED

The auxiliary fuels used were electricity and solid fuel for the central fireplace.

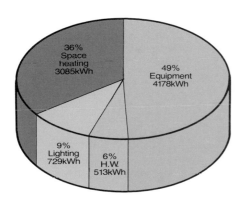

MONTHLY SPACE HEATING DEMAND AND SUPPLY

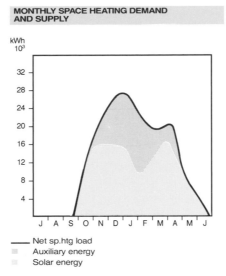

Net sp.htg load
Auxiliary energy
Solar energy

MONTHLY AVERAGE TEMPERATURES

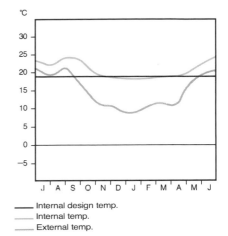

Internal design temp.
Internal temp.
External temp.

Occupants liked the inside of the building, particularly the daylighting but were less appreciative of the external appearance.

PROJECT DATA

House

Volume	326 m³	
Floor area	145 m²	
Roof area	96 m²	
External wall area	164 m²	(excl. window area)
Window area: total	20 m²	10% of wall area
south	16.2 m²	8% of wall area
north	0.2 m²	
Trombe walls	7.5 m²	

Thermal Characteristics

U value: roof	0.4 W/m²K
floor perimeter	0.95 W/mK
external walls	0.6 W/m²K
Windows	
without roller shade	3.1 W/m²K
with roller shade	2.3 W/m²K
Mean U value	0.71 W/m²K
Global heat loss coefficient	330 W/K
Infiltration rate	0.3 to 0.9 ach (depending on wind)

External design temperature	−1°C
Heated floor area	70 m²
Heated volume	176 m³
Net heat load	0.35 GJ/m²
	96 kWh/m²

Site and climate

Altitude	sea level
Latitude	41.1°N
Longitude	8.7°W
Average ambient temp: Jan	8.5°C
July	20.5°C
Degree days (base 18°)	1615
Global irradiation on horiz.	5312 MJ/m²
Sunshine hours	2667

Cost

Building: Local currency	6 million P.Esc
	- 37500 ECU
Solar features (estimated)	10%

LA SALUT CREDITS

Client
Community of owners

Architects
Francesc Rius i Camps,
c/ Sant Cugat, 1-3, F.
08024 Barcelona

Contractor
E.G.O.E.S.A.
(No longer in business)

Services Contractor
Instalaciones Lafe,
C/Feliv, 30,
08026 Barcelona

Monitoring
Direccio Gral. d'Energia,
Dept, d'Industria i Energia,
Generalitat de Catalunya,
Diagonal, 449, 7th Floor,
08036 Barcelona

Escola Tecnica Superior d'Arquitectura del Valles,
Universitat Politecnica de Catalunya,
PO box 508, Terrassa,
Barcelona

Commission of the European Communities

● Narrow fronted, four storey terraced houses demonstrate the advantages of combining passive solar gain, thermal storage and high levels of insulation.

● Passive solar gains provide 67% of the annual space heating load.

● Full width, two storey sunspace provides warm air which circulates through the house in a convective loop.

● The sunspace provides a private interior/exterior space on a densely populated, overlooked site.

LA SALUT

BARCELONA
CATALUNYA SPAIN

Project Background

La Salut is a project of six, 4 storey terraced houses in Barcelona. They are sited on a south facing hillside and have a two storey sunspace attached to the front of each house to provide passive solar gains and an amenity for the inhabitants.

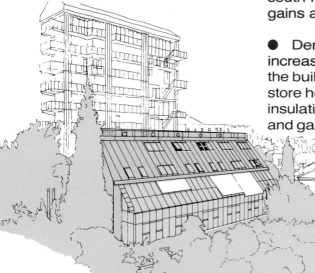

DESIGN OBJECTIVES

The client was a building co-operative whose brief was simply to provide six, 4/5 person houses. The architect, who was to be a future inhabitant, decided to take advantage of the site and incorporate passive solar and energy saving features into the design, within the approved cost limits. An additional objective was therefore to provide some useful experience for passive solar design in future and to draw conclusions on the cost effectiveness of the design. As the district is densely populated, and the site overlooked, another aim was to provide as much privacy as possible, yet have a communal landscaped garden. This led to a decision to attach sunspaces to the houses to provide a private interior/exterior transition space between house and garden, and which could also act as passive solar collectors.

ENERGY SAVING FEATURES

● South orientation of the terrace and internal planning to place principal rooms on the south side.

● Sunspace attached to south face to provide solar gains and additional insulation.

● Dense construction to increase the thermal mass of the building and thus its ability to store heat, with high levels of insulation in the roof, north wall and gable wall.

● Solar gains circulated to other parts of house by warm air operating in a convective loop from the sunspace up through the house and back down the stairway.

● Shading by the use of roller blinds to prevent excess gains.

SITE AND CLIMATE

The site is in the La Salut district of Barcelona which is characterised by narrow sloping streets and a curvilinear layout. The rectangular site, which is 1200m^2 in area, is carved out of the hillside in a series of terraces. The six houses have been built on the highest terrace, and have panoramic views across Barcelona toward the sea on the south side. On the north side, they are protected by the vertical face of the hill and by a tall block of flats.

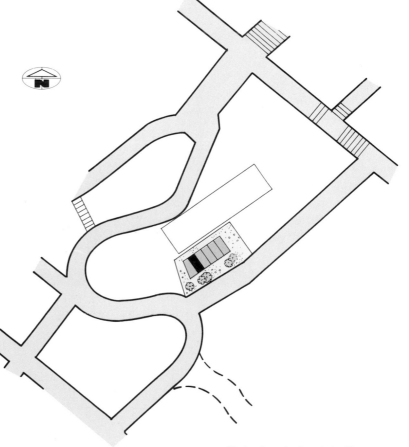

The local area is characterised by steep narrow streets in a curvilinear layout.

Design Details

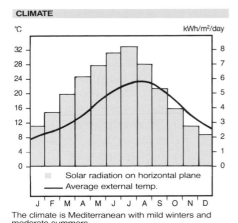

CLIMATE

The climate is Mediterranean with mild winters and moderate summers.

With the Mediterranean Sea in front, a protective range of 400-500m high hills at the rear and a river on either side, Barcelona has a climate of mild winters, and summers with moderate temperatures but relatively high humidity. The average annual temperature is 15.9°C, with a fluctuation of 32°C between the annual minimum and maximum. There are 1235 degree days (18°C base).

The microclimate is very favourable for solar design, the site is unobstructed to the south and sheltered on the north. Temperatures between 0.6°C and 2.1°C higher than those of the nearest weather station have been observed.

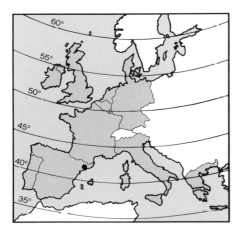

PLANNING

Having sited the terrace at the top of the sloping site to obtain the best views and solar exposure, the space at the rear (north) side of the terrace is very constricted. As the frontage of the houses is quite narrow, the habitable rooms have been placed on the outside, and the bathroom and staircase in the centre. This gives a layout in which little space is wasted in circulation areas.

On the second and third floors the roof slopes back on both north and south sides. On the north side, this has the advantage that the rooflights provide more light into the bedrooms at the rear where the cliff face and flats overlook the terrace. On the south side, the effect is to reduce the apparent height of the building as seen from the garden. This effect is enhanced by the double height sunspace which has both the ground and first floors opening onto it, giving the appearance of being only one storey. This play in proportions is also evident on the north elevation, where each level has a different material on the outside.

CONSTRUCTION

The construction is basically traditional with a timber pitched roof, and masonry cavity walls. However, more insulation is used than is normal and the south wall at the rear of the sunspace is 100mm thick concrete in order to increase the thermal storage capacity of this part of the building. Part of the north wall and the roof have an outer covering of 30mm polyurethane metal sandwich panels. Internally, all the north wall has 40mm of polystyrene insulation and the roof has 20mm of polystyrene with a 70mm air space. The floors are 230mm concrete on corrugated metal sheets. The sunspace is made of a

The sunspaces are carefully designed and integrated into the overall structure.

galvanised steel frame with 6mm single glazing. The timber rooflights are double glazed and are fitted with opaque blinds.

PASSIVE SOLAR DESIGN

There are four aspects to the passive solar design:-

● Direct gain;
● Sunspace;
● Convective loop for distribution of the warm air;
● Thermal mass.

Direct gain takes place through the doors and windows which open into the sunspace and through the windows of the upper two floors which are set at 45° in the roof.
The two storey sunspace

Design Details

The central, stairway forms the return air path in the convective heating loop.

GROUND FLOOR

FIRST FLOOR

SECOND FLOOR

THIRD FLOOR

extends over the complete width of the houses, and has a vertical section beneath the 45° roof. Single glazing is used and the floor and walls provide thermal storage. There are vents at the top of the sunspace for distribution of the warm air.

A convective loop is set up to distribute the heat around the house, the warmed air in the sunspace rising to the top and passing through the open windows of the upper floor. The air circulates from the upper rooms down the central stairway and back along the ground floor and through the door into the sunspace. Further convective loops can also be induced by opening vents from the sunspace to the upper two floors, again using the central stairs for the return air.

Thermal mass is provided in the floors (230mm concrete), the south facing wall (100mm concrete) and the internal walls. There is 6.5m³ of thermal mass within the sunspace, on

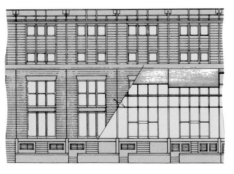

SOUTH ELEVATION
The roof slopes back on the second and first floors, reducing the apparent height of the building.

NORTH ELEVATION
This effect is enhanced on the north side by the use of different material for the first storey.

which the sun falls directly and a further 80m³ of mass within the house.

Overheating in summer is controlled in a number of ways. Blinds within the sunspace reduce the heat entering and manually opened vents in the roof of the sunspace, together with the doors, provide ventilation. The house is ventilated by opening the kitchen windows (north face) and the attic skylights thus producing air movement via the stairs. The high thermal mass of the house also moderates summer temperatures.

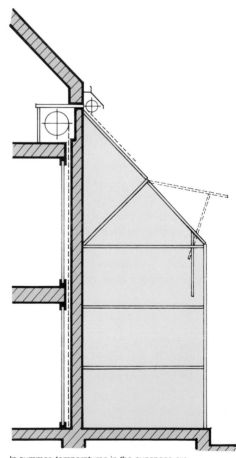

In summer, temperatures in the sunspace are controlled by external blinds and vents in the roof, in conjunction with open doors and windows below.

AUXILIARY HEATING SYSTEMS

Four houses have conventional gas boilers and radiators, with two different heating zones, one for the north side and the other for the south side. Apart from a thermostat on the boiler, all control is manual. The other two houses have electric panel heaters controlled by individual thermostats.

OPERATING MODES

When heating is required, the blinds in the sunspace are raised and the internal doors and windows are opened to make the convective loop. The damper between the sunspace and the upper two floors can also be opened to allow warm air to circulate to the top of the house. The doors and windows (and the damper) are closed at night to stop reverse circulation.

In summer, during the daytime, the sunspace is isolated from the house by closing the interconnecting doors and windows. The blinds in the sunspace are drawn and the external doors and roof vents opened. The attic skylights are opened and a through draught induced from the north side by opening the kitchen windows. At night, the doors and windows to the sunspace can be opened to provide cross ventilation.

CONTROLS

All control over passive solar gain, ventilation and the auxiliary heating system is manual, with the exception of the boiler thermostat and the electric heater thermostats. The gas heating systems provide separate zone control (again manually operated) for the north and south sides of the houses, to maximise the use of the solar gains.

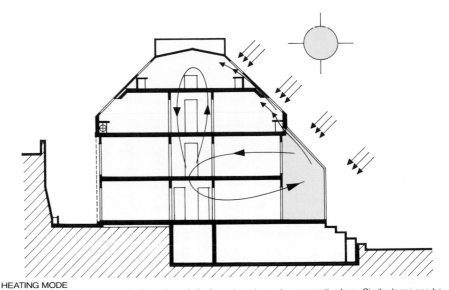

HEATING MODE
Warmed air from the sunspace circulates through the lower two storeys in a convective loop. Similar loops can be set up in the two upper storeys.

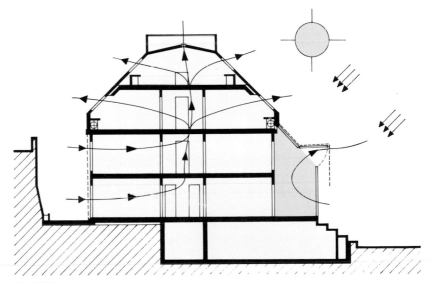

COOLING MODE
The sunspace is isolated from the house. Cool air is drawn up from the north face of the house to be exhausted through the skylights.

The sunspace forms an extension to the living room on the ground floor.

Performance Evaluation

MONITORING

One of the gas heated, middle terrace, houses was monitored over a period of 8 months from October 1985 to June 1986. Continuous recordings of temperatures were made outside and at five points inside the house, together with readings of gas and electric meters. A heat meter recorded the auxiliary heating used. Intermittent measurements have also been made with additional temperature probes, a solarimeter and two anemometers.

suffered from slow response and poor control, which has lead to a certain amount of discomfort for occupants. The electric systems installed in the other two houses are thought to be more satisfactory.
In general, the need for manual control of both the passive systems and the auxiliary heating system, has caused some problems for occupants.

PERFORMANCE OF PASSIVE SYSTEMS

The thermal performance of the overall design proved to be better than originally predicted:-

However the upper convective loop, in which warm air passes from the sunspace through the duct to the upper two storeys did not work well. The air flow through the duct was demonstrated early on in the monitoring to be very small and so the damper on the duct was left closed and only the lower convective loop was used to distribute the warm air.

COMPARISON WITH CONVENTIONAL DESIGN
The design uses 87% less energy compared to a conventional design.

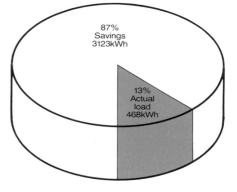

87%
Savings
3123kWh

13%
Actual
load
468kWh

CONTRIBUTION TO ANNUAL SPACE HEATING DEMAND
The solar contribution to the total space heating demand was 67%.

Opening the door and windows into the sunspace allows the circulation of warmed air into the house.

USER RESPONSE

The response from the occupants towards the design of the house has been generally favourable. The two main areas of concern have been some overheating in summer and the auxiliary heating system.
The shading in the sunspace was considered inadequate and could be improved, and more ventilation is needed to reduce peak temperatures and thus improve comfort.
The gas heating installed in the four houses was a conventional system and

● The solar contribution to the total heating load was 67%;

● Compared to a conventional design, the house saved 87% of the auxiliary heating load.

The good performance of the house is believed to be due to a combination of:-

● High insulation standards;
● Well distributed thermal mass;
● The well defined convective loop to distribute the solar gains.

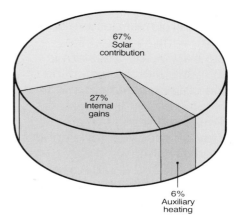

67%
Solar
contribution

27%
Internal
gains

6%
Auxiliary
heating

AUXILIARY FUEL USED

The fuel used for space heating was very low at 7% of the total fuel used

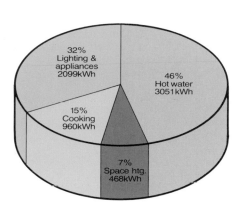

32% Lighting & appliances 2099kWh
46% Hot water 3051kWh
15% Cooking 960kWh
7% Space htg. 468kWh

NET MONTHLY SPACE HEATING DEMAND AND SUPPLY

Solar gain supplied most of the net heating load.

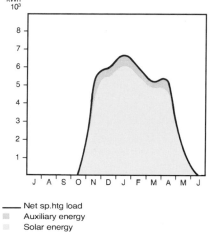

— Net sp.htg load
▢ Auxiliary energy
▢ Solar energy

MONTHLY AVERAGE TEMPERATURES

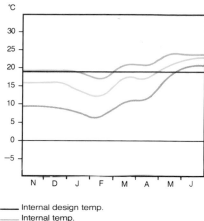

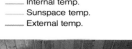
— Internal design temp.
— Internal temp.
— Sunspace temp.
— External temp.

COST OF BUILDING AND SOLAR DESIGN

Total cost 8m PTA — 1982 prices. The additional costs of the solar features only account for 6% of the total cost.

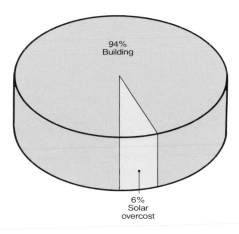

94% Building
6% Solar overcost

COST EFFECTIVENESS

The passive solar features, the sunspace and the increased thickness of concrete wall, cost 500 000 pesetas (3704 ECU's) on top of the basic house cost of 8M pesetas (59 260 ECU's). The annual saving in gas was 19 654 MJ, for the monitoring house, worth 37 207 pesetas, giving a simple payback period of 13 years. Taking into account the amenity value of the sunspace, the payback period is very reasonable.
If the original project had used the electric panel system instead of the gas system, the saving in capital cost would have almost equalled the cost of the passive measures.

The attic is lit by skylights in both north and south sides.

PROJECT DATA (Monitored house)

House
Volume	445.00 m³
Floor area	174.30 m²
Roof area	66.80 m²
External wall area	22.20 m²
Window area: total	11.60 m²
south	3.30 m²

Sunspace
Volume	54.00 m³
Floor area	11.30 m²
Glass area: roof	15.80 m²
wall	16.20 m²
Effective aperture	27.30 m²

Thermal Characteristics
U value: roof	0.34 W/m²K
floor	0.64 W/m²K
external walls	0.38 W/m²K
Windows	3.00 W/m²K
Conservatory glazing	5.70 W/m²K
Mean U value	1.40 W/m²K
Global heat loss coefficient	255.00 W/K
Infiltration rate	0.50 ach

External design temperature	3.00 °C
Heated floor area	174.30 m²
Heated volume	445.00 m³
Annual net heat load	0.107 GJ/m²
	(29.7 kWh/m²)

Site and climate
Altitude	40 m
Latitude	41°N
Longitude	0°W
Average ambient temp: Jan	7.5°C
June	20.8°C
Degree days (base 18°C)	1235 days
Global irradiation on horiz.	5266 MJ/m²/yr
	(1463 kWh/m²)
Sunshine hours	2439 hr/year

Costs
Building	Ptas 8,000,000	ECU 59,260
Solar features	Ptas 500,000	ECU 3,704

LES BASSES FOUASSIERES PROJECT CREDITS

Client
S.A.H.L.M. Le Val De Loire
13, Rue Bouche Thomas - Zac Sud
49000 Angers

Architects
C. Parant J.R. Mazaud A. Enard
S'pace S.A. 4, Rue D'Arcueil
94250 Gentilly

Site Architect
P. Mornet
45, Rue La Fontaine - BP 755
49007 Angers cedex

Energy Consultant
M. Cabanat - B. Sesolis
72, Rue Pixecourt
75020 Paris

Services Engineer
B.E.T. Ertib (A. Kantardjian)
112, Rue De Charenton
75012 Paris

Heating Plumbing Mechanical Ventilation Electricity
Etablissements Sipec,
41, Rue Alberic Dubois
49000 Angers

Shell Construction (Concrete Works)
Entreprise Bonnel
3, Rue Du Stade
49330 Chateauneuf Sur Sarthe

Carpenter
Entreprise Brechet
49370 Saint-Clement De La Place

Services Contractor
Technical Checking (Bureau De Controle)
Socotec Angers
122 Rue Du Chateau D'Orgemont - BP 1040
49000 Angers

Urban Office (Amenageur)
Sodemel
11, Avenue Turpin De Crime - BP 2445
49024 Angers Cedex

Monitoring Organisation
Centre D'Etudes Techniques De L'Equipment De
L'Ouest (C.E.T.E.)
Laboratoire Regional D'Angers
23, Rue De L'Amiral Chauvin BP66
49135 Les Ponts-De-Ce Cedex

Commission of the European Communities

● A combination of passive solar features in an estate of houses reduces heating bills by 37%.

● Careful design ensures that all main rooms face south for direct solar gain. 90% of glazing is on the south facade.

● A two storey sunspace with internal balcony, provides a pleasant living space and warmed ventilation air to the whole house.

● Trombe wall panels provide heated ventilation air directly to living rooms and bedrooms.

LES BASSES FOUASSIERES

ANGERS
FRANCE

Project Background

Les Basses Fouassieres is a development of twenty seven, 3 and 4 bedroom family houses, constructed in short terraces, each one incorporating a two storey sunspace and Trombe wall panels.

OBJECTIVES

The project stemmed from an architectural competition to build low energy housing. The client, an organisation providing low rent accommodation, required high comfort housing, with a 50% reduction in fuel use when compared to a house of the same volume, with standard thermal loss and typical distribution of windows. A pleasant environment, good facilities and high levels of comfort were considered more important than strict economic requirements, a budget of 40,000 French francs (£4,000 approximately) per dwelling being allowed for the innovative features.

orientations between south-east and south-west. 90% of the window area is on the south facade.

● Two storey sunspaces provide insulation and solar heated ventilation air to the principal rooms, by direct connections. The solid walls between the sunspace and the rooms act as a thermal store.
● Trombe wall panels are also provided, fixed to the outside of the south facing solid concrete wall, with ducts and a mechanical ventilation system supplying the warmed air to the adjacent rooms, and bathrooms and toilets.

SITE AND CLIMATE

The site lies in a new suburb to the west of Angers, a town 300 kilometres south-west of Paris. It has an elongated form, from north to south and slopes gently down to the east. The site is protected on the west side by mature trees 10 metres high and on the east has views over the old town of Angers and the adjacent lake, the 'Lac du Maine'.
The area has a moderate climate, typical of the Loire valley and is approximately 15 metres above sea level. It suffers from no unusual weather conditions.
The average ambient temperature in January is 5°C, and in July 18.4°C, with 2610 degree days (18°C base).
There are 2000 hours of sunshine per year, with a mean global irradiation of 1374 kWh/m².

The houses have a flexible layout giving variety while maximising solar aperture.

ENERGY SAVING FEATURES

● All main rooms, including all the bedrooms, benefit from direct solar gain, having

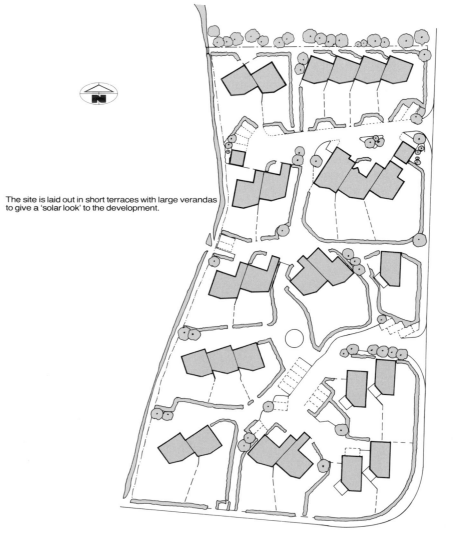

The site is laid out in short terraces with large verandas to give a 'solar look' to the development.

Design Details

CLIMATE

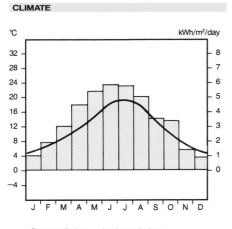

°C / kWh/m²/day

Legend:
- Solar radiation on horizontal plane
- Average external temp.

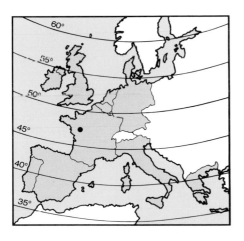

CONSTRUCTION

The basic construction is traditional, with 200mm external walls of concrete block with 100mm of polystyrene insulation externally, and roof insulated with 160mm of glassfibre, under a natural slate finish.

The only unusual structural feature is the south facing wall. This is constructed of 300mm poured concrete to act as a solar heat store within the sunspace and the Trombe wall panels which cover a large part of the south elevation.

PASSIVE SOLAR DESIGN

There are three passive solar aspects - the direct gain through the windows, the sunspace and the Trombe wall panels.

90% of the glazing in the house is located on the south side, with the remainder on the north side. Thus all the main rooms (being located on the south side of the house) benefit from the maximum direct solar gain without increasing the total amount of glazing in the house above typical levels. Heat loss on the north side is thus also

The Trombe walls are painted in dark colours to harmonize with the inside of the sunspace.

PLANNING

The site was layed out as a mixture of detached and semi-detached houses, and short terraces of three and four houses, to allow all houses to face south. There are three sizes of house, (with 4, 5 and 6 main rooms) but a total of 14 different plans arranged so that all main rooms were located on the south sides. Stairs and storerooms are located on the north side to act as a buffer. External garages are also located on the north side to gain maximum benefit from the insulating effect.

Exposed areas of the south wall are externally insulated with 100mm of polystyrene. All windows are double glazed in wood frames, but the sunspace is single glazed. A mechanical ventilation system is used to distribute the heat gains around the house, and can be used for cooling in the summer.

minimised.

The south facing sunspace covers the full height of the house, two storeys, and has direct access to the living rooms and bedrooms. Some of the bedrooms open onto a balcony within the sunspace, and the whole provides an extra, interconnecting living space. The mechanical ventilation system distributes

Design Details

the heat entering the main rooms to other parts of the house.

The vertical part of the sunspace consists of aluminium glazing bars fixed to a wooden frame, which gives an average area of 34 square metres of single glazing. The roof of the sunspace is a continuation of the roof of the main house and thus, being opaque, gives some protection from overheating in summer. The 300mm thick concrete wall between the house and the sunspace acts as a heat store, as does the solid floor, which is covered with sandstone flags. Heat stored during the daytime is slowly released into the house at night.

Heat reflective, insulated blinds were provided on both the windows and the walls of the sunspace. The window blinds are used to reduce heat loss at night in the heating season and the wall blinds reduce the loss of stored heat from the wall into the sunspace at night.

Summer overheating is prevented by natural ventilation, achieved by louvred vents at the top of the

The single storey Trombe wall panels supply heated air to the adjacent rooms.

sunspace and by manually opening the doors and windows.

The Trombe wall panels (or solar wall collectors) are vertical, single storey, single glazed panels, attached to the massive south facing wall of the house, with a 90mm air gap between the glazing and the wall. Air entering through automatically controlled vents at the bottom of the panel, is heated by the greenhouse effect and rises through 75mm sloping holes into the adjacent rooms. The mechanical

ventilation system then draws this warmed air to the bathroom and toilet.

The inside of the collector is painted a dark colour to harmonise with the other paintwork and to improve heat absorption. Reflecting roller blinds are used inside the collector both at night to reduce heat loss and in summer to prevent overheating.

Approximately 10 square metres of collector is provided in each house, with different panels supplying ground and upper floors.

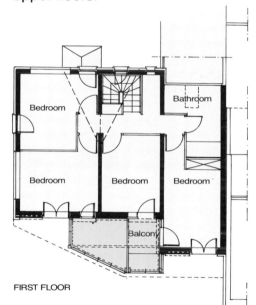

FIRST FLOOR

The sunspace provides an additional interconnecting living space.

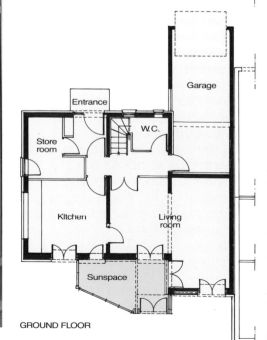

GROUND FLOOR

All living rooms face in a southerly direction.

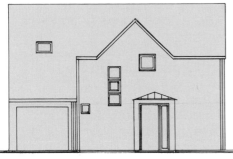

NORTH ELEVATION
Less than 10% of the glazing is on the north elevation.

In the summer the blinds are lowered as required, to keep the sun from the sunspace and Trombe walls, reducing the heat gain in the house. Positive venting of the sunspace is achieved by louvre vents at the top and by opening the doors and windows as necessary.
The mechanical ventilation system can also be reversed to provide summer ventilation.

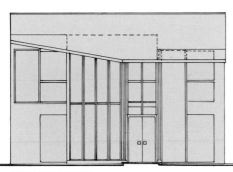

SOUTH ELEVATION
90% of the glazing is on the south side.

AUXILIARY HEATING SYSTEMS

Auxiliary heating is provided by thermostatically-controlled electric convectors in all rooms. A maximum-load reducing controller is incorporated to cut off the bedroom heaters if the total load exceeds 12kW.

OPERATING MODES

In winter, in the daytime all blinds are raised to allow the sun to enter the sunspace and the Trombe wall panels. The vents at the bottom of the Trombe walls open automatically when the temperature is high enough to provide useful heating in the house, and warm air passes into the house. In the evening, the roller blinds on the windows of the sunspace and inside the Trombe wall panels are lowered to reduce the loss of stored heat. The reflective blind on the wall inside the sunspace is also lowered to reduce heat loss from the massive wall to the conservatory.

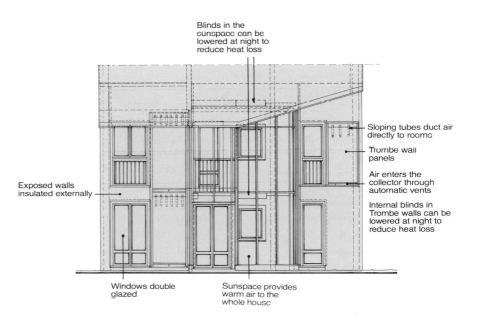

Blinds in the sunspace can be lowered at night to reduce heat loss

Sloping tubes duct air directly to rooms

Trombe wall panels

Air enters the collector through automatic vents

Internal blinds in Trombe walls can be lowered at night to reduce heat loss

Exposed walls insulated externally

Windows double glazed

Sunspace provides warm air to the whole house

SOUTH ELEVATION
— Heating mode

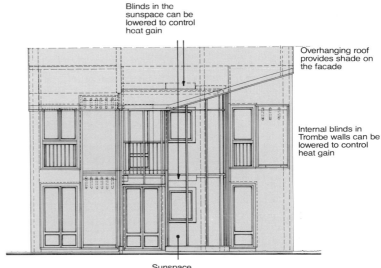

Blinds in the sunspace can be lowered to control heat gain

Overhanging roof provides shade on the facade

Internal blinds in Trombe walls can be lowered to control heat gain

Sunspace

SOUTH ELEVATION
— Non-heating mode

Performance Evaluation

MONITORING

Monitoring was carried out between October 1983 and May 1985, with data recorded on a micro-computer located in a garage on the site. Half hourly measurements were made of:- electricity consumption; auxiliary heating consumption; hot water consumption; mechanical ventilation electricity consumption; internal house temperature; temperatures in the sunspace and in the wall between the sunspace and the house; and the heating contribution from the Trombe wall panels.

Temperature sensors were originally placed in the mechanical ventilation system but since it was found that occupiers were frequently not using the mechanical system, the sensors were moved to corridors or bedrooms.

A weather station was set up on the site and half hourly recordings were made of external temperatures, solar radiation and wind speed and direction.

Inhabitants liked the sunspaces and made full use of them.

USER RESPONSE

A questionnaire was distributed to the inhabitants and 16 were completed.

The occupiers generally liked their houses and found the temperatures comfortable. The sunspaces were well liked and well used as an extra living space for dining and sitting, and many people grew plants in them. Of the people who returned the questionnaires, nearly half felt that their fuel bills were low, and most of the remainder felt them to be normal. Three quarters expressed the desire to live in another 'solar house', if they ever moved.

The design and use of the roller blinds caused problems and, particularly in the Trombe walls, the occupants did not seem to use them correctly. Many became damaged and inoperable, and it is accepted that a revised system is needed.

In general terms, the occupiers appreciated the southerly orientation, the insulation of the structure and the sunspace, but did not perceive the Trombe walls as 'real solar collectors'. Difficulty in operating the internal blinds correctly may well have contributed to this lack of enthusiasm.

Occupiers thought the houses looked 'curious and (even) unattractive' from the outside, though the sunspace did indicate the houses were 'solar houses' and different from 'normal houses'. The internal appearance of the houses was much better liked.

PERFORMANCE OF THE PASSIVE SOLAR FEATURES

● Solar gains contributed 31% of the total space heating requirement, incidental gains another 16% and auxiliary heating 53%.

● The solar gains thus reduced the space heating bill by 37%.

● Temperatures in the sunspace averaged 8°C higher than the external temperature on cold sunny days, and 5°C higher on cold overcast days. The temperature gradient between the floor and roof of the sunspace varied between 1.3°C on cold days to 3.5°C on hot days.

However, some aspects of the design were not successful:-

● The provision of the thermally massive south wall of the house was very costly and not as effective as the designers had hoped.

● The use of manually operated blinds for reducing heat loss at night was not a success, many became damaged in use and partly because of this, the occupants did not make proper use of them.

● For these reasons, the useful solar gain was not as high as predicted by the designers.

ENERGY FLOW

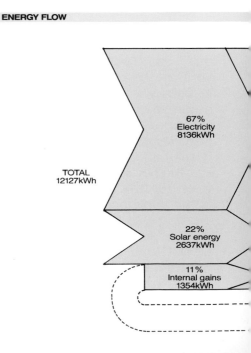

TOTAL
12127kWh

67%
Electricity
8136kWh

22%
Solar energy
2637kWh

11%
Internal gains
1354kWh

CONTRIBUTIONS TO ANNUAL SPACE HEATING DEMAND

Annual gross heating load for the average house at Les Basses Fouassieres is 8430 kWh (30.3 GJ).

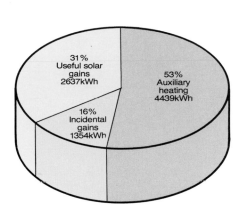

- 31% Useful solar gains 2637kWh
- 16% Incidental gains 1354kWh
- 53% Auxiliary heating 4439kWh

Solar gain reduced the heating bill by 37%.

MONTHLY SPACE HEATING DEMAND AND SUPPLY

kWh 10³

- ——— Net sp.htg load
- ▉ Auxiliary energy
- ▢ Solar energy

MONTHLY AVERAGE TEMPERATURES

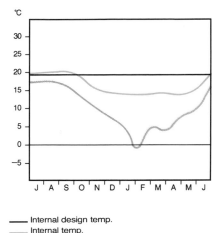

°C

- ——— Internal design temp.
- ——— Internal temp.
- ——— External temp.

AUXILIARY FUEL USED

Annual auxiliary fuel used per house at Les Basses Fouassieres is 8136 kWh (29.3 GJ).

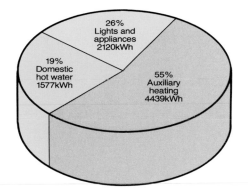

- 26% Lights and appliances 2120kWh
- 19% Domestic hot water 1577kWh
- 55% Auxiliary heating 4439kWh

COST EFFECTIVENESS

● The simple payback time for the whole package of passive solar measures is estimated at 13.6 years. This does not take into account the additional amenity value of the sunspace.

● The solar measures cost 40,000 French francs, adding 10% to the cost of the houses.

● The typical annual saving on the fuel bill for a family, is nearly 3000 French francs, a saving of around 37%.

COST OF ENERGY SAVING MEASURES

The total cost per house at Les Basses Fouassieres was FF 439,300.

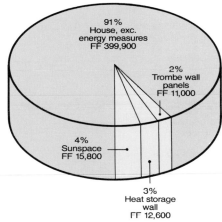

- 91% House, exc. energy measures FF 399,900
- 2% Trombe wall panels FF 11,000
- 4% Sunspace FF 15,800
- 3% Heat storage wall FF 12,600

FF40,000 were allowed for the extra cost of the passive solar measures.

- 18% lighting & Appliances 2120kWh
- 13% Domestic hot water 1577kWh
- 69% Heating 8430kWh

PROJECT DATA

House (5 room)

Volume	251.50 m³	
Floor area	60.00 m²	
Roof area	57.80 m²	
External wall area	145.60 m²	(excl. window area)
Window area: total	23.80 m²	16% of wall area
south	21.20 m²	90% of wall area
north	2.60 m²	10% of wall area

Sunspace

Floor area	12.00 m²
Wall glass area	34.00 m²

Site and climate

Altitude	15 m
Latitude	47°5′N
Longitude	1°36′W
Average ambient temp: Jan	5°C
July	18.4°C
Degree days (base 18°)	2610
Global irradiation on horiz.	1374 kWh/m²
Sunshine hours	2000hr/year

Thermal Characteristics

U value: roof	0.32 W/m²K
floor	0.85 W/m²K
external walls	0.42 W/m²K
windows	2.60 W/m²K
Mean U value	0.72 W/m²K
Global heat loss coefficient	
(excl. ventilation)	206.60 W/m²K
Infiltration rate	23.80 m³/hr
External design temperature	7°C
Heated floor area	99 m²
Heated volume	240 m³
Net heat load	146 kWh/m² per annum

Costs (1982 prices)

Building (27 houses)	FF 10,797,468	ECU 1,558,526
Average per house	FF 399,906	ECU 57,723
All solar features,		
Per house	FF 41,000	ECU 5,918
Sunspace	FF 15,800	ECU 2,280
Heat storage wall	FF 12,600	ECU 1,819
Trombe walls	FF 11,000	ECU 1,588

MAROSTICA CREDITS

Client
CO. VE. CO. (Consorzio Veneto Cooperative)
Cooperativa Marostica
c/o Lorenzo Vivian
Via Prof. Consolaro 39
36063 Marostica

Architects
COOPROGETTO s.c.r.l.
A. De Luca, M. Mamoli, R. Marzotto,
G. Scudo, P. Stella
Via Calderari 9
36100 Vicenza

Energy Consultant
L.I.F.E. s.c.r.l. — Ing. T. Costantini
Casa Solare
02040 Salisano
(Prov. di Riete)

Services Engineer/Consultant
Ing. G. Rossi
Via Palladio 24
30175 Venezia (Marghera)

Services Contractor
Miranda
No longer trading

Monitoring Organisations
ENEA (Comitato Nazionale per lo Sviluppo
dell'Energia Nucleare e delle Energie Alternative)
with CO. VE. CO. consultants
Ing. G. Rossi & Arch. G. Scudo
Veale Regina Margherita 125
00198 Roma

Commission of the European Communities

- Large development of 40 dwellings incorporates extensive use of direct gain and thermosyphoning solar wall panels, with roof mounted active solar water heating collectors.

- Passive solar components supply 30% of the net space heating load.

- Solar air heating panels designed for the scheme now mass-produced at low cost.

- Adaptation of 'Barra-Costantini' system. Air circulates through solar panels, via ducts in 'thermal ceiling', into rooms and back to panels. Concrete ceiling stores some of the heat.

- Passive solar system may be operated as a solar chimney for summer cooling of dwelling.

MAROSTICA

MAROSTICA
ITALY

Project Background

The scheme consists of four separate buildings; three rows of terraced houses comprising 24 dwellings in all, and one four storey housing block containing 16 flats. Construction was completed in 1984, and monitoring of the energy performance has been carried out for an eighteen month period.

Each flat has a double glazed extension onto the open plan living/dining room. This 'bay window' harmonises with the general facade, although it is an unusual feature.

DESIGN OBJECTIVES

A co-operative housing association named "Marostica" commissioned the project to provide accommodation for around 155 people. The scheme, highlighting maximum energy efficiency, would offer a mix of dwelling sizes and maintain a certain degree of flexibility over the internal layout of the single units.

The principal objective was to build low cost housing in which innovative passive solar components could be incorporated at costs acceptable for public housing schemes. The major challenge of the design was to examine and produce a "Barra-Costantini" passive solar system that could be integrated easily into current building processes.

ENERGY SAVING FEATURES

● Three parallel rows of two storey terraced houses and a four storey block of flats each facing north/south and spaced sufficiently apart to minimise winter overshading. Most principal rooms, and in particular the living room, are planned to face south.

● Wall mounted passive solar air heating panels (Barra-Costantini) are used on the whole scheme.

● Flats have a double glazed extension to the living area which increases the area of glazing on the south.

● Active solar water heating collectors are provided on the roofs of all four buildings.

● Other built-in energy features applied throughout include double glazing of all windows, draughtstripping, and floor and loft insulation.

SITE AND CLIMATE

The site is located in Marostica, a small town in northern Italy, some 15km from Vicenza. The 6500m² plot is in Panica, an area of new development. The site is fairly rectangular with the

CLIMATE

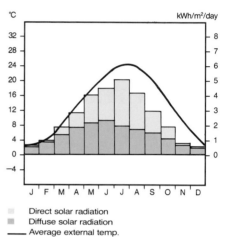

Direct solar radiation
Diffuse solar radiation
Average external temp.

long axis running north/south and gently sloping at 5° towards the south. It has good solar access. To the north there is a hill, and to the south across the access road there are two

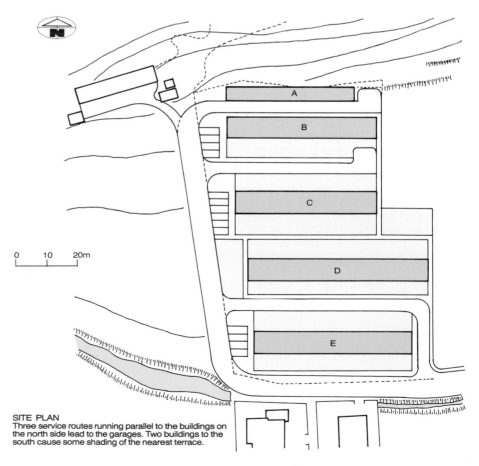

SITE PLAN
Three service routes running parallel to the buildings on the north side lead to the garages. Two buildings to the south cause some shading of the nearest terrace.

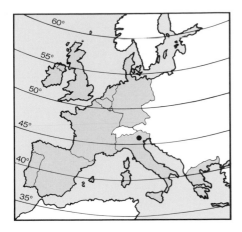

buildings. To the east is a view of the beautiful scenery and the medieval "Rocca di Marostica", with its ancient crenellated walls marking the slopes of the Pausolino hills.

Marostica, at 105m above sea level, is located at the foot of the "Prealpi Vicentine" (the plateau of Asiago). Immediately to the south of the first range of hills, the surrounding area is fairly flat and protected from the alpine winds. The climate is temperate continental, with 2340 degree days on a 19°C basis and an average winter solar radiation of 5.5MJ/m²day.

PLANNING

The buildings have been carefully spaced as a result of a detailed study of solar geometry, to avoid shadows falling onto the solar panels during winter months. The tallest building has been placed at the north end of the plot and all the roof pitches are chosen to minimise solar obstruction.

DESIGN DETAILS

The terraced houses are two storey dwellings, each with a basement. On the ground floor, entrances to both the north and south are given equal importance. The kitchen/dining/living area has been planned to allow different arrangements. On the first floor are either two or three bedrooms and a bathroom.
In the multifamily building, each flat has a double glazed extension onto the open plan living/dining room. The kitchen is a separate room, always located on the north side. Again, sizes vary, incorporating either two or three bedrooms.
The appearance of all four buildings is characterised by the south elevation consisting entirely of windows and solar panels which are unified by the use of the same red steel framing. The framing is used as a thin trimming applied to the glazing of the solar panels to soften the impact of their extensive surface area, which would otherwise appear entirely black. The result helps to distinguish the windows from the passive components. The "bay window" extension harmonises with the general facade design of the apartment block, although it is an unusual feature.
The north elevation is designed to avoid the austere feeling common amongst climate-respecting architecture, despite two-thirds of the glazing

being on the south facade. Active solar collectors for domestic hot water are integrated into the south slope of all the roofs, at an angle of 45°.

South elevation of terraced houses. Red steel framing is used as a thin trimming to the glazing of the solar panels.

CONSTRUCTION

Emphasis was placed on the need to choose a fairly simple semi-industrialised system, in which the passive components and the building processes could easily be integrated. Both types of dwelling are built with a "banches et predalles" structure (reinforced concrete walls running east/west and a prefabricated horizontal load bearing structure running north/south). The modules of the concrete slab measure 1.2 x 7.0m. To give a lighter component, the predalle is produced with a series of parallel ducts filled with polystyrene. To transform this

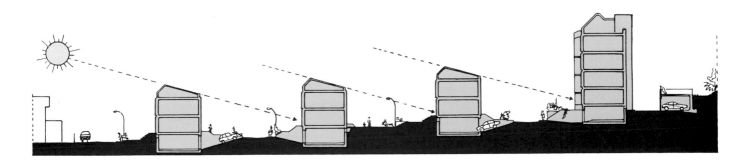

All the roof pitches are chosen to minimise solar obstruction.

Design Details

component into a "thermal ceiling", hollow steel ducts replace some of the insulating ducts. Steel beams support the roof which is covered with copper sheeting.

On the south facade, the upper and lower part of the walls were perforated for the air circulation system. A special joint was designed to allow the flow of air at a right angle between the solar air heating panel and the thermal ceiling.

● a thermosyphoning air panel incorporated into the south facade, this consists of a single pane of glass, an air space, a dark coloured aluminium sheet, a second air space in front of 60mm insulation and the load bearing wall;

● a thermal ceiling for distribution, through ducts incorporated into the horizontal structure, and for heat storage;

South elevation of terraced houses, appearance characterised by facade consisting entirely of windows and solar air heating panels.

south elevation of multifamily building. Solar features are 'bay window' extensions, large area of south facing glazing, solar heating panels and solar water heating collectors on roof.

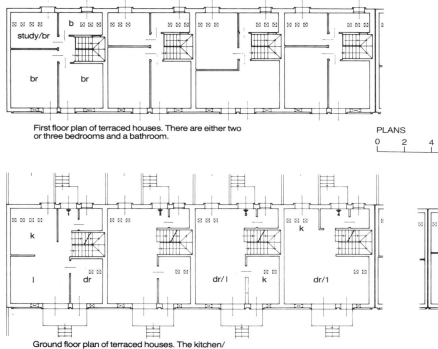

First floor plan of terraced houses. There are either two or three bedrooms and a bathroom.

PLANS
0   2   4   6m

Ground floor plan of terraced houses. The kitchen/dining/living area has been planned to allow different arrangements.

Typical floor plan of multifamily building highlighting the glazed extensions, each one serves two flats.

PASSIVE SOLAR FEATURES

Integration of the thermal and structural building components, the key to the passive solar design, was the result of co-operative work carried out by the design team and a manufacturer. Starting from a purpose-made solar panel, the team designed and built a production prototype which is now mass-produced at a low cost by the manufacturer.

The passive solar system is an application of the "Barra-Costantini" system, which is composed of the following elements:

● control valves for the inlet and outlet of air.

The south facade is governed by the need for a large black surface area of air panels, and the inlet and outlet air valves have imposed a certain layout on the rooms. Each terrace of houses has 190m² of solar wall panels and the multistorey block has 335m².

Internal layouts are planned so that most habitable rooms, and in particular the living room, face south. This maximises the use of direct gain. In addition, the apartment block features 100m² of double glazed 'bay window' extensions to increase the collection area for solar gains.

All the windows are double glazed. Unusually, the roller blind boxes are installed externally providing an overhang for partial shading of the glazed surface. They also reduce thermal bridging of the lintel. Natural ventilation is promoted since all units have openings to the north and south. The limited depth of the buildings and the absence of overshading ensure good daylighting levels.

AUXILIARY HEATING SYSTEM AND CONTROLS

Each of the 40 dwelling units has its own gas boiler, which serves as a back-up for both

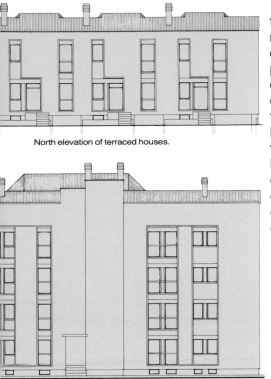

North elevation of terraced houses.

North elevation of multifamily building.

ELEVATIONS
0 2 4 6m

through the return opening. At night, a plastic membrane closes the return opening preventing reverse air circulation, while the heat stored during the day is radiated from the ceiling to the room space. During the summer, natural ventilation can be induced by keeping the inside lower damper open, closing the outside lower damper and opening the outside upper damper. In this way the system acts as a solar chimney. This arrangement is not essential in the temperate climate of Marostica.

A compact butterfly valve, which was both easy to install and operate, was used to simplify the whole system. The return air openings were reduced to one per solar panel, thereby easing the constraints upon the use of the interior spaces caused by the passive system.

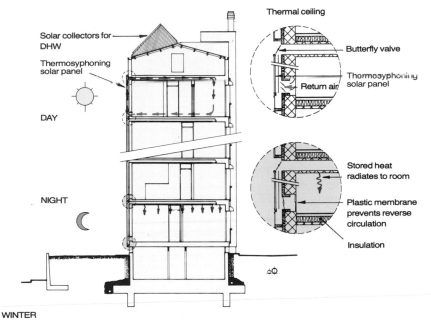

Solar collectors for DHW
Thermosyphoning solar panel
DAY
NIGHT
WINTER

Thermal ceiling
Butterfly valve
Thermosyphoning solar panel
Return air
Stored heat radiates to room
Plastic membrane prevents reverse circulation
Insulation

space and water heating. There is a heater supplied with thermostatic control in each room. On the south side, these heaters are placed just above the return air openings to the solar panels to promote the airflows. The passive system controls are manual, the dampers beneath the heaters are opened and closed as required.

As no mechanical ventilation is provided, opening the windows can cause disturbances to the airflow patterns induced by the convective loop.

OPERATING MODES

In winter, during the day, the air heated in the solar panels flows through the ducts in the concrete ceiling. The air heats up the concrete structure, becoming cooler before entering the room. Here it mixes with the room air and is convected back to the panel

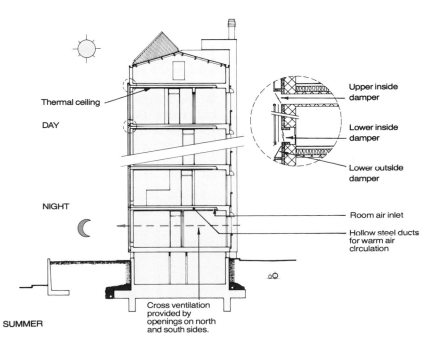

Thermal ceiling
DAY
NIGHT
SUMMER

Upper inside damper
Lower inside damper
Lower outside damper
Room air inlet
Hollow steel ducts for warm air circulation

Cross ventilation provided by openings on north and south sides.

Performance Evaluation

MONITORING

During 1985/86 the homes were monitored for an 18 month period. Three dwellings were monitored, two terraced houses and one flat. A datalogger and over 50 sensors were installed to record:

● the external microclimate,
● the air temperature and velocity in the passive solar system,
● the temperature and relative humidity in the rooms.

Meters were installed to collect data on:

● the fuel consumption for space heating,
● the delivered energy from the active solar water heating collectors.

One of the units was monitored more intensively to assess:

● the energy performance of the convective loop system,
● the global energy balance.

On the south side, the heaters are placed just above the return air openings to the solar panels, to promote the air flows.

PERFORMANCE OF SOLAR FEATURES

● The energy required for space heating has been reduced to just 59% of the demand of a comparable house built to normal standards.

South facade showing thermosyphoning air panel with damper and external roller blind with box.

● Solar gains contributed 26% to the total space heating requirement, useful internal gains another 14% and auxiliary energy 60%.

● 30% of net space heating load was met by useful solar energy although at the design stage the predicted savings attributable to passive components were 50%.

● Average total annual fuel bills were low: 600,000 lire for a four person unit for space and domestic water heating in 1986.

● 39% of the domestic water heating load was met by roof mounted active solar collectors.

COMPARISON WITH CONVENTIONAL DESIGN

169 200kWh (609GJ) would be required to heat a terrace of eight houses built to a conventional design.

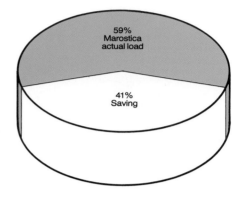

59% Marostica actual load

41% Saving

The design reduced the space heating load to 99 700 kWh (359 GJ) for the terrace, a saving of 41%.

AUXILIARY FUEL USED (PRIMARY ENERGY)

111 700 kWh

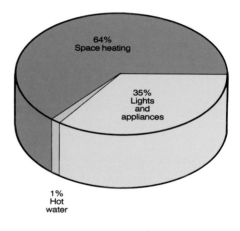

64% Space heating

35% Lights and appliances

1% Hot water

Auxiliary fuel used for space heating is gas.

ENERGY FLOWS ASSOCIATED WITH SPACE HEATING (SH)

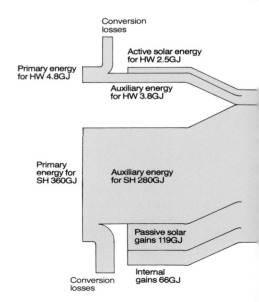

Conversion losses

Active solar energy for HW 2.5GJ

Primary energy for HW 4.8GJ

Auxiliary energy for HW 3.8GJ

Primary energy for SH 360GJ

Auxiliary energy for SH 280GJ

Passive solar gains 119GJ

Internal gains 66GJ

Conversion losses

CONTRIBUTIONS TO TOTAL SPACE HEATING REQUIREMENT

129 200kWh (465GJ) Terrace D

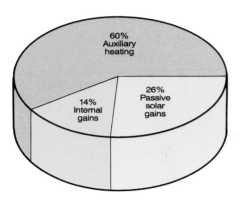

Passive solar gains contributed 26% (33 100 kWh) to the total space heating requirement. Auxiliary energy only accounted for 60% (77 800 kWh).

COST OF BUILDING AND SOLAR ON-COST

The total project cost L2 850 million in 1984.

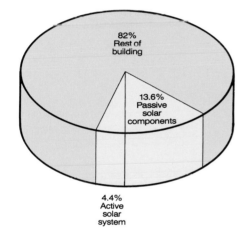

Passive and active solar systems accounted for L387 million and L126 million respectively.

WATER (HW)

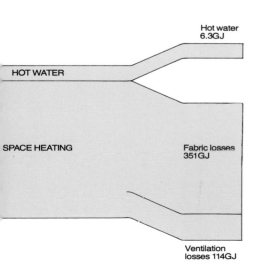

NET MONTHLY SPACE HEATING DEMAND AND SUPPLY

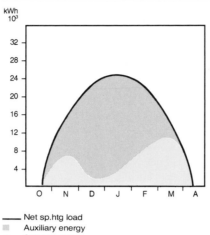

—— Net sp.htg load
▦ Auxiliary energy
▦ Solar energy

COST EFFECTIVENESS

The full cost of building the housing scheme in 1984 was 2850 million lire. More than 13% of this was spent on the passive solar system:- the thermo-syphoning solar panels, the air distribution system, and in the case of the flats, the glazed extension to the living room area. Nevertheless, the anticipated payback period is only 12 years, assuming an inflation rate equal to the discount rate.

MONTHLY AVERAGE TEMPERATURES

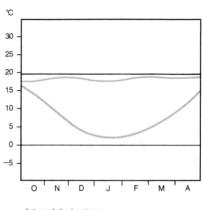

—— Internal design temp.
—— Internal temp.
—— External temp.

View from south facing living room, overlooking north face of adjacent terrace.

PROJECT DATA

Building

Total volume of housing scheme	13 400m³

Multifamily Building

Volume	5 045m³
No of floors	4
No of flats	16
Total floor area	1 552m²
Total roof area	386m²
Windows: total area	363m²
south	102m²
bay window extensions (south)	100m²
(east & west)	50m²
north	94m²
east & west	17m²
Solar air heating panels: total area	335m²
Solar water heating collectors: total area	45m²

Terrace of Houses (E)

Volume	2,772m³
No of floors	2 + basement
No of units	8
Total floor area	800m² + basement
Roof area	415m²
Windows: total area	154m²
south	102.5m²
north	51.5m²
Solar air heating panels: total area	187m²
Solar water heating collectors: total area	24m²

Costs (1984 prices)

Building (entire scheme)	L2850 million
	(2 192 000 ECU)
Passive solar system:	
Air heating panels (total area 915m²)	L305 million
Thermal ceilings	L59 million
Lowered ceilings in bathrooms and corridors	L23 million
Total cost	L387 million
	(298 000 ECU)
Active solar system	L126 million
	(97 000 ECU)

Thermal

U value roof	0.47W/m²K
floor	0.72W/m²K
external walls	0.41W/m²K
windows	1.80W/m²K
Mean U value	0.89W/m²K
Global heat loss coefficient Terr. D	2225W/K
Infiltration rate	0.50ac/h
External design temperature	−6°C
Heated floor area	4 003m²
Heated volume	13 400m³
Net heat load (heated area)	83kWh/m²

Site and Climate

Altitude	105m
Latitude	45° 45′ N
Longitude	12° 27′ E
Average ambient temp: Jan	5°C
July	24°C
Degree days (base 19°C)	2340 degree days
Global irradiation on horizontal	1317 kWh/m²

HOOFDDORP CREDITS

Client
N V Bouwfonds Nederlandse Gemeenten
Haarlem Regional Office
Professor Eijkmanlaan 2
2003 E J Haarlem

Architects

Bakker & Boots	Hopman
Koperwick 3	Oude Delft 257
1742 Schagen	2611 HE Delft
Kristinsson	Kol & Lindeman
Noordenbergsingel 10	De Hork 14
7411 SE Deventer	1531 NS Cuijk
Tauber	Van Ringen
Wendelaarstraat 58	Zwarte Ruiter 10
1814 GS Alkmaar	9351 NN Leek

Housing and Energy Conservation Group (WEB)
Eindhoven University of Technology
P O Box 513
5600 MB Eindhoven

Energy Consultants
NV Bouwfonds Nederlandse Gemeenten
Westerdorpstraat 66
3871 AZ Hoevelaken

Management Office for Energy Research (PEO)
Leidseveer 35
3511 SB Utrecht

Construction Consultant
Van Rossum BV
Delflandplein 1
1062 HP Amsterdam

Building Contractor

Produktiestroom BV	Bouwbedrijf A Pronk BV
Parklaan 2	Oostwal 128
1406 KL Bussum	1749 XP Warmenhuizen

Services Contractor
Unica Installatietechniek BV
Brink 10A
8021 AP Zwolle

Slootweg BV Deventer (no longer trading)

Monitoring Organisation
Task Group FAGO TNO/TPD
Eindhoven University of Technology

NV Bouwfonds Nederlandse Gemeenten
Hoevelaken

12

Commission of the European Communities

HOOFDDORP

HOOFDDORP
NETHERLANDS

Project Background

As part of the Dutch national research programme on the rational use of energy in the built environment (REGO), a field trial of low energy single family houses was set up.
The project involves 56 public sector subsidised ("Premium-A") houses and is located in Hoofddorp near Amsterdam. Seven architects each designed a block of low energy housing for the Energy Park, for which the brief included the requirement of a mean annual space heating demand of about 500m³ of natural gas (16.5GJ). The result is six rows of terraced houses, eight per row, plus one row of eight duplex apartments (maisonettes).
The innovative energy features were funded equally by the development corporation, by the Government's Management Office for Energy Research (PEO) and by the homeowners. Most of the houses were completed by the start of the 1984/85 heating season.

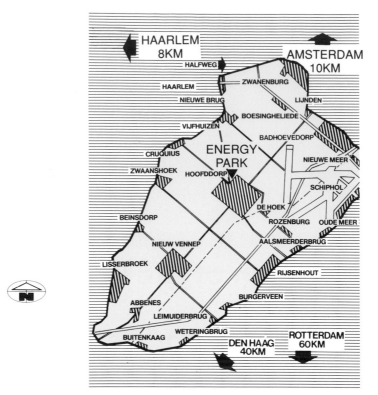

The site is on the northern edge of Hoofddorp, the principal town of the polder of Haarlemmermeer.

DESIGN OBJECTIVES

The main purpose of the Energy Park was to determine the interrelationships between energy saving measures and construction, services and architecture. The aim is for the dwellings to provide an example of what may be attainable in energy efficient single family housing by the end of the eighties, through a combination of:

- the drastic reduction of fabric and ventilation heat losses;
- the integration and optimisation of passive and active solar energy systems;
- the application of high efficiency heating systems.

With this in mind, almost all current Dutch construction techniques are represented; traditional brickwork, prefabricated components, cast and lightweight concrete and timber frame.
The large diversity in construction types, systems and energy saving measures means a direct comparison of the different houses is not possible.

ENERGY SAVING FEATURES

● Five of the terraces are designed around a south facing orientation, and the other two are independent of orientation.

● Integral sunspaces are incorporated into the apartment designs, and two of the house designs have attached sunspaces.

● Three types of active solar energy systems are employed.

● Extra insulation has been placed in the cavity walls, roof, ground floor and party walls in every case.

● Extensive measures were taken to reduce air infiltration.

● Each architect chose a glazing standard which exceeds simple double glazing.

● The traditional surface to volume ratio was varied in at least three designs.

● Three different warm air heating systems and a more conventional, though advanced, radiator system, were specified.

CONCLUSIONS

The purpose of this project was to explore the optimum energy efficient balance of solar, conservation, auxiliary heating and ventilation options through the different designs selected for the Energy Park. In this respect, it is the mix of designs that constitutes the true value of the project, and to treat the house types individually does not do full justice to the significance of the scheme.
The average annual fuel consumption for space heating in the Energy Park over the 1985/86 heating season was 21GJ (approximately 7GJ higher

than was predicted). This was a saving of more than 43GJ compared to the average consumption of a Dutch terraced house. Individual designs achieved up to 80% fuel savings compared to a house of the same size built to conventional standards.

The predicted, relatively small, contribution from the solar energy system appears to agree well with the measurements. Sunspaces have an additional benefit in terms of the improved comfort and amenity which the occupants experience.

Each of the designs has a combined energy and mortgage bill that is comparable with, or lower than, the average for Premium-A houses that have been built in the last five years. At current fuel prices, the most cost effective measures are simple direct gain systems with better insulation and improved construction details, combined with advanced, conventional heating systems. However, in a number of cases, the "experimental" features are shown to be feasible for standard building practices, at acceptable, or even zero extra costs.

SITE AND CLIMATE

The site is on the northern edge of Hoofddorp, the principal town of the polder Haarlemmermeer. Schiphol, Amsterdam Airport, and a growing number of related industries are located in this polder, once Lake Haarlem. These boost an extensive housing programme in and around Hoofddorp. The Energy Park is on the edge of the town, in an area designated for the construction of 800 houses per year between 1981 and 1995. The polder is completely flat and 4m below sea level. Although the prevailing winds are south-westerly, most frosty winds are north-easterly. The heating season runs from mid-September to mid-May. There are 2280 degree days (15.5°C base) or 3140 degree days (18.3°C base).

The plot has unlimited solar access, nothing overshadows it except some trees planted along a dike which also act as a windshield against the westerly winds.

PLANNING

The 1.4 ha site is located in a corner between the flood dike across Haarlemmermeer and the Hoofddorp bypass. Six of the rows are oriented 15° east of south, one 50° east of south and one 75° west of south. Other than achieving a density of about 40 houses per hectare, and attempting to comply with the Passive Solar Guidelines for the region, no special emphasis has been placed on urban design. The Passive Solar Guidelines came into being in 1983, and specify 70% south orientation and a 17° obstruction angle.

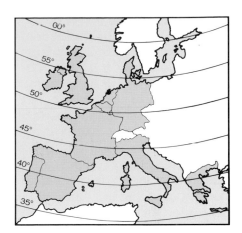

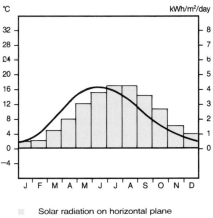

CLIMATE (Schiphol)

Solar radiation on horizontal plane
Average external temp.

The Energy Park site viewed from the east.

Design Details

In the five terraces with a north-south orientation the living room and most of the bedrooms face south. Generally, the kitchen is an extension of the living room, but faces north. Whether or not the entrance on the north side of the house is the main entrance, it always has a draught lobby. With the exception of the apartments, each dwelling is designed so that the attic can be converted into a fourth bedroom if desired.

Four of the rows in the Energy Park, those designed by Bakker & Boots(B), Kristinsson(K), Van Ringen(R) and Tauber(T), are based on conventional layouts, although B employs a sloping north face and R a sloping south face. Hopman's design (H) has a shallow but wide floor plan to maximise solar exposure. The team from Eindhoven University of Technology (W) selected a deep, narrow floor plan, to minimise both the surface to volume ratio and the area of facade (which is relatively expensive to build). W also chose a design with a sloping south facing wall.

Kol & Lindeman designed the only row with separate dwellings on the ground and upper floors (L1 and L2). The floor plans for these apartments are very unconventional. L1 has an all glass facade with a two storey sunspace behind it, onto which one of the bedrooms has a balcony. L2 starts half way along the first floor where the service areas and bedrooms are located, and on the second floor there is a wide living room with an attached sunspace.

CONSTRUCTION

The houses are all built on concrete piles 9m to 12m deep. The ground floors are mostly constructed from reinforced, or hollow core concrete, over a crawl space. Approximately

Five of the terraces face south, one faces south-east and the other has an east-west orientation.

100mm polystyrene is used to insulate the floor slab. Foam glass is used between the floors and beams which are supported on the top of the piles. Intermediate floors are also insulated in all but K, L1 and L2, to allow for lower temperatures in the bedrooms than in the living room.

The load bearing walls are made of in-situ concrete at R and sand-lime bricks in B,K and W. H and T use a timber frame construction, and the load bearing walls in the apartments are aerated concrete.

In each row, at least 40mm polystyrene is used in the party walls to isolate the dwellings from each other. The front and back walls are made of prefabricated panels with an external skin of brick or timber, in all but K, which is entirely brick. Cavity walls are insulated with either polyurethane or mineral wool, the thickness of the insulant varying between different designs. The resulting exterior wall U values range between 0.22 W/m²K and

0.33W/m²K.

All the roofs use prefabricated roof trusses, but they are insulated to different thicknesses with a range of materials; 175mm mineral wool at K, 140mm mineral wool at T, 130mm polyurethane at L1 and L2 and 90mm polyurethane in the rest of the designs. All the roofs are tiled except for the collector areas. Each architect took pains to prevent thermal bridges and used some form of vapour barrier, although no one used a continuous one.

A range of different glazing types were used by the architects, all of them choosing to improve upon standard double glazing. K used double glazing combined with insulating shutters. Triple glazing is used for W, T and the north facing windows of L2, and double glazed, low emissivity greenhouse glass is used for the sunspaces in L1 and L2. Gas filled, double glazing with low emissivity coating is used in all the rest of the designs. The only recorded construction problems were associated with the requirements for the closed loop solar-cavity system in K's design, and with the use of aerated concrete at L1 and L2 (which required a specialist contractor to be brought in). Many of the designs met Scandinavian standards of airtightness, but in all except H, the airtightness was worse during the second heating season than it had been prior to occupation. For a number of houses, this was probably due, at least in part, to alterations made by the inhabitants.

SOLAR DESIGN

● Each of the designs makes use of direct solar gains by having a greater than normal percentage of glazing on the south face. The only special feature is a clerestory, used in W, over the full width of the living room.

● Sunspaces are used in three out of the seven rows and one row has the provision for a sunspace.

● Solar collectors are integrated into the designs of K, R and T. All three are air heating collectors covering most of the south facing roof area.

Garden orientation seems as important to the occupiers as any other solar feature. All the rows except T and W have southerly oriented gardens. North facing gardens are attached to the terrace designed by T whilst W has gardens which are east-north-east facing. Both of these designs have a border on the southernmost side which separates the living room from the street.

VENTILATION & AUXILIARY HEATING SYSTEMS

Due to the airtightness of the dwellings, there was a need for mechanical ventilation. Six of the seven designs experimented with a combined air heating and ventilation system. B, L and H use an identical system: - one unit combining warm-air heating, domestic water heating, mechanical ventilation and heat recovery. There are also separate heaters for the living room, master bedroom and other bedrooms. K, T and R use a combination of different units for these functions. W uses a room sealed boiler unit for both domestic hot water and the low temperature radiator system. In this design, the ventilation air enters the house through vents in the window sills, and is mechanically exhausted from the kitchen, WC and bathroom.

All the designs employ thermostatic controls for the heating system and manual control for the ventilation system. The systems and equipment used were the most advanced available at the time the dwellings were constructed. However, in some cases, the final stages in their development had not yet been reached. This was an acceptable condition, as the project was an R&D exercise. Unfortunately, the necessary extra work adjusting and modifying the equipment proved to be very costly. Although all the systems worked reasonably well, none of them constitute a decisive breakthrough in services technology, and it would appear that there is still considerable room for improvement.

Bakker & Boots designed a terrace of houses with a sunspace across the full width of the south facade of each house.

Kristinsson made the whole of the south facing roof into a solar collector.

60% of all glazing is on the south side in Tauber's design. Roof-mounted solar collectors preheat both the ventilation air and the domestic hot water.

The layout of the Energy Park gave Hopman's terrace an orientation 50º east of south and so the sunspaces become only an optional feature.

Bakker and Boots (B)

The structural separating walls in this design are made of traditional sand-lime bricks. The front and back walls are brick outer skin over prefabricated panels. The houses have painted red-cedar cladding on the upper half of the side walls and red concrete tiles over the prefabricated roof construction. The basic floor plan is 5.4m by 8m, excluding the porch and full height cupboard on the entrance side. The house has three bedrooms on the first floor and the potential for a fourth bedroom in the attic.

Nearly all the windows in the house are double glazed using low emissivity coated glass. There are thermal shutters on both the kitchen window and the windows on the end walls.

SOLAR DESIGN

There is a single glazed sunspace across the full width of the south face. The living room opens onto this through 5m² of glazed doors and windows and the ratio of glazing to living room floor area is 21%. Only 24% of the 10.8m² windows are on the north side.

The sunspace has two thermostatically-controlled fans which can be used to circulate air through the living room. It has a pair of folding doors to the outside and two ventilation windows in the sloping roof.

PERFORMANCE OF PASSIVE SOLAR DESIGN

The sunspace produces only marginal fuel savings, but its 12m² add a comfortable 40% enlargement to the living room and kitchen area without incurring any fuel penalties.

Whilst the occupants greatly enjoyed the sunspace, its usefulness would have been increased had it been double glazed.

Based on a normalised (48 dwellings) project price (which does not represent the actual costs incurred in this R&D exercise) the selling price of the house would be 153 655 Gld. This is only about 2.5% more than a comparable standard Building Code house would cost (in both cases, including a land cost of 23 140 Gld and 19% tax).

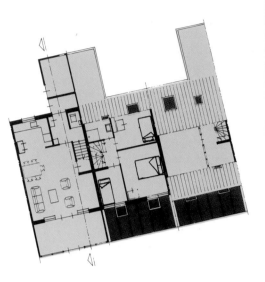

CONTRIBUTIONS TO THE ANNUAL SPACE HEATING DEMAND

5 520kWh

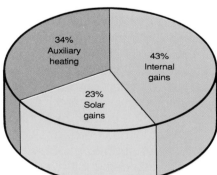

- 34% Auxiliary heating
- 43% Internal gains
- 23% Solar gains

Kristinsson (K)

In Kristinsson's design, the bearing walls are traditional sand-lime bricks, and the structure is clad with brick. The basic floor plan measures 4.95m by 8.40m. The living room is 21.2m² and opens onto the south facing garden through a glazed storm door. It has larger than usual windows, giving a percentage of glass to living room floor area of 20%. The separate kitchen serves to isolate the living room from the north side of the house. There are three bedrooms on the first floor and a storage room in the attic. A combined enclosed porch and full height cupboard are attached to the north facing entrance to the house.
All 10m² of glazing are double glazed and nearly all windows have insulating shutters that can be operated from the inside. Only the shutters on the living room windows have to be operated from the outside.

SOLAR DESIGN

The concept stems primarily from a heavily insulated, direct gain design that has been used before by Kristinsson. Here, the window area on the south side of the house is 72% of the total. An experimental collector has been added as part of the concept of a "solar cavity". In this system, air moves between black-painted roofing and two layers of polycarbonate, to a duct in the cavity of one party wall. A 120W fan then moves the air down to the crawl-space under the house, along and up through the cavity in the other party wall and back into the collector again. The heat from the air in this closed loop system is transmitted through the cavity walls into the rooms.

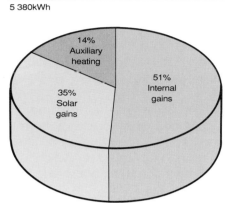

CONTRIBUTIONS TO THE ANNUAL SPACE HEATING DEMAND
5 380kWh

- 14% Auxiliary heating
- 51% Internal gains
- 35% Solar gains

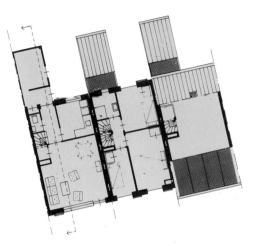

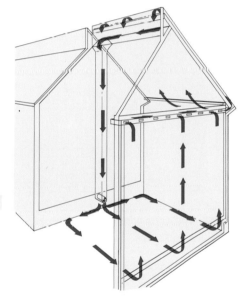

Section showing air movement in "solar cavity" ducting system.

PERFORMANCE OF SOLAR DESIGN

Most of the energy savings in this design are due to the direct gain windows and the energy conservation measures, rather than to the solar cavity system. If these are separated out, the project confirms that savings due entirely to the solar cavity only marginally pay the interest on the cost of this system.
In total, solar energy contributed just over a third to the gross space heating load. One criticism of the design is that the very small heating unit used was extremely slow to heat the heavy mass of the house.

Tauber (T)

This Scandinavian-inspired design uses a mostly prefabricated timber frame construction combined with a concrete ground floor to provide internal mass. The lower storey is clad with brick in line with Dutch building traditions. The floor plan is 5.75m by 8.10m. There are three bedrooms on the first floor and space for an optional fourth bedroom in the attic, which is where all the heating equipment is housed. The heating system includes an active solar system, a heat exchanger and the auxiliary system. To prevent the attic overheating, a cabinet was placed around the components and a thermostatic vent was introduced to outside. An extra skylight was placed in the roof to provide daylight in the attic. All 10.3m^2 of glazing in the house are triple glazed.

CONTRIBUTIONS TO THE ANNUAL SPACE HEATING DEMAND

9 235kWh

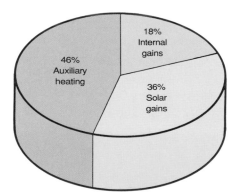

- 18% Internal gains
- 46% Auxiliary heating
- 36% Solar gains

SOLAR DESIGN

● 60% of all glazing is on the south side. The 2.9m^2 of south facing window in the living room is equivalent to 10% of its floor area.

● An active solar air-heating collector system preheats both the ventilation air and an 80 litre water storage cylinder which supplies domestic hot water.

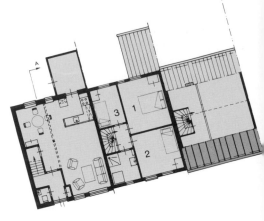

PERFORMANCE OF THE DESIGN

Solar energy contributed 36% to the gross space heating load and user response to the house itself was good. However, some aspects received a moderate to poor rating, the most notable of which was the auxiliary heating equipment, a warm-air system. Separating out the savings due to conservation measures, it is apparent that the additional annual savings directly attributable to the active collector system are less than 5% of its cost. The normalised selling price of the house is 154 865 Gld, compared to 142 655 Gld for a similar house constructed to Building Code standards, giving an 8.5% on-cost for the trial houses.

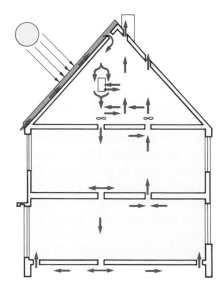

The roof-mounted active solar collectors preheat both ventilation air and the domestic hot water via a heat exchanger.

Hopman (H)

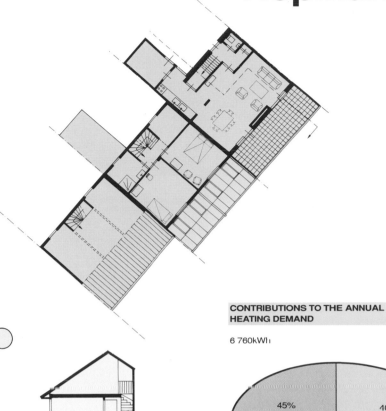

Like Tauber's, this design uses a mostly prefabricated timber frame construction in conjunction with a concrete ground floor which provides internal mass. Facing brick is used on the walls at ground floor level in keeping with Dutch building traditions.

Instead of the 5m by 8m floor plan commonly used, Hopman chose a basic floor plan 7.2m wide and 6.4m deep. On the ground floor the living area is 27.5m^2 and there is a porch with a full height cupboard attached to the entrance. The first floor comprises two large bedrooms, a bathroom and a 2m by 2m workroom. The auxiliary heating system is sited in the attic, which also provides storage space. All 7.2m^2 of glazing in the house are triple glazed.

SOLAR DESIGN

In addition to energy conservation measures, the preliminary design included an attached sunspace across the full 7.2m width of the house. Unfortunately, the layout of the site gave these houses an orientation 50° east of south so the sunspaces became optional features only, and were not included by the builders. None of the homeowners has as yet retrofitted a sunspace, although a brickwork garden feature could be used as a structural separating wall, should they wish to take up the opportunity. 68% of the glazing in the houses faces south easterly as a result of the change in orientation.

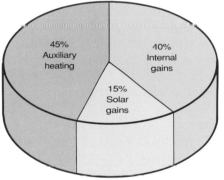

When the layout of the Energy Park gave this terrace an orientation 50° east of south, the sunspaces were dropped from the design.

PERFORMANCE OF THE DESIGN

This is an example of a design in which insulation measures are the chief means of achieving a low energy house.

The brick walls jutting into the garden could become structural walls for a sunspace if retrofitted.

Kol & Lindeman (L1 & L2)

Lindeman proposed a terrace of duplex apartments to achieve high density housing, hence this design is unlike the single family houses in the rest of the Energy Park. Both the layout and the choice of aerated concrete as a construction material are highly unconventional. The apartment block is clad with brick and timber, whilst the structural columns and beams are steel. The basic floor plans measure 7.4m by 14.2m. L1 has an all glass south facade creating a two-storey sunspace. Behind this are the living room and kitchen on the ground floor, and three bedrooms on the first floor. L2 begins half way along the first floor on the north side, where the service areas and three bedrooms are to be found. On the second floor, the living room and kitchen area occupy the full width of the apartment, and there is a sunspace on the south side.

L1 has no north facing windows and those in L2 are triple glazed, 2.4m^2 in the bedrooms and 2m^2 in the living room.

L1 has a two-storey sunspace. On the ground floor, glazed doors and windows open onto the sunspace and at the upper level there is a balcony in front of one of the bedrooms.

SOLAR DESIGN

● L1's integral two-storey sunspace uses nearly 37m^2 of low emissivity double glazing.

● The sunspace adjacent to the living room in L2 encloses the hall and stairway and acts as a large skylight for the service area on the first floor.

● The roof over bedrooms and sunspace in L1 serves as a terrace for L2.

● Ordinary greenhouse blinds are used in both sunspaces to prevent overheating.

● The ratios of glazing to living room floor area for L1 and L2 are 30% and 32% respectively.

Adjoining the sunspace on the ground floor, the kitchen and living room in L1 have 9m^2 of single glazed windows and doors. Another 9m^2 of single glazed bedroom windows open onto the sunspace on the first floor and one of the bedrooms has a balcony onto the sunspace.

The sunspace glazing in L2 is made up of 16m^2 of vertical and 17m^2 of sloped glazing of the same type as is used in L1. The adjacent living room windows measure nearly 9m^2 and are single glazed.

CONTRIBUTIONS TO THE ANNUAL SPACE HEATING DEMAND

5 930kWh

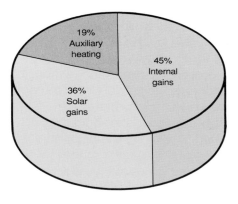

19% Auxiliary heating
45% Internal gains
36% Solar gains

L1 is a duplex apartment on the ground and first floors.

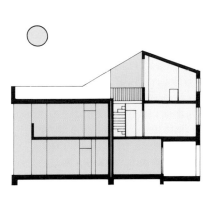

PERFORMANCE OF PASSIVE SOLAR DESIGN

For L2, the solar contribution to the gross space heating load is 38%, and for L1 it is 36%. However, this experimental design confirms calculations that only marginal additional fuel savings can be ascribed to the sunspaces, over and above those produced by the conservation measures and direct gain. It also shows that investments in innovative floor plans, however desirable, cannot be justified on energy grounds alone. Additionally, the building experienced difficulties evening out temperature extremes. The amount of single glazing used in the project probably represents the upper limit for solar gain exploitation in the heat gain versus heat loss balance existing in this climate. For L2, the glass cover over the hall and stairway (both of which require heating) actually leads to a greater fuel consumption than would a facade built according to standard regulations. Despite this, the sunspaces were highly rated in the user surveys.

Another significant consideration relevant to Lindeman's project (and Hopman's) is the effect that stark, high, north walls have upon the quality of urban design.

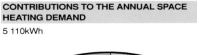

CONTRIBUTIONS TO THE ANNUAL SPACE HEATING DEMAND
5 110kWh

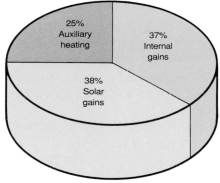

25% Auxiliary heating

37% Internal gains

38% Solar gains

L2 is situated on the first and second floors.

L2 has a sunspace across the full width of the apartment on the south side.

Van Ringen (R)

This design, in line with common building practice in Holland, is constructed from in-situ concrete, with prefabricated elements in both the facades and the roof, and clad with brick. The house has a basic floor plan 5.2m by 8m and an extra porch and full height cupboard attached to the entrance. On the first floor there are three bedrooms and a bathroom, whilst the attic contains the heating equipment and provides storage space.

All 10m^2 of window in the house are gas filled, low emissivity coated double glazing.

SOLAR DESIGN

● 72% of all glazing is on the south face of the house.

● Attached to the living room is a 3m by 2m, single glazed sunspace.

● The roof has a 62° pitch to accommodate the 17.4m^2 air collector designed to preheat ventilation air.

The 26.3m^2 living room has 4.8m^2 of south facing glazing, of which 3.5m^2 open onto the sunspace. This gives a glazing to living room floor area ratio of 18%.

Due to both the steep roof pitch and the presence of the collector equipment, the north side of the roof would have to be modified if the attic were to be used as a fourth bedroom.

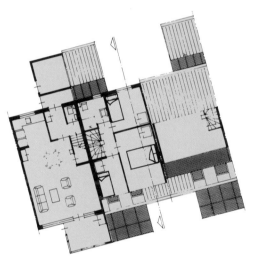

CONTRIBUTIONS TO THE ANNUAL SPACE HEATING DEMAND

5 175kWh

29% Auxiliary heating

42% Internal gains

29% Solar gains

PERFORMANCE OF THE SOLAR DESIGN

The overall solar contribution to the gross space heating load is 29%.

Once the savings attributable to direct gain and energy conservation measures have been deducted, the monitoring confirms calculations that neither the collector nor the sunspace save sufficient energy to repay the interest on the capital cost.

User response to the sunspace has also been moderate because of the limited space it provides.

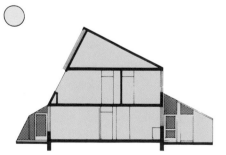

Eindhoven University of Technology (W)

This design by the Housing and Energy Conservation Group at Eindhoven University of Technology is constructed from traditional sand-lime bricks with prefabricated elements used in the walls and roof. The front and back walls are clad with brick and timber and the roof is tiled.
The design aims to minimise the surface to volume ratio. The arguments in favour of this approach concern not only the need to save energy but also the desire to reduce the facade area which is relatively expensive to construct. The 4.65m by 10.34m floor plan comprises an open-plan living room/kitchen on the ground floor, three bedrooms and a bathroom on the first floor, and the heating equipment and storage space in the attic. The total glazed area is 9.8m^2.
The entrances on both the south and north sides of the house have enclosed porches attached.

SOLAR DESIGN

● 70% of total glazing is on the southernmost side of the house (which faces south-west due to its position in the Energy Park).

● A sloping clerestory along the living room ceiling compensates for the narrow, deep floor plan and provides sufficient daylight in the living room.

The ratio of window to floor area in the living room is nearly 25% but without the clerestory it would have been less than 9%. The clerestory glazing is the

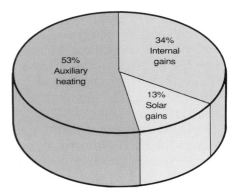

CONTRIBUTIONS TO THE ANNUAL SPACE HEATING DEMAND
8 580kWh

53% Auxiliary heating
34% Internal gains
13% Solar gains

same type as that used in the majority of the windows - gas filled, low emissivity double glazing.

PERFORMANCE OF PASSIVE SOLAR DESIGN

The solar contribution to the gross space heating load is only 13%, acceptable for this orientation. The normalised selling price of the house is 146 365 Gld, whereas a comparable standard house would cost 143 275 Gld. Hence, this design represents an increased cost of only just over 2% compared to a standard house.

Performance Evaluation

MONITORING

Prior to monitoring, the "Physical Aspects of the Built Environment" group of Eindhoven University of Technology used their own simulation programme (KLI) to perform energy calculations on the final designs. Monitoring started in the second half of 1984 and came to a formal end in May 1986. Measurements began just before each terrace was occupied so that the parameters for the energy model could be validated in an unoccupied situation. A number of tests on airtightness, thermal behaviour, equipment efficiency, etc, were carried out on one terraced house of each design. After occupancy, monitoring consisted of continuous reading of the temperatures and relative humidity in the living room, bedrooms, attic and sunspace, for one house in each row. The actual energy consumption is derived from monthly readings which the homeowners recorded on special data sheets. The success of the monitoring is therefore largely due to the co-operation of the residents.

The third aspect of the monitoring was a survey in which the homeowners were asked their opinions on their houses.

USER RESPONSE

Information on occupant response was gathered by means of a number of written enquiries. In general, the occupants were appreciative of the designs, 70% of the total responses gave a rating of excellent or good and only 3% said they were poor. However, some house types were considerably better liked than others.

PERFORMANCE OF PASSIVE SOLAR DESIGNS

When assessing the contribution to the gross space heating load made by solar gain, it is important to note the extent to which this load has been reduced compared to standard Building Code designs. Since the internal gains provide a high proportion of the gross heating load, the solar contribution appears small. However, as a proportion of the net load, the solar contribution is more significant.

In many of the Energy Park designs, around 40% of the space heating is met by useful internal gains. Excluding the two rows with principally east-west orientation, the solar contribution to the gross heating load varies between 23% and 38%, but as a proportion of the net space heating load, the solar contributions are between 40% and 71%.

Average thermostat settings in the calculations, 19-21°C for the living room and 14-18°C for the bedrooms, were similar to the actual 85/86 averages, of 18-21°C and 13-19°C respectively. More than 60% of the houses were occupied all day.

COST EFFECTIVENESS

The project received extra subsidies to cover the development costs and the costs associated with the small number of dwellings per design. With the subsidies, the average cost of the houses remained below the compulsory cost ceiling for Premium-A housing. To establish the costs under normal market conditions, a "normalised" cost was derived. A reasonable market penetration with no extra subsidies or development costs was assumed, combined with a project size of 48 houses per design. For insulation, glazing and conventional (improved efficiency) heating and ventilation options, this gives "normalised" figures below the cost ceilings. For the rest of the experimental features however, the normalised costs remain at or above the cost ceilings imposed for public housing schemes.

Air collectors are not yet economically feasible but are technically sound, and sunspaces, whilst they cannot be justified in terms of fuel savings alone, are generally enjoyed by the occupants.

Kol & Lindeman's duplex apartments have integral sunspaces.

In addition to the sunspaces in Van Ringen's design, the roof has a 62° pitch to accommodate air-heating solar collectors.

A sloping clerestory along the living room ceiling compensates for the deep, narrow floor plan in the Eindhoven University design.

PROJECT DATA

Building	B	K	T	H	L1	L2	R	W
Width (m)	5.12	4.61	5.49	6.92	7.4	7.4	4.84	4.37
Depth (m)	7.46	7.72	7.5	5.9	5.89	4.0	8.2	9.82
Net area (m²)	106	94	105	97	103	88	101	101
Living area (m²)	55	55	64	64	62	50	43	65
Service area (m²)	51	39	41	34	42	38	58	36
Window area: total (m²)	10.77	9.95	10.31	7.22	18.31	37.32	10.06	9.78
southern most	8.16	7.14	6.18	5.82	18.31	33.00	7.02	6.86
northern most	2.61	2.81	4.13	1.40	0.00	4.32	3.04	2.92

Sunspace								
Floor area (m²)	12.1				9.5	9.6	6.8	
Glass area: total (m²)	23				37	33	8	
vertical	10				37	16		
sloped	13					17	8	

Thermal characteristics (W/m²K)	B	K	T	H	L1	L2	R	W
U value: exterior wall	0.33	0.24	0.25	0.25	0.22	0.22	0.33	0.29
roof	0.30	0.25	0.26	0.33	0.31	0.31	0.30	0.30
floor	0.30	0.33	0.36	0.32	0.26	0.26	0.30	0.30
windows								
lower floor	1.80	2.90	2.10	2.10	1.90	1.90	1.80	1.80
upper floor	1.80	2.90	2.10	2.10	2.10	2.10	1.80	1.80
sunspace glazing	5.7				1.9/5.7	1.9/5.7	5.7	
Infiltration rate (@50Pa)	3.8	2.7	3.6	4.0	3.9	4.5	1.9	2.6
External design temp	-10ºC	-10ºC	-10ºC	-10ºC	-10ºC	-10ºC	-10ºC	-10ºC
Heated floor area (m²)	106	94	105	97	103	88	101	101
Heated volume (m³)	314	297	345	341	266	267	322	312
Net heat load (kWh/m²)	52	57	88	70	58	58	51	85

Site and Climate

Altitude	-4 m	
Latitude	52º N	
Longitude	4º E	
Average ambient temp: annual	9.4 ºC	
Jan	2.3 ºC	
July	16.6 ºC	
Degree days (base 18.3ºC)	3140	days
Global irradiation on horiz	1167	kWh/m²
Sunshine hours	1549	hrs/yr

The average annual fuel consumption for space heating in the Energy Park over the 1985/86 period was 21GJ. Individual houses achieved upto 80% savings compared to a house of the same size built to conventional standards.

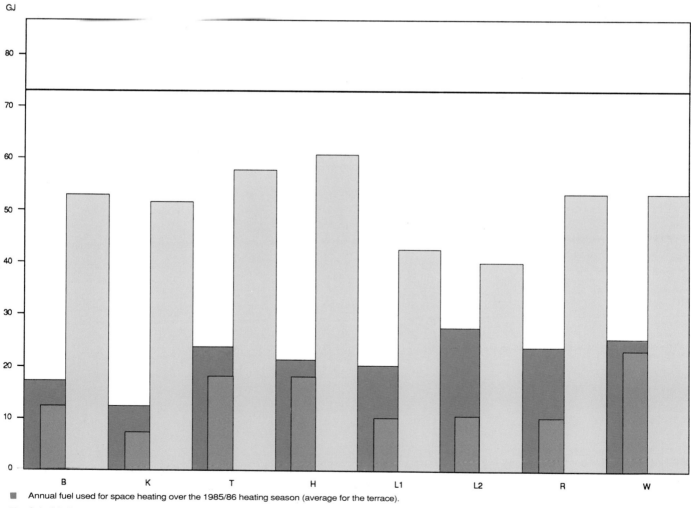

GJ

B   K   T   H   L1   L2   R   W

■ Annual fuel used for space heating over the 1985/86 heating season (average for the terrace).

■ Calculated average annual fuel used for space heating.

□ Annual fuel used for space heating in the same dwelling built to Dutch Building Standards.

— Annual fuel used for space heating in an average Dutch terraced house.

NB. These figures are not directly comparable with those in the pie-charts as the charts include conversion efficiencies.

LIEVRE D'OR CREDITS

Client
OPHLM de la Ville de Dreux
22 Rue des Gaules
28150 Dreux

Architects
Groupe Aura
SCPA Laumonnier
Meninger Portron
50 Rue du Fauborg
St Martin
75012 Paris

D et M Perinic
12 Rue JB Potin
92170 Vanves

J Beluard
20 Rue des Capuchins
28103 Dreux

Service Engineer
ETC
7 Place Franz Liszt
75010 Paris

Energy Consultant
M Raoust Ingenieur Conseil
SCPA CLAUX PESSO RAOUST
70 Blvd Magenta
75010 Paris

Building Contractor
Entreprise Delavera
9 Quai du Roi
45000 Orleans

Monitoring Organisation
Group Ramses (CNRS PIRSEM)
Centre Universitaire d'Orsay
Batiment 208
91405 Orsay Cedex

Commission of the European Communities

- Large estate of 19 apartment blocks, comprising 593 dwellings retrofitted with a mix of sunspaces, solar wall collectors (Trombe walls) and insulation.

- Architectural and energy improvements integrated to revitalise a 1960's estate with poor physical and social conditions.

- Overall reduction in energy consumption of nearly 50%.

- Sunspaces contribute 26% to the net space heating load per flat, where fitted. In other flats, solar wall collectors make a lesser contribution to space heating and are not cost effective.

LIEVRE D'OR

DREUX
FRANCE

Project Background

Sunspaces attached to some existing buildings were built as separate structures and were then linked to the main building.

Le Lievre d'Or is an estate of 19 four to eight storey apartment blocks comprising 593 dwellings, built between 1965 and 1967. The development is a typical result of the town planning policies of the 50's and 60's, designed to meet the heavy demand for housing brought about by the population influx related to industrial development. The estate is in Dreux, a town with 33,000 inhabitants which is an important centre for the electro mechanical and car industries. The population of Dreux has doubled over the past 20 years.
In 1979, as a result of the serious deterioration in physical and social conditions, the high rate of occupant turnover and high heating bills, the estate owners, Office Public d'Habitations a Loyers Moderes (OPHLM), decided on an extensive refurbishment programme. The refurbishment includes the introduction of sunspaces and wall collectors as well as insulation, all integrated into a major architectural improvement of the estate.

DESIGN OBJECTIVES

There were two principal design objectives:-

● to improve the appearance of the estate;

● to reduce heating costs.

Sociological and architectural aspects were to be integrated and residents consulted throughout the refurbishment.

The extra costs associated with the energy saving measures were met by the French Housing Ministry and the French Agency for Energy Management (AFME).

ENERGY SAVING FEATURES

A variety of energy saving measures were introduced:-

● Improvement of the heating systems, including new boilers and controls, lagging pipework and fitting thermostatic radiator valves in the individual flats.

● Insulation of roofs, ground floors and walls;

● Installation of double glazed windows;

● Draughtproofing of windows and doors;

● Installation of kitchen and bathroom extract systems;

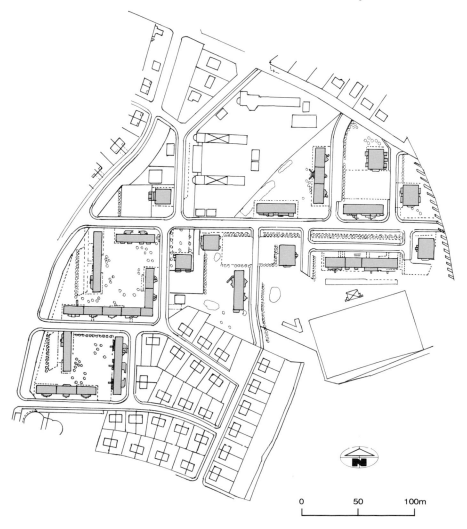

0   50   100m

A total of 19 blocks of flats were included in the refurbishment.

Design Details

- Addition of sunspaces to south facades;

- Construction to form Trombe walls on 'blind' south facades;

- Provision of increased window areas on south facades.

SITE AND CLIMATE

Dreux is located 80km west of Paris, at the intersection of the rivers Blaise and Eure on the Beauce plain. The Lievre d'Or estate is 1km from the centre of Dreux and includes a school, a small shopping centre and other local shops.

The climate is characterized by very low rainfall (51cm over the whole year). There are 2626 degree days on average per year (base 18ºC) 1800 hours of sunshine.

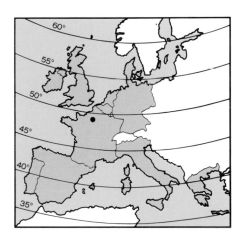

CLIMATE

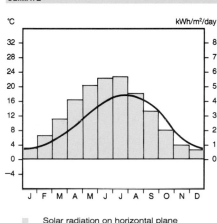

Solar radiation on horizontal plane
Average external temp.

A major visual improvement of the estate was required

CONCLUSIONS

Everyone considers the refurbishment to be a success:- the client, the municipality, the designers and the inhabitants. There has been a reduction in vandalism (it is now the best area of Dreux in this respect) and a significant reduction in occupant turnover.

The energy consumption has on average been reduced by nearly 50% and the appearance of the area has been greatly improved in architectural terms.

PLANNING

Careful design and implementation of the refurbishment were necessary with full occupant consultation since the work was carried out with "tenants in place".

Before renovation, all facades were "sad, grey and uniform", and entrances were difficult to find.

Architectural features, in the form of sunspaces, balconies, extensions, extra windows and colour, have been incorporated into all facades. The entrances have been improved so that their location is clearly shown by the architecture of the facades. Some private gardens have been made for lower flats, and other facilities, such as drying rooms and bicycle and pram stores, have been introduced.

CONSTRUCTION

The existing walls of the blocks were constructed from hollow autoclaved breeze-blocks. The extensions, to increase the size of flats and for the sunspaces, were built from in-situ concrete as independent structures with separate foundations and linked to the main building with flexible fittings.

Bored pile foundations were used for the extensions, and these were difficult to place due to the presence of many underground services. Careful detailing was necessary to ensure the watertightness of extensions.

External insulation was applied to all the exposed walls combined with a variety of coloured finishes.

Design Details

A variety of coloured finishes were used to brighten up the external appearance.

absorbing surface) and insulated on the inside, in the flat. Hot air from the collector is directed into the flat via an automatically controlled vent. In summer a vent at the top of the collector allows the hot air to escape. 11.3m^2 of collector have been allowed for each flat, though several flats receive warmed air from the same Trombe wall. No ducting was used to move the solar heated air around the flats, all movement is passive; through the windows from inside the sunspace and though the vents from the Trombe walls.

PASSIVE SOLAR DESIGN

A number of passive solar measures have been used on various flats within the estate:-

● Enlargement of south facing rooms (38 dwellings) and an increase in window size (double glazing used).

● Addition of sunspaces to south facing flats (141 dwellings).

● Construction of Trombe walls from 'blind' south facades (32 dwellings).

The sunspaces were constructed as separate, but linked, structures. They are built from aluminium framing with single glazing and are between 6m^2 and 8m^2. They provide a buffer zone for the existing walls, preheated ventilation air for adjacent rooms and additional space for the flats. Summer overheating is reduced by the overhanging roofs.

The Trombe walls provide solar heating through grilles to 32 dwellings. The wall is painted black on the outside (forming the

0 1 2 3m

The sunspaces transform the appearance of the south elevation.

Trombe wall

Additional space was provided in the flats by the extensions and sunspaces.

Extensions to some south facing living rooms provided an opportunity to increase the area of glazing.

0   2   4   6m

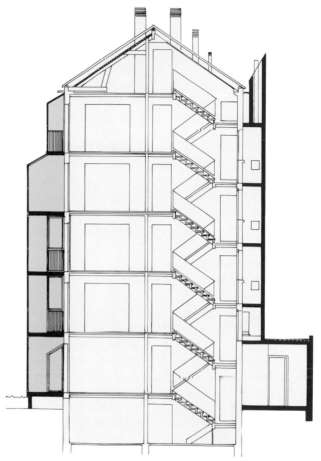

Direct gain and convective air movements provide the solar heating to the flats.

OPERATING MODES AND CONTROLS

The sunspaces provide solar heated air for the flats by natural movement through the internal windows and doors. In summer, the sunspaces are ventilated by opening windows. No blinds were provided to reduce gains. When no warm air is available from the sunspace the internal doors and windows are closed. In the heating season, the Trombe walls provide warmed air, when available, through automatically controlled vents to the flats. These vents close when no warmed air is available. In summer, the vents to the flats are manually closed and a vent at the top of the collector allows the unwanted hot air to escape.

AUXILIARY HEATING SYSTEMS

The existing gas boilers which provided heating for a whole block of flats have been renewed, pipework has been lagged and new controls, including thermostatic radiator valves, have been installed in all flats. The controls overcome the previous problem that one third of the flats were underheated and two thirds overheated. Domestic hot water is provided by individual boilers in the flats.

The aesthetic improvements are considered very successful.

Performance Evaluation

MONITORING

Extensive monitoring has been carried out at the site since 1981. This has been at two levels:-

● Global monitoring of fuel consumption per block (15 blocks), and monitoring of meteorological conditions;

● Detailed monitoring of individual flats to examine the performance of the solar features.

Occupants appreciate both the increased space and the warmth of the sunspace.

The monitoring was carried out by the National Scientific Research Centre (CNRS) using a central data acquisition system. Data analysis was carried out using a program (CALECO) originally developed by the Energy Efficient Building Group at the Lawrence Berkeley Laboratories (California, USA) and a simulation model has been developed to operate in parallel with the data analysis which gives an hour by hour comparison between measured and calculated data.
The results discussed are based on the global monitoring and the detailed monitoring of seven flats in block 19, which were retrofitted with sunspaces. Some monitoring of control flats has also been carried out.

USER RESPONSE

The inhabitants of the estate are reported to be very satisfied with the refurbishment. The dwellings are larger, much more comfortable and the combined rent and service charges (including heating) are lower than previously. Architecturally, the appearance of the estate is greatly improved, particularly by the added sunspaces. The tenants appreciate this as well as the extra space and warmth provided by the sunspaces.
It appears that where the flats have solar wall collectors the occupants do not fully understand them, nor use them well.
A further endorsement of the success of the scheme would seem to be the reduced turnover of occupants, down from 210 changes in 1978 to only 60 in 1982.

PERFORMANCE OF PASSIVE SOLAR FEATURES

Global monitoring of the blocks showed a reduction of 48% in fuel consumption between 1980 and 1983, when the refurbishment was completed. Much of this was due to the insulation and the new heating system. Consumption has risen again slightly since 1983, due to colder winters and possibly less energy conscious use of the sunspaces (occupants keeping connecting door and windows open).
Detailed monitoring of block 19 (a block to which sunspaces were added) showed a solar contribution of nearly 20% to the gross, or 26% to the net space heating load. Overall, the flats

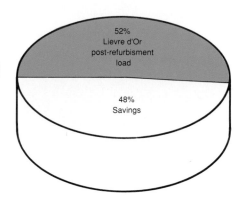

COMPARISON WITH PRE-REFURBISHMENT CONSUMPTION

52%
Lievre d'Or
post-refurbisment
load

48%
Savings

For the whole estate, the energy savings were 48% compared to the consumption before refurbishment.

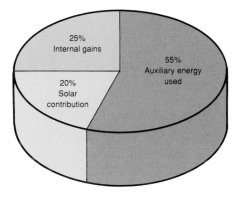

CONTRIBUTIONS TO ANNUAL SPACE HEATING LOAD

25%
Internal gains

55%
Auxiliary energy used

20%
Solar contribution

For an individual flat with a retrofitted sunspace, solar gains provided 20% of the gross space heating load.

with sunspaces are estimated to save 55% of energy consumed, compared to the situation before renovation. Of these savings, 6.7% are attributed to ventilation preheat and 24% to the insulating effect of the sunspace. There is no record of sunspaces overheating in summer.
The Trombe walls were estimated to provide the equivalent of 1500 kW during the heating season to each flat, a similar amount to that provided by the sunspaces, ie, around 20% of the gross space heating load. However, this has not been confirmed by the monitoring due to failure of

COST OF FUEL USED ANNUALLY

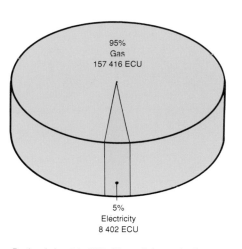

95%
Gas
157 416 ECU

5%
Electricity
8 402 ECU

For the whole estate, 95% of the cost of space heating came from gas usage.

COST OF BUILDING AND SOLAR DESIGN

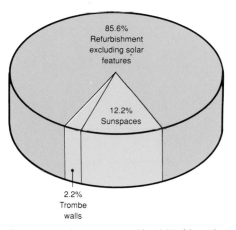

85.6%
Refurbishment excluding solar features

12.2%
Sunspaces

2.2%
Trombe walls

Overall the solar features accounted for 14.4% of the total refurbishment cost.

measurement probes. Distribution of warm air to different flats is poor, with flats on the lower floors receiving cooler air than those on the top floors. Generally, the performance of the Trombe walls is considered poor. No overheating of the inside wall has been recorded.

The performance of the increased areas of south facing glazing in the enlarged flats has not been specifically monitored either, but is not thought to be good due to the lack of sufficient thermal mass in the floors and the absence of insulating shutters to reduce heat loss at night.

NET MONTHLY SPACE HEATING DEMAND AND SUPPLY

Single flat in block 19, with sunspace.

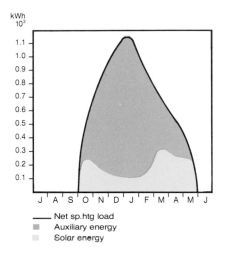

kWh
10³

J A S O N D J F M A M J

— Net sp.htg load
■ Auxiliary energy
□ Solar energy

COST EFFECTIVENESS

Since the sunspaces were added for architectural, spatial and energy reasons, no cost effectiveness calculations are possible based on the energy savings alone.

The solar wall collectors were added primarily for energy saving reasons, and the return on the capital investments of 15 300 FF per flat (where they were installed) is very poor. On the estimated annual savings of 342 FF, the simple payback time is about 36 years. Methods of reducing the capital costs are being investigated.

MONTHLY AVERAGE TEMPERATURES

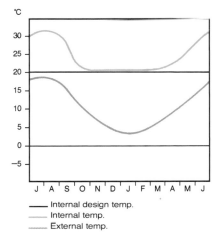

°C

J A S O N D J F M A M J

— Internal design temp.
— Internal temp.
— External temp.

PROJECT DATA				Mean U value	0.73	W/m²K
				Global heat loss coefficient	166	W/K
Building Characteristics				Infiltration Rate	Not known	
- 4 room flat with sunspace in block 19				External design temperature	-7	°C
				Heated floor area	71	m²
Flat				Heated volume	180	m³
Volume		180	m³	Net heat load	85	kWh/m²
Floor area		71	m²			
External wall area		66	m²			
Windows:	Total area	9	m² 100%	**Site and Climate**		
	South	4.8	m² 53%	Altitude	10	m
	North	0	m²	Latitude	48° 46'	N
				Longitude	2°1'	E
Sunspace				Average ambient temp: Jan	2.9	°C
Volume		15.5	m³	July	17.8	°C
Floor area		6.3	m²	Degree days (base 18°C)	2626	days
Wall area:	Glass	16.8	m²	Global irradiation on horiz	1127	kWh/m²
	Solid	6	m²	Sunshine hours	1800	hr/yr
Thermal Characteristics				**Costs**		
U value:	Roof	0.62	W/m²K	Building refurbishment		
	Floor	0.60	W/m²K	(typical flat)	45 268 FF	6 501 ECU
	External walls	0.56	W/m²K	Sunspaces	15 839 FF	2 275 ECU
	Windows	2.6	W/m²K	Trombe walls	15 297 FF	2 197 ECU
	Conservatory glazing	3.4	W/m²K			

BAGGESENSGADE CREDITS

Client
Andelsboligforening Baggesensgade 5
(Housing Co-operative)
Baggesensgade 5
2200 Copenhagen N.

Architect
F. Stein
Housing Laboratory
School of Architecture
Royal Academy of Arts
Kongens Nytorv 1
1050 Copenhagen K.

Energy Consultant
Technological Institute
Heating Department
Gragersensvej
2630 Tåstrup

Project Engineer
Ole Vanggaard
Consulting Engineer
Hårbøllevej 64
4792 Askeby

Contractors
Bybyg Aps
St Kongensgade 108
1264 Copenhagen K.

Monitoring Organisation
Erwin Petersen
Technological Institute
Heating Department
Gragersensvej
2630 Tåstrup

14

Commission of the European Communities

BAGGESENSGADE

COPENHAGEN
DENMARK

● Retrofit glass south facade creates sunspaces or open balconies for flats in a five-storey block.

● Clever design locates the floors of the sunspaces 450mm above the floor level in the flats giving greatly improved daylighting and views from the flats.

● Building now uses only 66% of the auxiliary energy it required prior to the retrofit, solar gains contribute 27% to the gross space heating load.

● Fuel savings increased from almost zero in the first heating season to 34% in the second year of monitoring, due to education of the residents in the use of their sunspaces.

Project Background

Renovation of the old south facade of the block was a planning requirement.

A glass facade has been added to the south elevation of a five-storey block which was in need of renovation. The glass skin creates a 10m² sunspace for each of the flats on the first to fourth floors. On the fifth floor an open balcony is created.The ground floor is allocated for commercial use. In 1985, the project was awarded a prize by the City of Copenhagen as one of the best buildings architecturally.

OBJECTIVES

As part of a general urban renewal programme for the neighbourhood, the city required the rear, south face of the apartment block to be renovated. The residents, who had already built a conservatory at ground level, decided they would like an "extended" version of this familiar and much used room covering the entire south facade of the building, in preference to replacement of existing windows and renovation and insulation of the masonry facade. The flats are not privately owned as such, all the inhabitants are members of a housing co-operative.
The project was the first of its type in Denmark, so the aim was to gain experience in the technical, economic and functional aspects of this approach to refurbishment.

SITE AND CLIMATE

The building is in a district of Copenhagen which is undergoing extensive urban

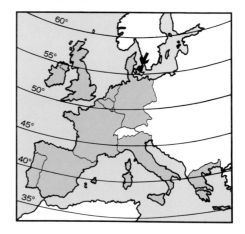

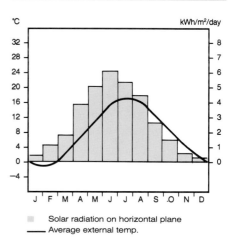

CLIMATE (Copenhagen)

Solar radiation on horizontal plane
Average external temp.

renewal. The buildings to the rear have been cleared and this allows solar radiation to penetrate each floor on the south face of the block. As the site was already "overbuilt" according to the Building Code, it was necessary to apply for a dispensation for the works. The climate is the urban climate of a city. The area experiences

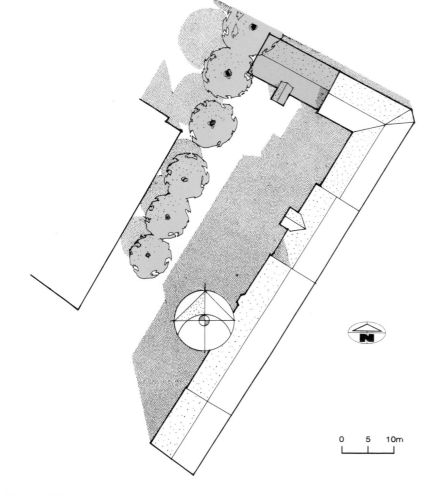

0 5 10m

Adjacent buildings and mature trees reduce the period during which the building has direct solar exposure.

Design Details

The new glass facade is a separate structure and creates sunspaces for the flats in the block.

a coastal temperate climate with mild winters and relatively cool summers.

The microclimate is the result of several influences - a high building to the east and north, a row of deciduous trees and a church tower to the west. These appreciably reduce the period during which the building has direct solar exposure. At the same time, these obstructions offer protection against winds from every direction except the southwest, the predominant winds. The strength of the wind from this direction is increased as it funnels between the physical obstructions.

CONCLUSIONS

The project has been received with great interest and enthusiasm by professionals and individuals alike, and consequently, future refurbishment schemes are likely to involve similar retrofit solutions. Significant energy savings were achieved when occupants learnt to use the system efficiently.

DESIGN DETAILS

The facade is the result of many, often conflicting, requirements. In energy terms, it would be desirable to have as much transparent area as possible, whilst the architect and the client wanted to give the new facade its own identity with a pattern of thicker window frames and smaller subdivisions. Wood was chosen in preference to metal according to a desire for more "friendly" materials to co-ordinate with the existing structure.

The main objectives of the project were to investigate the feasibility of building in such a confined area without the use of heavy machinery (there was no space on the site), and to cause as little disturbance as possible to the occupants. Both of these objectives were successfully achieved.

CONSTRUCTION

The new facade is supported on larch wood columns and has floors constructed of:

- 40mm magnesite screed;
- 20mm plywood;
- cavity formed by 170mm timber framework;
- 10mm cement fibreboard as fireproofing.

Ventilation air passes through the cavity and into the sunspace. Wind stability is achieved by attaching the decks to the corners of the building and to the central stair tower.

PASSIVE SOLAR DESIGN

The new glass skin is 1.5m in front of the existing building and creates a 10m^2 sunspace for each flat. The sunspace saves energy in two ways:

- by supplying direct and indirect solar gains to the heated spaces to offset the space heating demand;

- by providing a buffer zone with the external environment to partially insulate the flats against the wind.

Construction is of larch wood columns with single glazing.

Design Details

In addition, the sunspace adds useful space to the flats.

One or more windows in the existing south facade have been replaced with doors onto the sunspaces according to each individual occupant's wishes. With the exception of the ground feature of the passive solar design. Light-coloured floors and ceilings also increase the amount of reflected light in the flats.

As the new facade is only single glazed, there are large fluctuations in both temperature

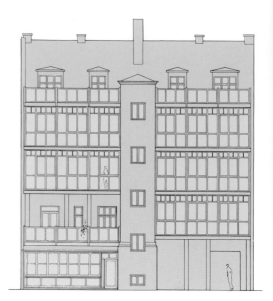

The appearance of the building is transformed by the new facade.

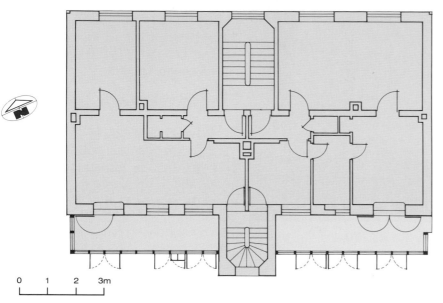

All rooms on the south side open onto the sunspace, the choice of doors or windows was left to the individual.

and first floors, there are two small flats (70m^2) per floor. The introduction of the sunspaces has resulted in several of the occupants in these particular flats converting the three secondary rooms along the south facade (kitchen and two small bedrooms) into the main living space.

The deck between the existing building and the new glass facade is placed approximately 450mm above the floor level of the flat. The reason for this change in level is to allow as much direct sunlight as possible to enter the existing flat, and to provide as unobstructed a view as possible from the inside. The glass in the lower section of the new facade is necessary to provide a good view from the lower level inside the flat. The raised decks result in a great deal of daylight being reflected onto the ceilings in the flats, and this is an added

and humidity within the sunspaces. In winter, the temperature in this zone can drop below 0°C, whilst just a short sunny spell, of say only 30 minutes, is sufficient to provide the flats with useful solar gains. Single glazing was chosen by the clients because they wished the sunspaces to have a close relationship with the outside. The existing windows are double glazed and to have more than three layers of glass between the inhabitants and the external environment was considered unacceptable.

The sunspaces are a welcome and very flexible addition.

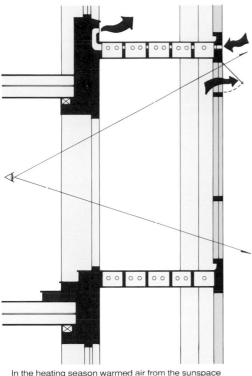

In the heating season warmed air from the sunspace is convected into the flats. Excess warm air is vented to the outside in summer.

CONTROLS

Approximately two thirds of the glass facade is openable window and, in addition, there are ventilation windows at the top. Even when all the windows are closed, there is still some fresh air intake as the structure,

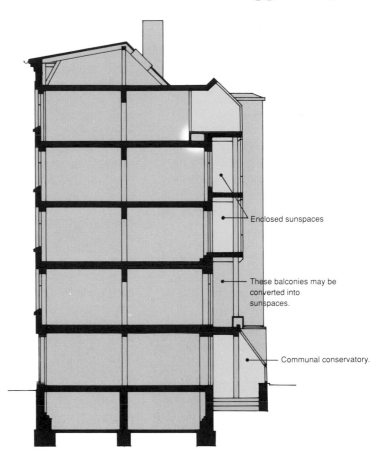

Enclosed sunspaces

These balconies may be converted into sunspaces.

Communal conservatory.

On one side of the first floor, there is an open balcony rather than an enclosed sunspace.

Two thirds of the new glass facade is openable and there are small ventilation windows at the top.

by design, is not totally sealed. In addition to this "planned leakage", the deck is ventilated in such a way that fresh air passes through it into the sunspace. These measures reduce condensation on the inside of the glass facade. One problem is that the windows tend not to be sufficiently clean, due to difficulty with access. Several occupants have installed shading devices to protect both them and their plants from excessive solar exposure, and to provide some privacy. It is likely that automatic opening devices will be installed in several sunspaces where the occupants are often away from their flats in the summer.

OPERATING MODES

Between autumn and spring, the sunspaces can provide useful solar energy both directly and indirectly. Solar heated fresh air flows into the flats through open doors and windows, whilst the existing heavyweight masonry facade stores solar gains for release later in the day.
Due to the changeable weather conditions typical of a Danish summer, the storage factor is also very important in this season.

AUXILIARY HEATING SYSTEM

The building is connected to the municipal district heating network. All of the radiators have thermostatic valves and thus are automatically shut off when passive solar gains are available.

Performance Evaluation

MONITORING

The apartment block was monitored for two years, 1985-1987. The total energy consumption for the building was measured and consumptions for individual flats were then calculated based on readings taken from digital heat meters installed on the radiators within each flat.

Temperatures were measured at low level within the flats, in the glazed balconies and outside. More extensive monitoring took place for short periods.

The sunspace structure was constructed with minimum disruption to the occupants.

USER RESPONSE

All the occupants are very pleased with their new sunspaces which are a welcome and very flexible extension to the fairly small flats. The raised deck with three steps up to it has given the small flats a new spatial quality. The response from the surrounding neighbourhood has also been enthusiastic, and the five floor conservatory has been nicknamed "the dolls house". However, not all the inhabitants are equally energy conscious with respect to use of the sunspaces. The result is that some of the flats have very high energy savings, whilst in others the savings are very low, or even negative.

PERFORMANCE OF PASSIVE SOLAR DESIGN

The conventional way to modernise such a block would be to repair and replace the windows, draughtstrip throughout and insulate and renovate the masonry facade. The resulting annual saving in energy would be approximately 12000 kWh.

Over the 1985/86 heating season, monitoring revealed only very small energy savings associated with the sunspaces. This was because the residents were not using them appropriately. The inner pane of the existing double glazed windows had been removed, since single glazed windows are generally easier to handle, and the doors between the flats and sunspaces were often left open on days when the temperatures in the sunspaces were low. Monitoring over the 1986/87 heating season showed that there had been a great improvement in performance, and the addition of the sunspaces had produced 34% savings (21600 kWh) compared to the consumption prior to refurbishment.

These savings were due partly to the sunspaces acting as buffer spaces, in general the air temperature in them is 5-10°C higher than ambient, and this reduces heat loss through the south facade. In addition, the sunspaces provide useful solar gains directly through open doors and windows on sunny

COMPARISON WITH PRE-REFURBISHMENT CONSUMPTION

The auxiliary space heating load prior to refurbishment for all the flats was 63 900kWh.

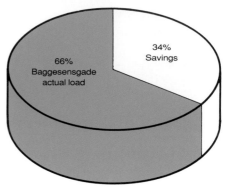

Since the new glass facade has been built, the new consumption is only 42 300kWh.

AUXILIARY FUEL USED ANNUALLY

Total annual fuel used is 73 700kWh for the flats.

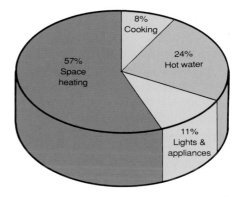

days in spring and autumn, whilst solar gains stored in the masonry facade offset any space heating load in summer. Solar gains are estimated to provide 27% of the gross space heating load in the flats as retrofitted.

COST EFFECTIVENESS

The purpose of this experimental project was to assess the usefulness and the energy saving potential of sunspaces when used in the refurbishment of flats. The cost of the sunspaces per

CONTRIBUTIONS TO TOTAL SPACE HEATING DEMAND

Total annual space heating demand is 80 930kWh.

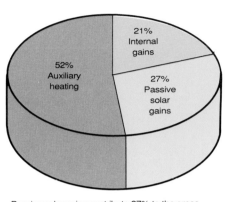

Passive solar gains contribute 27% to the gross space heating load.

MONTHLY SPACE HEATING LOAD

For all the flats

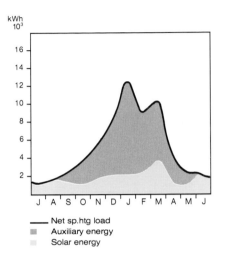

— Net sp.htg load
▦ Auxiliary energy
▨ Solar energy

MONTHLY AVERAGE TEMPERATURES

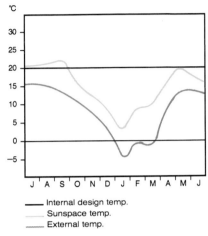

— Internal design temp.
— Sunspace temp.
— External temp.

flat was kr 89 000, whereas the cost of conventional refurbishment would have been kr 40 000. However, the architect believes that if another similar retrofit were to be undertaken, the costs would be much reduced, approximately kr 65 000 per flat instead. Even though the cost of space heating is relatively low as it is provided by a district heating scheme (very common in large towns in Denmark), the annual savings amount to approximately kr 840 per flat.

The sunspaces also have considerable value as increased space since they are inhabitable for about three-quarters of the year. A "normal" extension would cost approximately kr 5 500/m² to build. An additional incentive for this type of refurbishment in Denmark is the availability of loans at very low interest rates.

From the amount of interest shown in the project, it would appear that sunspaces are a viable way of improving the quality of the many small inner city flats, whilst achieving reduced heating costs.

OVERCAST WINTER DAY (16 January 1987)

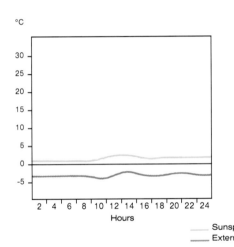

Hours

SUNNY SPRING DAY (21March 1987)

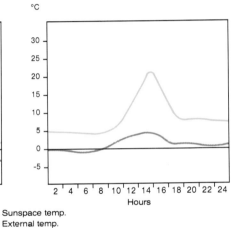

Hours

— Sunspace temp.
— External temp.

PROJECT DATA

Building				Global heat loss coefficient		
Volume		1700	m³	(excluding workshop on ground floor)	760	W/K
Floor area		620	m²	Infiltration rate	0.5	ac/h
Roof area		140	m²	External design temperature	-12	°C
Windows:	total area	125	m² 100%	Heated floor area	620	m²
	south	65	m² 52%	Heated volume	1700	m³
	north	60	m² 48%	Net heat load	68	kWh/m²
	south covered					
	by sunspace	40	m²	**Site and Climate**		
				Altitude	0	m
Glazed balconies				Latitude	56	°N
(excluding existing balconies)				Longitude	12	°E
Volume		140	m³	Average ambient temp: Jan	-1	°C
Floor area		50	m²	July	16	°C
Glass wall area		90	m²	Degree days (base 17°C)	2909	days
				Global irradiation on horiz	1015	kWh/m²
Thermal characteristics				Sunshine hours	1500	hr/yr
U value:	roof	0.45	W/m²K			
	external walls	1.0	W/m²K	**Costs** (1985 prices)		
	insulated gable			Glazed balconies	kr 710 000	90 000 ECU
	end walls	0.34	W/m²K			
	windows					
	(double glazed)	3.0	W/m²K			
	sunspaces					
	(single glazed)	7.0	W/m²K			

ECOLE PRIMAIRE DE TOURNAI CREDITS

Client
Ministère de l'Education Nationale
Fonds des Bâtiments Scolaires de l'Etat (FBSE)
Direction provinciale du Hainaut
Chemin de Fer, 433
7000 Mons

Architects
Prof Jean Wilfart, with C Rahier, F Staquet,
M Huygh, M Xhoffer, B Detollenaere, JP Reygaert.
Centre d'études et de recherches du FBSE
Rue Montoyer, 57/59
1040 Brussels

Energy Consultants
A Bluth, G Clerdent
FBSE
Rue de Serbie, 42/48
4000 Liège

J Alsteen
FBSE
Chemin de Fer, 433
7000 Mons

Building Contractor
DHERTE SA
Rue Lieutenant Cotton, 4
7880 Flobecq

Services Contractor
DRUART SA
Ch. de Bethléem, 9
7000 Mons

Monitoring Organisation
Centre de Recherches en Architecture
Université Catholique de Louvain
Place du Levant, 1
1348 Louvain-la-Neuve

for: Ministère de la Région Wallonne
    Inspection Générale de l'Energie
    Avenue Prince de Liège, 7
    5100 Jambes

Commission of the European Communities

● School designed to be "climate respecting" in both construction and use, encourages pupils to respond to the natural environment.

● One large central sunspace and four smaller sunspaces attached to classrooms, provide solar gain directly to teaching spaces.

● Active roof-mounted air-heating collectors provide warm air directly to the heating system when needed, excess heat is transferred to pebble and water stores.

● Passive solar gains provide 30% of the space heating and the active solar system provides a further 21%, however the electricity consumption for the fans is high.

ECOLE PRIMAIRE DE TOURNAI
TOURNAI
BELGIUM

Project Background

The school has two wings, each with five classrooms; three on the ground floor and two on the first, and sunspaces are attached to the ground floor classrooms. This is the west wing.

PROJECT BACKGROUND

Ecole de Tournai is a "state of the art" primary school built and monitored as part of a competition organised by the Directorate for Energy and New Technologies, part of the Ministry for the Walloon Region. It is designed to combine the desire for a low energy building with the spatial requirements of a new teaching philosophy. The 10 classes, 250 pupils in all, have been in the school since September 1985.

OBJECTIVES

For the past ten years, the Ministry of Education has been wanting teachers to experiment with radical new methods. Ecole de Tournai is designed specifically to suit this new style of teaching and the layout has been planned accordingly. The school is zoned and the particular areas in use at any one time are governed by the external climate. In addition, the building aims to make good use of solar gains via both passive and active systems.
It is hoped that the school will show the pupils how to respond to, rather than ignore, climatic fluctuations and the natural environment in general and thereby encourage them to be more energy conscious.

ENERGY SAVING FEATURES

● A wide, centrally-placed sunspace is incorporated into the building on the south side.

● Four smaller sunspaces are connected to the six ground floor classrooms.

● Direct solar gains are stored in the heavyweight walls and floors.

● 143m^2 of roof-mounted active air-heating collectors contribute directly to the space heating load.

● A 49m^3 pebble store in the east wing and a 4m^3 water store in the west wing store any excess solar energy collected by the panels.

● A compact building form and high insulation levels minimise heat losses.

SITE PLAN
The school has unrestricted solar access, and the surrounding buildings and trees protect it from the wind.

- The north facade is partially below ground and has very few windows.

- All windows have low emissivity coated double glazing except the sunspaces which are single glazed.

- External blinds are fitted to the central glass roof to prevent overheating.

SITE AND CLIMATE

The school is located on the edge of the old town centre of Tournai, in the middle of a block, on a 0.65 ha site. The surrounding houses and trees protect the school from noise

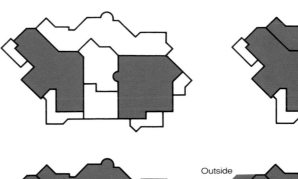

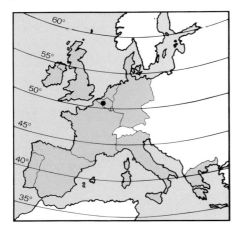

CLIMATE (Chièvres)

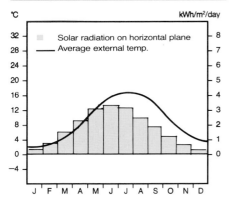

and wind, but are sufficiently far away not to restrict solar access. The site is almost flat, but the building takes advantage of the slight slope and is built partially below ground to the north. The climate is temperate, humid south-westerly winds are the

Zones used depending on temperature. The central sunspace, the four smaller sunspaces, and the central space (including the library) do not have any auxiliary heating and are only occupied when they are sufficiently warm. In summer, the open air theatre and part of the garden are also used.

prevailing winds for most of the year, but in spring cold, dry north-easterly winds are equally important. There are on average 1542 hours of sunshine a year. The mean monthly maximum daytime temperature is 21.7°C in July and 4.5°C in January, and there are 2310 degree days (on a 15°C base).

PLANNING

The internal planning of the school does not follow the conventional layout of corridors with self-contained classrooms on both sides, instead there are a variety of spaces; standard classrooms, rooms only for individual or teamwork, and areas with specialised functions.

DESIGN DETAILS

The two-storey central space, which houses the library, is the hub of the building around which the rest of the school is organised. Surrounding it there

Entrance to the school. The design takes advantage of the slightly sloping site, and the north side is built partially below ground.

Design Details

are two wings, to the east and west, each with five classrooms, three on the ground floor and two on the first floor.
These classrooms are interconnected and attached to them are the small sunspaces which are used as natural science laboratories. The large sunspace in the centre of the school rises in tiers to the top of the building and opens onto every storey.
Within the four floor levels, there are workrooms, a photographic laboratory, a video room, a staff room for student teachers, and a multipurpose hall in the basement, connected to an open-air theatre.

CONSTRUCTION

The load bearing walls are made from heavyweight concrete blocks. External walls are cavity walls insulated with mineral fibre (U-value 0.36 W/m^{2}K). Floors are made from prefabricated concrete slabs covered with sandstone flags in the classrooms and with carpet in the circulation spaces. In the five sunspaces, the floors are

South-east elevation. The ground floor classrooms are adjacent to sunspaces which collect solar gains.

cast concrete covered with black stone tiles.
The roof is a deep timber structure with 225mm of glass fibre insulation and zinc waterproofing. Security single glazing is used in the sunspaces and low emissivity coated double glazing is used for the external windows and the windows between the classrooms and the sunspaces.

PASSIVE SOLAR DESIGN

The building has a highly glazed south facade due to the presence of the central sunspace and the smaller sunspaces, whilst the north

The central sunspace rises in tiers to the top of the building and opens into every storey.

facade is partially below ground and has limited openings.
The way the school is planned produces different comfort zones. The five sunspaces and the central space do not have any form of auxiliary heating. Therefore, the sunspaces are only occupied when the

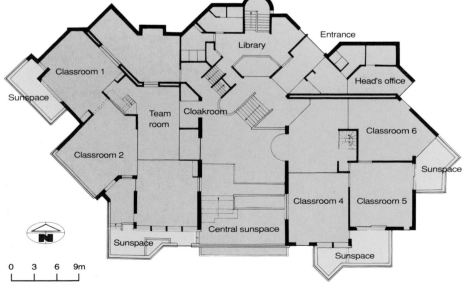

GROUND FLOOR PLAN
The utility spaces, the service areas and some of the workrooms are located on the north side and act as buffer spaces for the classrooms on the southern side.

On sunny days in winter, the doors between the classrooms and sunspaces are opened as soon as the sunspaces are warm enough.

temperature within them is sufficient. The central space, on the other hand, has an almost constant temperature due to the neighbouring heated spaces and the central sunspace.
The utility spaces, the service areas and some of the workrooms are located on the northside and act as buffer spaces. Protected by these buffer zones, and opening onto the sunspaces are the classrooms and their associated workrooms, which require more constant temperatures.

AUXILIARY HEATING SYSTEM

Auxiliary heating is provided by a warm-air heating system. Air is heated in the 143m^2 south facing solar collectors on the roof, and if necessary, further heated by the four gas-fired boilers.
On warm days, if the building requires no heating, the heat from the collectors is stored in the pebble store and the water store, both of which are in the basement.

The warm air circulates through cavities in the internal central double wall and in the precast concrete slabs before reaching the outlets. Hence, heat is radiated from the walls and floors as well as being supplied as warm air. The whole heating system is microprocessor controlled.

OPERATING MODES

In winter, on cold days, only the classrooms are occupied. On sunny days, as soon as it is warm enough to do so, the doors to the sunspaces are opened and warm air enters and heats the classrooms. The unheated library and sunspaces are only occupied when their temperatures permit it.
During the summer, the whole

The smaller sunspaces are used as natural science laboratories when they are warm enough to be occupied.

school, the garden and the small open-air theatre are used. To prevent overheating, the external roof-mounted sunspace blinds are lowered and the skylights opened. The connecting doors between the sunspaces and classrooms are kept closed, and the sunspaces are well-ventilated to prevent hot air entering the main school building.

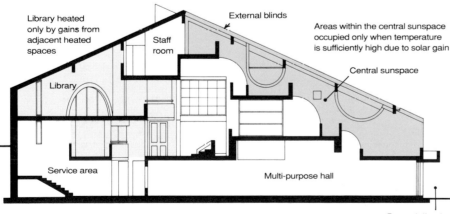

Library heated only by gains from adjacent heated spaces

Staff room

External blinds

Areas within the central sunspace occupied only when temperature is sufficiently high due to solar gain

Central sunspace

Library

Service area

Multi-purpose hall

Open-air theatre

North-south section through school.

Performance Evaluation

Classroom 4 showing window onto central sunspace.

MONITORING

The school was monitored from November 1985 to April 1987. Two factors determined the way in which the school was monitored; the presence of a computerised control system for the auxiliary heating, and the design of the building (two very similar wings connected by the central sunspace). The former allowed data concerning operating modes to be gathered, whilst the latter led to the choice of one wing, the eastern one, to be monitored.

Air temperatures were recorded at 17 locations in the east wing and the central sunspace. The surface temperature of the floor slab in the central sunspace and the air movement in the sunspace were also recorded. Three temperature sensors were placed in the solar collectors. Forty-eight temperature sensors were placed in the pebble store to determine the temperature gradient in three directions. The warm air heating system was also monitored and measurements were made of:- the air temperature in the cavity walls; the surface temperature of the floor slabs and the temperature inside the floor ducts (a total of 36 sensors).

Externally, air temperature and insolation on a horizontal plane were recorded. Gas consumption for space heating and the electricity use associated with each piece of equipment (pump, valves, etc) were measured. All the data were stored on mini-cassettes and processed by computer.

USER RESPONSE

The pupils and their teachers are enthusiastic about the school design in terms of the quality of spaces it provides and their ability to meet the requirements of the teaching philosophy. Sometimes, there was confusion as to the diversity of possible options, but then a detailed "owners manual" was written to help them operate the building properly. There were also problems with noise at first, due to the connections between classrooms on different floors, but these have now been overcome by sealing the noise paths.

PERFORMANCE OF PASSIVE SOLAR SYSTEM

● The school shows 43% savings compared to a conventional design, despite some operational problems at the beginning (the comparison is based on a survey of all Belgian schools). In future, the performance should be improved due to a better understanding of how to operate both systems.

● Solar gains contribute 51% to the gross space heating load (30% passive solar, 21% active solar), incidental gains 5% and auxiliary heating only 44%.

● The system of ducting warm air through cavities in the walls and floor is not very successful as these elements have too high

COMPARISON WITH CONVENTIONAL DESIGN

From a survey of all Belgian schools, 416 240kWh would be required to heat the primary school if it had been built to a conventional design.

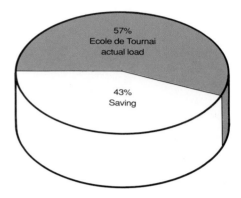

The actual fuel used by the space heating system and the fans delivering the solar heated air was 237 340kWh.

AUXILIARY FUEL USED ANNUALLY
247 340kWh

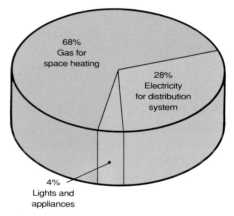

an inertia. The building takes a few days to reach comfortable temperatures after a period with no heating.

● The warm air circuit in the precast concrete slabs was very long and so the air lost too much heat to the floor, leaving the air temperature at the outlet too low. This problem was overcome by creating a by-pass directly to the air outlet.

● The water store has not proved very useful due to losses in the various heat exchangers producing air that is generally too cold. The pebble store does work well, but its heat capacity is insufficient, compared to the thermal mass of the school, to

CONTRIBUTIONS TO TOTAL SPACE HEATING LOAD
266 750kWh

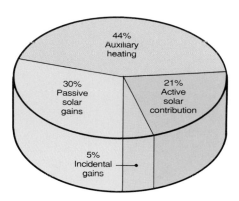

Solar energy contributed 51% (136 540kWh) to the gross space heating load.

COST OF FUEL USED ANNUALLY
732 680BF (16 652ECU) in 1987

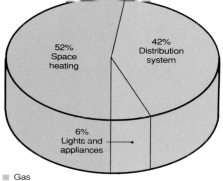

■ Gas
■ Electricity

Although there is a significant reduction in the delivered energy use, there is a cost penalty, 90 000BF in 1987, as gas for space heating is displaced by solar gains distributed using electricity.

provide other than "preheating" of the east wing for a couple of months in the autumn.

COST EFFECTIVENESS

It is difficult to evaluate the additional building costs related to the passive solar design and no specific payback period has been calculated. The school is considered a success in this respect, though the active solar system requires further improvement.
Despite a significant reduction in the overall delivered energy used by the school in comparison with a conventional design, there is a small cost penalty rather than a financial

NET MONTHLY SPACE HEATING DEMAND AND SUPPLY

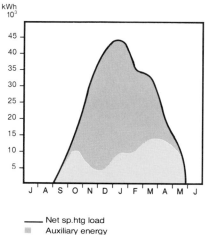

——— Net sp.htg load
■ Auxiliary energy
■ Solar energy

saving. This is explained by the fact that although gas for space heating is displaced by solar gains these gains are distributed by fans (ie, the active solar system). At present, ways of reducing the high electricity use associated with distribution are being investigated. The active system, including the two stores and the distribution network, was also the most expensive energy saving measure.

TYPICAL SUNNY WINTER DAY (February)

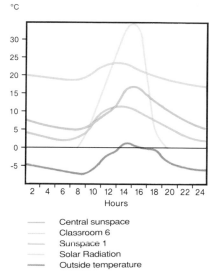

——— Central sunspace
——— Classroom 6
——— Sunspace 1
——— Solar Radiation
——— Outside temperature

View from the library overlooking central sunspace.

PROJECT DATA

Building excluding sunspaces			
Volume		7111	m³
Floor Area	total	2410	m²
	ground	1095	m²
Wall Area		508	m²
Roof Area:	opaque	860	m²
Glazed Area:	total	235	m² 100%
	south	127	m² 54%
Sunspaces			
Volume		774	m³
Floor Area		225	m²
Roof Area		292	m²
Glazed Area:	total	205	m² 100%
	south	93	m² 45%
Thermal Characteristics			
U Value	roof	0.19	W/m²K
	floor	1.00	W/m²K
	external walls	0.36	W/m²K
	windows	1.6	W/m²K
	sunspace glazing	5.8	W/m²K

Mean U value (excluding sunspaces)	0.9	W/m²K
Global heat loss co-efficient	4650	W/K
Infiltration Rate	0.29	ach
External design temperature	-10	°C
Heated floor area	1720	m²
Heated volume	5553	m³
Net heat load	131	kWh/m²
Site and Climate		
Altitude	50	m
Latitude	50° 37'	N
Longitude	3° 23'	E
Average ambient temp: Jan	4.5	°C
July	21.7	°C
Degree days (base 15°C)	2310	days
Global irradiation on horiz	926	kWh/m²
Sunshine hours	1542	hr/yr
Costs (1985 Prices)		
Total cost 75 000 000 BF	1 744 000	ECU

LOU SOULEU CREDITS

Client
OPHLM de la Ville D'Avignon
Residence les Remparts
12 bis Bd. Saint Ruf
84000 Avignon

Architects
SCP D'Architectes
Y Contandriopoulos C Simeray
42 Rue Farges
13008 Marseille

Energy Consultant
Groupe OTH

COMETEC
4 Rue Leon Poulet
13008 Marseille

OTH Mediterranee
5 Avenue de Lattre de Tassigny
84000 Avignon

Services Engineer
ESI
324 Bd Chave
13005 Marseille

Building Contractor
Entreprise Mourret
8 Rue Kruger
84000 Avignon

Services Contractor
Entreprise Moscati (No longer trading)

Entreprise Spic
2 bis Rue du Chateau
84700 Sorgues

CEPRA
28 Rue Sainte Catherine
13007 Marseille

Monitoring Organisation
TELENERGIE (OTH)
CETE Mediterranee BP 39
13762 Les Milles Cedex

Commission of the European Communities

- Public housing scheme is first built version of award-winning French design.

- Passive solar features include two-storey sunspaces attached to the "duplex" apartments, and a four-storey central atrium.

- Communal areas are located on the north side and have limited openings as this face is exposed to the famous Mistral in winter.

- Sunspaces preheat fresh air for the mechanical ventilation system, reducing the space heating load by 30%.

- Remarkably good thermal performance is achieved in winter, the solar contribution to the heat load reaches 80%, but at the expense of summer overheating.

LOU SOULEU

AVIGNON
FRANCE

Project Background

Lou Souleu (which means the sun in the local dialect) consists of 22 publicly-owned flats in a "climate-respecting" apartment block at "Le clos de Massillargues" in Avignon. This project is the first built version of an award-winning design called "ERGOS".

The majority of the flats in the four-storey building are "duplex" (maisonettes), only the studio apartments and the one three-bedroomed apartment are on a single level. Each duplex housing unit has an attached two-storey sunspace (which faces either south, east or west). In the centre of the block there is a four-storey atrium.

OBJECTIVES

The public office concerned with the construction and renting out of "moderately-priced" housing in Avignon manages 5800 dwellings. As part of their energy conservation policy they insulate during refurbishment and install condensing gas boilers. These measures give buildings a "3 star" rating, ie, an energy saving of 35% compared to standard buildings, and the public office is then entitled to Government subsidies. In new-build schemes, the office is wary of active solar systems but it favours passive solar designs if they are water and air-tight and if adequate measures are taken to prevent overheating in the summer. This particular project is small, their schemes usually involve between 90 and 200 dwellings.

The aim of the project from the point of view of the construction office was to test the "climate-respecting" design when occupied. For the architects and the energy consultant, Lou Souleu was an opportunity to build an "ERGOS" style block of flats, this design being the result of a national competition entitled "Habitat Original par la Thermique" (HOT), ie, architectural designs with good thermal performances. The design was predicted to save 50% of the fuel used for space heating and 55% of the fuel used for domestic water heating.

ENERGY SAVING FEATURES

● High levels of insulation reduce heat losses.

● A 57m^2 central atrium reduces heat losses and captures solar gains.

● Concrete walls and staircases store solar energy collected by the atrium.

● Two-storey sunspaces attached to almost every flat on either the south, east or west facades, capture direct solar gains and provide preheated ventilation air.

● 64m^2 of roof-mounted solar water heating panels arranged in six banks, preheat domestic hot water for all of the flats.

● Mechanical system reduces ventilation rates to the minimum levels necessary for comfort and hygiene.

● Communal areas are located on the north side of the block and north facade has very few openings, all of which are small.

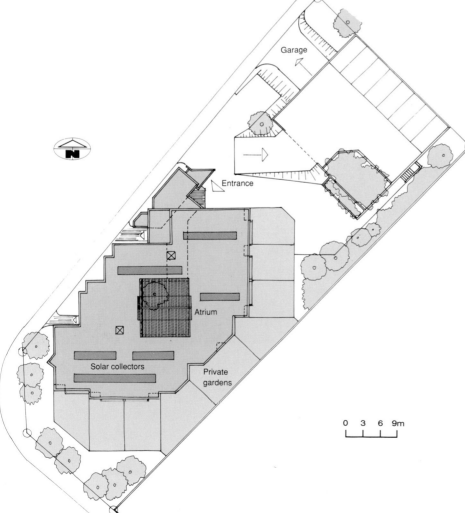

SITE PLAN
In the centre of the building there is a glazed internal courtyard (or atrium) onto which back the twenty two flats. Active solar collectors are mounted on the roof of the block.

Design Details

CONCLUSIONS

The project shows remarkably good thermal performance in the winter, particularly for the south facing dwellings. The solar contribution to the heat load reaches 80% and the overall payback period is estimated to be 8 years.

Unfortunately, in summer the sunspaces are uncomfortably hot in spite of the precautions taken to avoid overheating. The atrium was not a great success in terms of its contribution to energy savings in the winter, and it too caused problems in the summer. The payback period is too long for the atrium to be considered cost effective.

SITE AND CLIMATE

Le clos de Massillargues is located in the suburbs of Avignon which is the county town (chef-lieu) of the Vaucluse region.

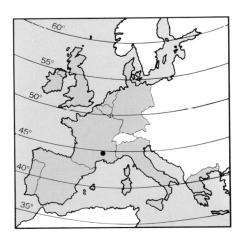

Avignon is 680km south of Paris, and in the fourteenth century it was the seat of the Pope and the capital of Christendom. These days it has 165,000 inhabitants. Lou Souleu is a 10 minute drive from the town centre, located in a low density residential area between the old town and modern tower blocks further out. Single family houses with gardens surround the "solar"

To the north of the apartment block are the communal areas, and a wall has been built in front of the main entrance to act as a windbreak.

apartment block. Facilities in the area include a 900-pupil school, a small shopping centre, a stadium and a swimming pool.

The climate in the region is generally very sunny, with an average of only 91 days of rain

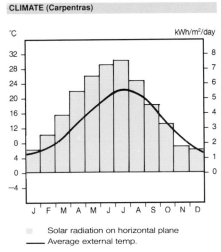

CLIMATE (Carpentras)

Solar radiation on horizontal plane
Average external temp.

per year. The famous Mistral sweeps the region between February and April, whilst September is the calmest month. During the monitoring period (1985/86), February was particularly cold, the temperature dropped as low as -10ºC, and it was not as sunny as usual. March, however, was warm and much sunnier.

DESIGN DETAILS

In the centre of the building there is a glazed internal courtyard onto which each flat backs. Access to the flats is via the courtyard on the ground floor, and at the upper level via an internal gallery. Except for the studio flats and the one three-bedroomed flat, all the apartments are duplex and have an internal metal spiral staircase. Another feature of the duplex apartments is the two-storey sunspace (floor area about 9m²) attached to the living room and facing either south, east or west. To the north of the block are the communal areas and a wall has been built here in front of the main entrance to act as a windbreak. Generally the north facade has very limited window openings. The south facade, on the other hand, has large windows and highly glazed sunspaces.

The central courtyard is covered with a glazed roof thereby creating an atrium. On the east and west elevations, the gable ends of the atrium roof are visible, whilst from the north and south sides the view is of the horizontal roof section.

Design Details

At the upper levels, access to the flats is via galleries within the atrium.

CONSTRUCTION

The apartment block is a concrete structure insulated with expanded polystyrene (EPS).

● The structural walls are 160mm reinforced concrete.

● The ground floor is a suspended floor of concrete above EPS insulation over precast hollow concrete slabs.

● The intermediate floors are 180mm reinforced concrete on thin precast slabs with 80mm EPS insulation and 10mm plaster beneath.

● The flat roof is a 160mm reinforced concrete slab (on precast slabs) with 80mm EPS insulation, finished with several layers of felt waterproofing, covered with loose chippings.

● Internal partitions are plastered 50mm bricks.

PASSIVE SOLAR FEATURES

The passive solar features of the block are:

● large areas of south facing window;

● single and two-storey sunspaces attached to most flats;

● a central atrium.

The sunspace collects direct solar gains and also preheats ventilation air for the dwelling. At the lower level the living room is separated from the sunspace by glazed doors, whilst at the upper level windows separate the bedrooms from it. High and low level openings are provided to allow ventilation and the regulation of solar contributions. To reduce summer overheating, the sunspace is fitted with internal roller blinds.

overheating in summer and improve thermal and visual comfort.

Both the sunspaces and the atrium are built from steel sections. The atrium has three principal steel girders with a metal walkway at the top. This provides access for maintenance of the internally-mounted motors, roller blinds and extract fans.

In addition to the passive solar system, there is an active solar water heating system, six rows of collectors are mounted at 45° on the roof. Three rows of panels ($32m^2$ of collector) supply domestic hot water to 11 flats, via a 1000 litre storage tank.

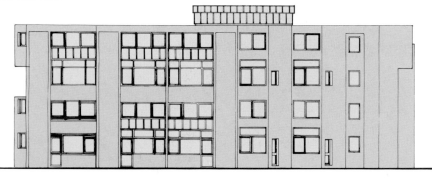

Large windows and sunspaces on the south facade collect direct solar gains, and the sunspaces also preheat ventilation air.

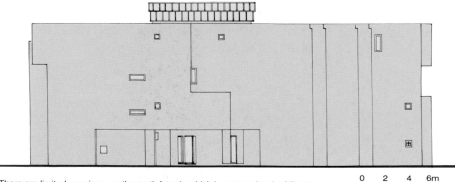

There are limited openings on the north facade which is exposed to the Mistral.

0   2   4   6m

The atrium reduces heat losses from the flats (as the air in the atrium is at a higher temperature than ambient) and it collects solar gains, which are stored in the concrete walls and staircases. Part of the glazed roof can be raised to provide ventilation, although in winter the roof is kept closed. Motorised sliding blinds fitted to the glazing reduce

AUXILIARY SYSTEMS

The auxiliary space heating system installed in the flats is standard electric convector heaters. For domestic hot water, to supplement the solar heated water there is another 1000 litre tank per 11 flats which is electrically heated. A mechanical ventilation system

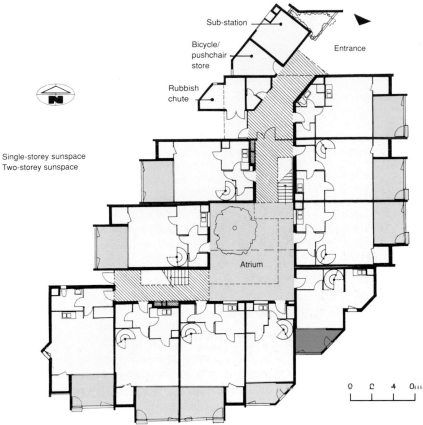

Single-storey sunspace
Two-storey sunspace

Sub-station

Bicycle/pushchair store

Entrance

Rubbish chute

Atrium

0   2   4   0m

GROUND FLOOR PLAN
The duplex apartments have two-storey sunspaces facing either south, east or west, and an internal spiral staircase. Access to all the flats is via the atrium.

spring and autumn, once the sunspace is sufficiently warm, the doors and windows to the rest of the apartment are opened, and solar gains displace some of the auxiliary energy (on peak electricity) used for space heating.

In summer, the internal sunspace doors and windows are kept closed, and the sunspace is vented through the external high and low level openings. Overheating is also reduced by lowering the internal roller blinds. In addition, part of the atrium roof is raised to provide ventilation, and internal blinds are drawn across.

CONTROLS

In the sunspaces, both the operation of the ventilation openings and the raising and lowering of the internal roller blinds are manual operations. In the atrium, raising and lowering of sections of the glass roof and operation of the blinds are automatically controlled by means of an internal temperature probe.

draws fresh air from the sunspaces, where it receives a degree of preheating. The air change rate is limited to the minimum which can achieve reasonable comfort and hygiene standards. The bathroom and toilet receive a constant supply, whilst the kitchen is fitted with a variable delivery outlet (between 30m³/h and 180m³/h).

OPERATING MODES

Throughout the heating season, the sunspaces preheat fresh air for the mechanical ventilation system. On sunny days in

The sunspaces and atrium are well liked by the tenants.

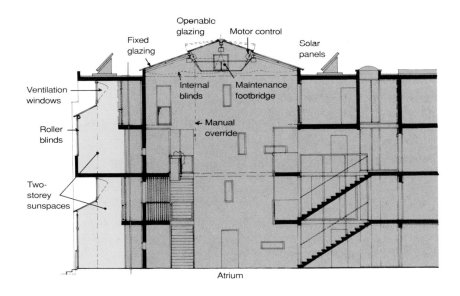

Openable glazing

Fixed glazing

Motor control

Solar panels

Ventilation windows

Internal blinds

Maintenance footbridge

Roller blinds

Manual override

Two-storey sunspaces

Atrium

NORTH-SOUTH SECTION
The sunspaces preheat ventilation air throughout the heating season, and solar gains contribute directly to the space heating load on sunny days in spring and autumn.

Performance Evaluation

To reduce overheating in the atrium in summer, part of the roof is raised to provide ventilation and the internally-mounted blinds are drawn across.

MONITORING

Two almost identical dwellings were monitored for a year (1985/86), the only difference between them was their orientation, one flat faces south whilst the other one faces east. 7500 hourly readings were collected over 355 days including meteorological data, internal temperatures, fuel consumption, opening times of doors and windows and the use of mechanical ventilation systems. One-off measurements of ventilation rates were also made.

USER RESPONSE

Many people would like to live in the Lou Souleu apartment block. Those who do live there like it and have a tendency to stay longer than would normally be expected. The sunspaces and atrium are well liked, and the building is judged to be aesthetically pleasing.

PERFORMANCE OF PASSIVE SOLAR DESIGN

The energy consumed in both of the flats was very low, but lower in the south facing flat. Since the inhabitants accepted temperatures as low as 15ºC in the dwellings, the actual consumption figures were adjusted assuming that the internal design temperature (18ºC) had been maintained. This allowed the energy used to be compared to conventional designs. For the south facing flat, the adjusted savings were 78%, only 1097kWh of electricity were used over the year. The average consumption figure for both flats is 1623 kWh, which

represents a 67% saving. The average solar contribution to the gross annual space heating load is 70%, with the sunspaces providing 30% of this load simply by preheating fresh air for the mechanical ventilation system. In the south flat, the solar contribution is fairly constant over the heating season, whilst for the east flat, the gains in autumn and spring are much more significant than those in winter.

The sunspaces and the atrium, however, were not entirely successful. Unfortunately, in the summer months the sunspaces and adjacent living spaces overheated with average temperatures in July in excess of 27ºC. In the atrium even higher summer temperatures were experienced, but fan induced ventilation did not take place during the monitoring period. The atrium design was unsuccessful in three other respects: - a high level of noise was produced by the motors which moved sections of the glass roof; the mechanized internal blinds were too delicate; and daily manual operation of openings and blinds was needed in summer due to

COMPARISON WITH CONVENTIONAL DESIGN

4917kWh would be required to heat a flat of the same size as the east and south facing monitored flats built to a conventional design.

CONTRIBUTIONS TO ANNUAL SPACE HEATING DEMAND

4910kWh

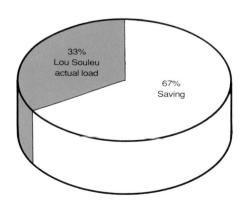

1623kWh was the adjusted average consumption figure for the two flats.

30% of the total load was supplied by preheating ventilation air in the sunspaces.

technical failures.
In addition, only a small amount of solar radiation was collected by the atrium in the heating season, and the air change rate in it proved higher than predicted (0.8 ac/h instead of 0.5 ac/h) as the glass roof was not sufficiently airtight.

COST EFFECTIVENESS

The cost associated with the solar features including the active system, (530 000 FF) was 10.8% of the total building cost in 1982. For the passive features only, sunspaces and central atrium, the on-cost was 6.3%.

The total energy saving is 3 300 kWh/yr per flat (taking an average of the south and east facing flats). As the cost of building (FF/m²) varies considerably from region to region, it is only possible to give a payback period for the block as built in Avignon. This figure, for the package of energy saving, passive and active solar features, is about 8 years.

Average for south and east facing flat.

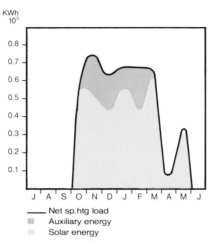

KWh
10³

— Net sp.htg load
■ Auxiliary energy
□ Solar energy

MONTHLY AVERAGE TEMPERATURES

For south facing flat.

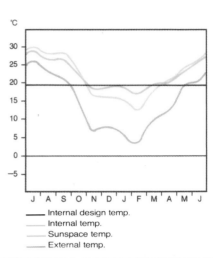

°C

— Internal design temp.
— Internal temp.
— Sunspace temp.
— External temp.

In the south facing flats, the solar contribution is fairly constant over the heating season, whilst for the east facing flats, gains in autumn and spring are much more significant than those in winter.

COST OF BUILDING AND SOLAR ON-COST

The total project cost FF 4.9M in 1982.

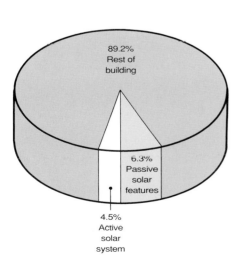

89.2% Rest of building

6.3% Passive solar features

4.5% Active solar system

The sunspaces and atrium cost 6.3% of the total project cost.

PROJECT DATA

Building				
22 Dwelling block				
Volume		4975	m³	
Floor area		2073	m²	
Duplex apartment (3 rooms south facing)				
Volume		178	m³	
Floor area		74	m²	
Roof area		74	m²	
External wall area		16	m²	
		(+ 23m² onto atrium)		
Window area:	total	23.4	m²	100%
	south	22.5	m²	96%
	north	0.9	m²	4%
Sunspace				
Volume		38.6	m³	
Floor area		9.1	m²	
Glass area		22.5	m³	
Atrium				
Floor area		57.6	m²	
Site and Climate				
Altitude		66	m	

Latitude		43.5°	N
Longitude		4.5°	E
Average ambient temp:	Jan	3	°C
	July	22	°C
Degree days (base 18°C)		1900	days
Global irradiation on horiz		1533	kWh/m²
Sunshine hours		2773	hrs/yr
Thermal characteristics			
Duplex apartment (3 rooms south facing)			
U value:	roof	0.43	W/m²K
	floor	0.41	W/m²K
	external walls	0.57	W/m²K
	windows	4.8	W/m²K
	sunspace glazing	4.8	W/m²K
Mean U value		1.0	W/m²K
Global heat loss coefficient		137	W/K
External design temperature		-7	°C
Heated floor area		74	m²
Heated volume		178	m³
Net heat load		58	kWh/m²

Costs (1982 prices)

Building (whole)	FF 4 930 200	ECU 711 141
Solar features	FF 530 000	ECU 76 448

ARONA CREDITS

Client
UPSE (Unione Piemontese Sviluppo Edilizio)
Via Cristoforo Colombo 17
10129 Torino

CIEN srl (Consorzio Imprese Edili Novaresi)
Viale Buonarroti 10
28100 Novara

Architect
Cooperativ T&A
Archh G Brusetti, S Franzosi, R Ripamonti
Via Vittorio Veneto 26
28041 Arona (NO)

Energy Consultant
SOFTECH srl
Via Cernaia 1
10121 Torino

Prof. L Matteoli
Dipartimento Scienze E Tecniche
Per I Processi Di Insediamento
(Formerly ITAC)
Facolta di Architettura
Polytecnico di Torino
Viale Mattioli, 39
10125 Torino

Services Consultant
Cooperativa T&A
Ingg G Falzotti, G Escuriale
Piazza Martiri 4
Novara

Building Contractor
Litobit (Compagnia Italiana Bitumi SpA)
Via Vitorrio Veneto 71
28041 Arona (NO)

Services Contractor
Sacchetti G & Figli (SNC)
Via Monte Nero 23
Arona (NO)

Monitoring Organisation
UPSE with the consultancy of Hi-tek srl (Torino)
Hi-tek srl
Via Cernaia 1
10121 Torino

Funding Support
CER (Comitato Edilizia Residenziale)
presso Ministero Lavori Pubblici
(Ministry of Public Works)
Piazzale Porta Pia
00100 Roma

CEC (Commission of the European Communities)
Wetstraat 200
1049 Brussels
Belgium

Commission of the European Communities

- Owner-occupied apartment block incorporates passive and active solar features with high levels of insulation.

- Thermostatically - controlled fans distribute solar heated air from sunspaces to bedrooms above, in duplex apartments.

- Passive solar gains contribute 20% to the net space heating load.

- 41% savings in primary energy for space heating recorded, compared to a conventionally built apartment block.

ARONA
LAKE MAGGIORE
ITALY

Project Background

As part of an extensive solar energy demonstration programme carried out by a consortium of builders (UPSE) in the Piedmont region of Northern Italy, a block of twenty-four apartments was built in 1984. The whole programme was supported by the Ministry of Public Works (CER) and by the CEC.

When completed, this particular scheme will include another apartment block, not as tall as the first, with twenty-five flats, located on the southern edge of the site. The two blocks will face each other enclosing a communal landscaped garden. However, unlike the first block, the second will not be designed along passive solar guidelines.

OBJECTIVES

The purpose of the project was to examine the technical and economic feasibility of a package of energy saving and passive solar measures. These were to be applied to a block of owner-occupied apartments built to a fairly high standard. The incorporation of the solar energy features into the building made it an "experimental housing scheme" and the extra costs associated with these features were therefore partly paid for by CER.

The brief required two different sizes of apartment; smaller flats for occupation by the elderly and/or disabled with special access arrangements, and larger ones for families. Also required were individual garages and cellars.

ENERGY SAVING FEATURES

The block includes the following energy saving features:-

● Principal rooms face south, and there is a sunspace extension to the living/dining area.

● Roof-mounted air heating solar panels preheat ventilation air in winter and contribute to domestic hot water production in summer.

● The building has high levels of insulation and cold bridging has been reduced.

● Windows are double glazed and fitted with blinds for increased insulation at night.

● The communal space heating system is individually controllable within each flat.

CONCLUSIONS

Of the seventeen low energy projects (480 dwellings) recently built around Turin as part of the UPSE programme, this multi-storey residential block is one of the most successful, in terms of its thermal performance, its cost effectiveness and the feedback from the inhabitants.

The energy saving measures, together with the passive and active solar energy systems, lead to a reduction of over 40% in the primary energy used for space heating compared to a conventional Italian building of the same volume (ie, built to the standards laid down in Law 373).

In winter, the air-heating solar panels mainly provide preheated ventilation air, as the collector area is unfortunately not large enough for there to be a significant contribution directly to the space heating system.

0 5 10 15m

SITE PLAN
The second block, yet to be built, will not obstruct the solar access to the existing block.

Design Details

SITE AND CLIMATE

Arona is a small city on the shores of Lake Maggiore, in the northern part of Piedmont. The lake has a moderating effect on the local climate and also determines the area's individual character.

Although it is in an urban area, the site generally has good solar access. However, to the south west another multi-storey apartment block cuts out the sun to some of the lower storeys in winter.

The climate in Arona (Lat 46°N, 212m above sea level) is relatively mild with many clear days and low winds. The annual average outside air temperature is 11.8°C, and there are 2400 degree days (19°C base).

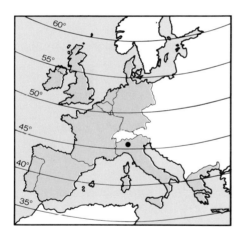

CLIMATE (Arona)

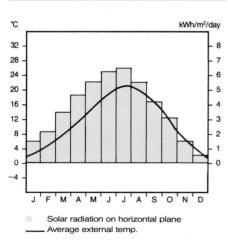

Solar radiation on horizontal plane
Average external temp.

An interesting south facade is produced by the sunspaces, balconies, blinds and awnings and by the use of colour.

PLANNING

The entire scheme will consist of two buildings facing each other along an east-west axis, and enclosing a common open area. The building to the north of the plot is a five-storey block and is designed to maximise solar gains. The second building, yet to be constructed, will border a car park to the south of the site and will have a shorter wing running along the western boundary. This three-storey building will not be based on solar principles and will, in fact, restrict solar access to the south facing garden of the existing block.

DESIGN DETAILS

The building has twenty-four units; eight are 60m² first floor flats allocated to the elderly, and the remainder are 92m² duplex apartments (maisonettes). The larger flats are approached on the north side by two pedestrian walkways on the second and fourth floors, whilst the "sheltered" flats have ramps. The living/dining rooms in all the apartments are located on the south and look out onto sunspaces.

The south elevation is characterised by large enclosed sunspaces and balconies. The lower row of duplex apartments have balconies in front of the sunspaces and the upper row of duplex apartments have the balcony above the sunspace in front of the two bedrooms. A dog-leg staircase in the centre of these flats leads to the bedrooms above. On the flat roof, active solar collectors span the full width. The heating plant is also on the roof housed in a pitched-roof plant room. (In Italy, the heating plant is usually in the basement.)

The north facade has a regular pattern of columns with the two pedestrian walkways running across. The east facade is almost blank enclosing the staircases and lift, whilst on the west face there is an open staircase.

CONSTRUCTION

The building is a combination of prefabricated elements and in-situ construction. The overall structure is designed to have considerable thermal inertia. Prefabricated, prestressed concrete walls (running north-south) and floors make up the

Design Details

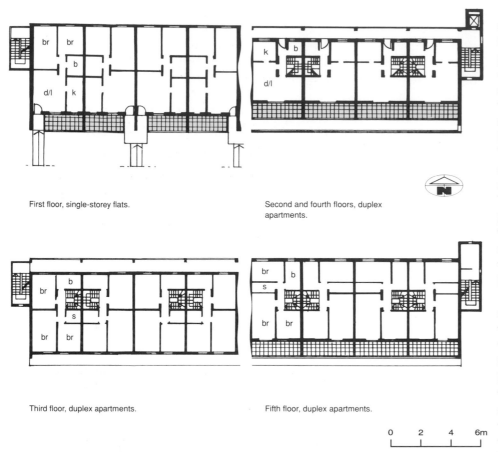

First floor, single-storey flats.

Second and fourth floors, duplex apartments.

Third floor, duplex apartments.

Fifth floor, duplex apartments.

0   2   4   6m

TYPICAL FLOOR PLANS
There are twenty-four dwellings in the block, eight are single-storey flats for the elderly/disabled and the other sixteen are duplex apartments for families

principal load-bearing structure. The load-bearing walls are 160mm thick panels at 6m intervals, defining the frontage of each apartment. The east and west outer walls are insulated with an external layer of 50mm of glass fibre. The horizontal load-bearing components are 1.2m x 6.0m and either 160mm or 200mm thick.

The north facing external wall is traditionally built from a double skin of hollow pot bricks with 60mm glass fibre cavity insulation. The south facing wall is the same, but the insulation is only 50mm thick.

All windows are double glazed although the sunspace glazing is single.

PASSIVE SOLAR DESIGN

Sunspaces are effectively integrated into the apartment block structurally, functionally and in terms of the overall appearance. These sunspaces

The duplex apartments are approached on the north side by two pedestrian walkways on the second and fourth floors. The double exposure allows good cross ventilation.

are large enough (1.8m x 6.0m in the duplex apartments) to provide a true benefit to the occupants and they are not simply spaces attached solely for energy reasons, which is often the case in Italian "solar" housing.

The sunspaces cover the entire south frontage of each apartment and are 1.8m deep. They have concrete floors to provide thermal mass. Between the sunspaces and the living room, there are large openings with double glazed doors, fitted internally with PVC roller blinds. In the lower set of duplex apartments (on the second and third floors), the sunspace has full height single glazing divided into eight sections. These can be folded back in a concertina fashion, four on each side, allowing the sunspace to be totally open to the balcony in front. Internal reflective venetian blinds are placed behind the glazing. The balcony itself is protected from the sun by a moveable canvas awning.

In the upper set of duplex apartments (on the fourth and fifth floors) the balcony is above the sunspace. Here, it is again possible to totally open up the sunspace, and so an iron railing has been fitted as a parapet for safety reasons.

In both apartment arrangements, thermostatically-controlled fans blow the solar heated air into the bedrooms through openings in the sunspace ceiling.

In the single-storey apartments, the living/dining area and the kitchen overlook the sunspace, and the two bedrooms are located to the north. Glazed doors open onto the sunspaces, and these are fitted with PVC roller blinds. No fans have been installed here as the sunspaces only supply solar gains to adjacent rooms on the same floor.

The level of natural lighting in all the apartments is good. The service areas are in the central part of the flats, so that all the habitable rooms receive better daylighting and have good exterior views. The entrances to all the duplex apartments are protected by the building overhang, and the double exposure allows cross ventilation.

In addition to the passive solar features, there is a roof-mounted active solar system consisting of 91m² of air collectors.

OPERATING MODES AND CONTROLS

In winter, direct solar gains enter the living spaces through the highly glazed south facade. When the air in the sunspace is warm enough, a differential temperature sensor automatically activates the fan which distributes the preheated air to the upper storey in the duplex apartments. Roller blinds are lowered at night, and on cloudy days in unused rooms. In summer, the venetian blinds inside the sunspace and the external awning are used as shading devices to prevent overheating and to control glare. The roller blinds, if correctly positioned, also improve summer comfort. The external glazing in the sunspaces has a range of different opening positions and can be used to enhance cross ventilation. At night, windows are open, roller blinds down and awnings retracted.

AUXILIARY HEATING SYSTEM

A communal gas-fired boiler (127.5kW rating) feeds a wet radiator system and the hot water tank, which is supplemented by the active solar system. The collectors

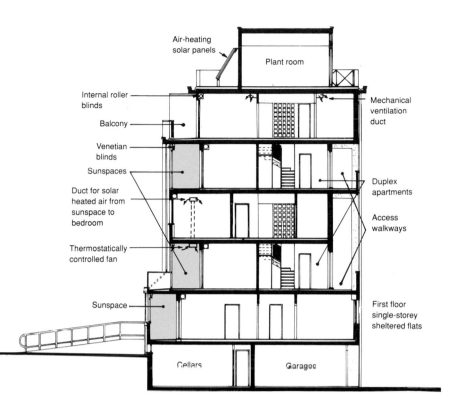

supply preheated air to a mechanical ventilation system in winter (there is an auxiliary back up) and contribute to hot water production in summer. It was originally intended that the collectors would also contribute directly to the space heating system via an air to water heat exchanger. In practice, this contribution is very small (only a few per cent) as the collectors have been undersized. Temperature sensors in the air outlet from the collectors determine the need for auxiliary heating of the ventilation air or the use of the air for heating the domestic hot water.

The south elevation is characterised by large enclosed sunspaces and balconies, the lower row of duplex apartments have balconies in front of the sunspaces, and the upper row have a balcony above the sunspace. Air-heating solar collectors are mounted along the full width of the block.

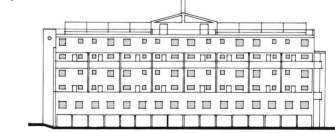

The north facade has limited openings. Garages are positioned on the north side at ground level and the plant room is on the roof.

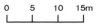

0   5   10   15m

Performance Evaluation

View of second floor sunspace with balcony in front. The glazed doors can be folded back so that the sunspace is totally open to the balcony.

MONITORING

The internal climate in various rooms was measured over the whole 1985/86 heating season, heat meters were installed on the auxiliary heating system and weather data were available from a nearby meteorological station. The level of monitoring undertaken here is fairly good.

USER RESPONSE

The owners of the apartments are very pleased with them. The duplex apartments were intended to be a modern version of the "cascina", (a type of farmhouse in the Po Valley) with a large living/kitchen area on the ground floor and the bedrooms on the upper floor. This link with tradition may explain the high level of acceptance of the "experimental" housing scheme in a small provincial city.

The contribution made by the sunspaces to the space heating demand is recognised by the occupants due to the presence of the thermostatically-controlled fan. The active system, on the other hand, is located on the roof and part of quite complicated heating plant, so the occupants are not as aware of the contribution it makes. The control system allows the occupants to increase the solar contribution from the sunspaces by reducing the temperature setting on the thermostat in the hall. This has made them generally more energy conscious.

PERFORMANCE OF PASSIVE SOLAR DESIGN

● Passive solar gains contribute 20% to the net space heating load, and active solar another 9%, due almost entirely to preheating of the ventilation air.

COMPARISON WITH CONVENTIONAL DESIGN

290 300kWh (1045GJ) primary energy would be required to heat the apartment block if it were built to conventional Italian Building Codes.

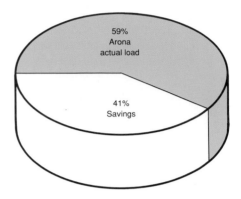

171 950kWh (619GJ) was the actual primary energy used for space heating over the 1985/86 heating season.

CONTRIBUTIONS TO THE ANNUAL SPACE HEATING DEMAND

The total annual space heating demand is 225 850kWh (813GJ).

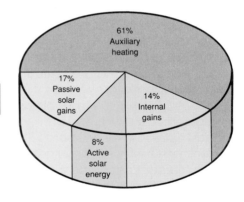

The active contribution is due almost entirely to the collectors preheating ventilation air.

● Overall, there is a saving of 41% compared to the primary energy used for space heating in a conventional apartment block built to the Italian Building Codes.

The system used here has been tested throughout the whole UPSE programme, which includes many passive and low-energy housing schemes in Piedmont. As yet, the occupants have not reported any major problems, and both the philosophy and performance of the system are considered a success.

ENERGY FLOWS ASSOCIATED WITH SPACE HEATING (SH) AND HOT WATER (HW) IN GJ

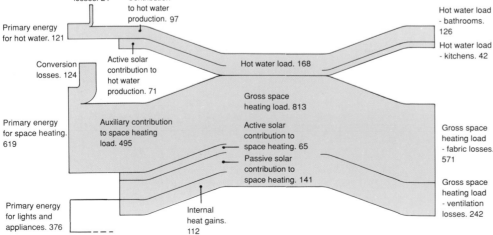

Passive solar gains contribute 20% to the net space heating load, and the active solar system contributes 9% and a further 42% to annual hot water production.

COST EFFECTIVENESS

The extra costs associated with the passive and active solar measures were relatively low. The passive system cost L 54M and the active system another L 64M out of the total cost of L 2 250M, ie, around 5%. The simple payback period of the full over cost (including the insulation) as compared to a reference building is 15 years, based on the value of the energy savings alone.

Since the sunspaces provide additional living space as well as energy savings, no calculation of the simple payback of the passive solar measures is poccible.

AUXILIARY FUEL USED (PRIMARY ENERGY)
310 000kWh (1116GJ).

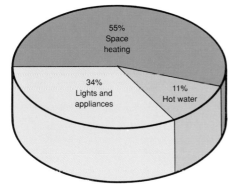

- 55% Space heating
- 34% Lights and appliances
- 11% Hot water

COST OF BUILDING AND SOLAR ON-COST
The total project cost was L2 250M in 1985.

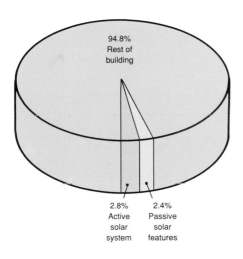

- 94.8% Rest of building
- 2.8% Active solar system
- 2.4% Passive solar features

NET MONTHLY SPACE HEATING LOAD
For the whole apartment block (24 dwellings).

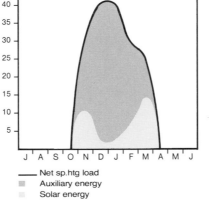

KWh 10³

J A S O N D J F M A M J

— Net sp.htg load
▩ Auxiliary energy
▢ Solar energy

MONTHLY AVERAGE TEMPERATURES

°C

O N D J F M A

— Internal design temp.
— Internal temp.
— External temp.

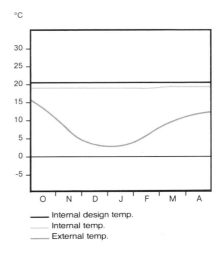

View from living room of sunspace and balcony beyond. The doors onto the sunspace are fitted with roller blinds, and venetian blinds are mounted inside the external sunspace glazing.

PROJECT DATA

Building

Total volume of housing scheme	9 678	m³
No. of floors excl. garage and cellars	5	
No. of flats	24	
Total floor area	3 460	m²
Total roof area	867	m²
Windows: total	289	m²
south	119	m²
north	97	m²

Sunspaces

Volume	592	m³
Floor area	220	m²
Glass area	321	m²

Active solar collector area 91 m²

Thermal

U value:	roof	0.57	W/m²K
	floor	0.65	W/m²K
	external walls north	0.47	W/m²K
	south	0.69	W/m²K
	windows with		
	night insulation	approx. 1.2	W/m²K
	sunspace		
	glazing	approx. 5.0	W/m²K

Mean U value	approx. 0.6	W/m²K
Global heat loss coefficient	4 285	W/K
Infiltration rate	0.5	ac/hr
Heated volume	7 263	m³
Heated floor area	2 326	m²
Surface/volume ratio	0.45	
Net heat load (heated area)	260.6	MJ/m²
	(72	kWh/m²)
External design temperature	-5	°C

Site and Climate

Altitude	212	m
Latitude	45° 36'	N
Longitude	8° 34'	E
Average ambient temp: annual	11.8	°C
January	2.5	°C
July	21.4	°C
Degree days (base 19°C)	2 400	days
Global irradiaton on horiz	1 365	kWh/m²
Sunshine hours	1 979	hrs/yr

Costs (1985 prices)

Building*	L 2 250 M	1 665 000	ECU
Active solar	L 63 M	46 620	ECU
Passive solar	L 54 M	39 960	ECU
Auxiliary heating system	L 190 M	140 600	ECU

(*active, passive and auxiliary systems are included)

LOS MOLINOS CREDITS

Client
Caja de Ahorros de Alicante y Murcia
San Fernando 40
03001 Alicante

Architect & Energy Consultant
Ignacio Blanco Lopez
Alameda 4
46010 Valencia

Building Contractor
Construcciones Planelles Hijos SL
San Juan 13
Crevillente
Alicante

Monitoring Organisation
Departament de Termodinamica
Facultat de Fisica
Universitat de Valencia
46100 Burjassot
Valencia

Under contract from:
Instituto de Energias Renovables - CIEMAT (Centro
de Investigaciones Energeticas, Medioambientales y
Tecnologicas)
Av Complutense 22
28040 Madrid

Commission of the European Communities

- Classrooms and laboratories of an Environmental Education Centre designed to demonstrate a range of passive heating and cooling systems.

- New passive component, "Blanco wall," provides heating and cooling and presents a white external appearance.

- Comfortable temperatures achieved throughout the year without auxiliary heating or cooling.

- Innovative building successfully integrated with local rural architecture.

- Savings associated with exclusion of an auxiliary heating system pay for the extra cost of the passive measures.

LOS MOLINOS
CREVILLENTE
SPAIN

Project Background

The project consists of the classrooms and laboratories of an Environmental Education Centre, in which the building itself is a didactic example of passive solar architectural systems. The building is carefully integrated into the rural architecture of the area and this has led to the development of new passive solar systems. The building was built in 1983 by the Caja de Ahorros de Alicante y Murcia as an extension to the existing centre.

OBJECTIVES

The aim was to actively demonstrate passive solar systems in use and to exclude the need for both auxiliary heating and cooling systems. In addition, it was thought essential that the building remain sympathetic to the mediterranean architectural style characteristic of the region.

1. Converted windmill (common room)
2. Converted windmill (dining area)
3. Windmill
4. Farm school
5. Classrooms and laboratories

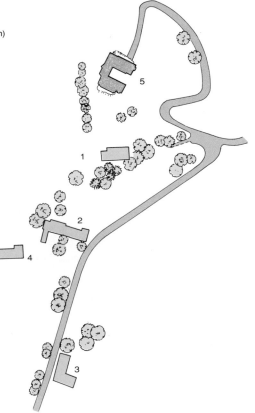

It is important that the classrooms and laboratories are complementary to other parts of the Environmental Education Centre, which are housed in renovated windmills.

ENERGY SAVING FEATURES

● The building was placed at the top of the south slope of a hill, with the north side earth-sheltered.

● Direct solar gain is captured through large south facing windows with wooden shutters for shading in summer, and only small ventilation openings are placed on the north facade.

● South facing "Blanco walls" provide both heating and cooling.

● Sunspace-corridor allows direct gains to adjoining classroom and storage of solar energy in water drums.

● Double glazed sunspace tower linking ground and first floors, houses a staircase surrounding a water tank to store solar gains.

● The building forms three sides of a square around a patio which remains open to cooling easterly breezes in summer.

● A fountain in the patio humidifies the surrounding air and thereby assists cooling.

● High levels of insulation are used in walls and roof.

● An active solar water heating system supplies all the hot water requirements.

SITE AND CLIMATE

CLIMATE (Alicante)

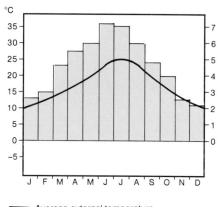

— Average external temperature
▪ Solar Radiation on a horizontal plane

The building is part of an Environmental Education Centre which occupies an area of 70 Ha. Other parts of the centre are housed in converted windmills, hence the name Los Molinos, the Windmills. The centre is located 50km along the N-340 road from Alicante to Murcia. The height of the site above sea level ranges from 150m to 300m and the classrooms and laboratories are located at the highest point. The climate is maritime mediterranean, summers are warm and winters are fairly cool. There is little rainfall in autumn and winter (October to February) and virtually none for the rest of the year. The monthly average temperature in January is 14.5°C, with

temperatures of 39ºC being reached in August. The annual average temperature is 21.9ºC. Solar radiation is high throughout the year.
The building is however subjected to strong winds and the surrounding brushwood vegetation offers little protection. The surroundings do not provide sufficient solar protection in summer either, so shading devices which also reduce glare were needed.

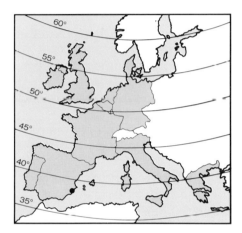

DESIGN DETAILS

One of the biggest problems in mediterranean architecture is how to provide adequate ventilation and cooling in summer. As white is mostly used for the external finish of popular architecture, an externally-white structure promoting cross-ventilation in summer, and collecting and storing solar energy in winter, has been specially designed and is integrated into the building. This structure has been named the "Blanco wall". Traditional passive systems such as direct gain, a sunspace, a patio, and water thermal storage have also been included in the building.

PLANNING

The building consists of the classrooms and laboratories arranged in three wings around a patio. The patio is fundamental to building's spatial organisation and receives cooling breezes from the east in summer. It also incorporates a pond and garden.
The north wing has two floors and is partially earth-sheltered on the north to protect it against the winter winds. This facade is windowless and has openings for ventilation only. On the south side of this wing, a sunspace-corridor is attached to the ground floor classrooms with a Blanco wall above. The south wing is only single storey and the south facade is also a Blanco wall.
The connecting west wing contains the hall, secretary's office, service areas and photographic laboratory.

CONSTRUCTION

The main construction is load bearing concrete block walls with structural timber floors and roofs. The north, east and west walls are insulated with 50 mm external fibreglass panels. The south facing walls are the Blanco walls, comprising tilted windows, moveable reflectors and mass walls (externally insulated with 50mm of fibreglass) or glazing and water thermal storage tanks.
The roof of the building is made from 50mm thick insulated fibre glass panels on a timber frame, externally protected by a covering of 70mm hollow bricks, cement plastered on the outside.
The suspended floors in the main building and sunspace-corridor are made from clay tiles, 40 mm thick, on steel joists.
Windows are single glazed with heavy timber shutters which act as solar shading devices in summer. The sunspace glazing is not fitted with shutters.
There were two main difficulties with the design and construction; the incorporation of unusual materials and new construction elements without incurring a significant increase in building costs, and the provision of thermal mass inside the building.

The building houses classrooms and laboratories in three wings around a patio. On the right is the sunspace tower with stairs leading to the first floor in the north wing.

Design Details

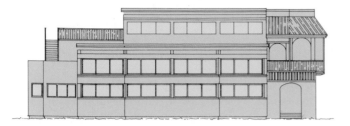

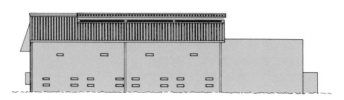

PASSIVE SOLAR DESIGN

The building has five elements of passive solar design:-

● direct solar gain;

● the Blanco wall system, providing both heating and cooling;

● a sunspace-corridor with water thermal storage;

● a sunspace tower with water thermal storage;

● a patio open to the easterly winds with an humidifying pond.

The large areas of south facing window allow direct gain into the classrooms. Shutters are provided for shading in summer. The Blanco wall system comprises 60° tilted windows, internal moveable alumimium reflectors and internal thermal storage. Sun entering the classrooms through the windows is reflected onto the thermal storage which also forms the south walls.
Two types of storage are used. In the single storey south wing, the concrete wall, below the main window, forms the storage. It is constructed from 250mm thick concrete blocks with 50mm of external insulation and tiled internally. In the top storey of the north wing, 3 thin water tanks form the storage. These

are 420mm thick, 1100mm high, 3700mm in length and with a volume of 1.7m³ each, located behind the glazing of the outer wall.
External reflecting shutters increase direct solar gain to the tanks when needed and are raised at night to insulate the tanks against heat loss to the outside.
The internal reflectors also rotate and form insulation for the tilted windows at night (they have 40mm of fibreglass behind the mirrored surface). In this position, the Blanco wall can be used as a solar chimney for summer ventilation, by opening the vents at the top. A black

roller blind fixed to the top of the reflector is pulled down over the reflector to increase solar absorption and thus increase the stack effect. Both the reflectors and the roller blind absorbers are fitted with counter-balance mechanisms, so that they are easy to operate. The sunspace-corridor attached to the south-facing ground floor of the north wing has a floor area of 22.4m² and a glazed area of 25m². Eighteen, 50 litre water tanks inside provide storage for solar gains, whilst the classroom behind receives direct solar radiation through the interconnecting glazed doors and windows. The active solar

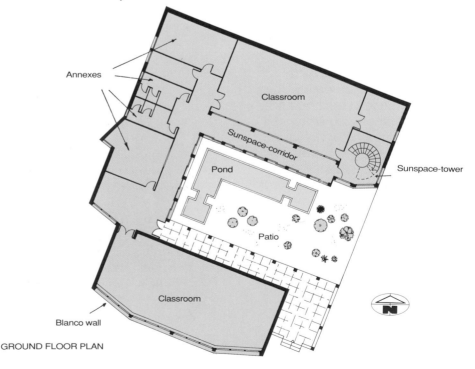

GROUND FLOOR PLAN

water heating system, comprising 7m^2 of collector panels, is mounted in the roof of the corridor.

In the sunspace tower there is a spiral staircase, connecting the ground and first floors of the north wing, which winds around a 7m^3 water tank (4.6m high x 1.4m diameter). This black painted steel tank acts as thermal mass whilst the surrounding black steel steps collect or dissipate solar gains

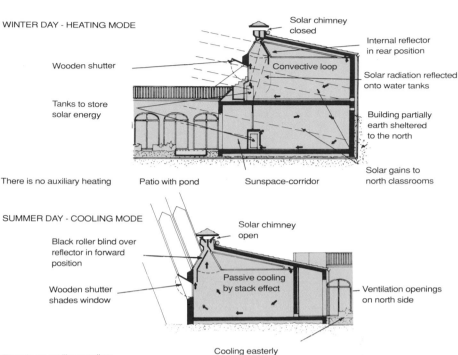

WINTER DAY - HEATING MODE

Solar chimney closed

Wooden shutter

Internal reflector in rear position

Convective loop

Solar radiation reflected onto water tanks

Tanks to store solar energy

Building partially earth sheltered to the north

Solar gains to north classrooms

There is no auxiliary heating — Patio with pond — Sunspace-corridor

SUMMER DAY - COOLING MODE

Solar chimney open

Black roller blind over reflector in forward position

Passive cooling by stack effect

Wooden shutter shades window

Ventilation openings on north side

There is no auxiliary cooling

Cooling easterly breezes in patio

Blanco wall in south wing.
Internal reflectors direct solar gains to concrete storage beneath the windows.

according to conditions.

The patio is a passive element commonly found in mediterranean architecture. It is open to the east to benefit from the prevailing summer breezes. The air is humidified by water from the 30m^2 pond. In extremely hot conditions, this water can also be used for evaporative cooling by directing it onto the roof tiles of the classrooms, from where it pours down channels and returns to the pond again.

AUXILIARY HEATING SYSTEMS

No auxiliary systems for heating, cooling or ventilation have been installed. Electricity is only used for lighting (via efficient fluorescent tubes) and for teaching aids (video recorders, slide projectors, etc).

Sometimes in summer, a small amount of electricity is used to operate the pump in the pond.

CONTROLS

All the passive systems are manually controlled corresponding to the didatic use of the building. Only the active solar water heating system is automatically controlled.

OPERATING MODES

The Blanco wall is operated in the following ways:-
On winter days the internal reflector panels are in the back position and are adjusted to reflect the sun onto the back of the storage walls and water tanks. The external reflector panels outside the water tanks are lowered. The ventilators in the solar chimney are closed but other internal ventilators are opened to encourage air circulation via the convective loop under the roof.

On winter nights, the internal reflector panels are swung forward to cover the tilted windows, thus providing insulation. The external reflector panels in front of the water tanks are closed.

On summer days, the black roller blind is drawn over the

Blanco wall in north wing on the first floor.
External horizontal reflector shutters direct solar gains to water tanks.

internal reflector panels which remain in the closed position against the tilted windows. The stack effect is increased by opening the ventilators in the

Performance Evaluation

solar chimney and north facade, thereby promoting cross ventilation. The external reflector panels in front of the water tanks remain in the upright, closed, position.

On summer nights, the solar chimney and north facing ventilators remain open.

The external shutters on the south facing windows allow the entry of low winter sun, but provide shading in summer. The shutters are lowered over the windows at night to reduce heat loss.

The only control on the sunspace-corridor is opening the windows to allow the ventilation of unwanted solar gains.

The sunspace tower collects solar gain in winter, which is stored in the water tank and stairs, and the high thermal mass moderates temperatures in summer. There are no control mechanisms.

The central patio operates as a buffer to winter winds (northerly) and is open to summer (easterly) winds which provide cooling ventilation air to the building. The pond is used in summer to humidify, and therefore cool, this ventilation air.

MONITORING

Monitoring took place between October 1986 and February 1988,by sampling every 2 minutes, and averaging and recording every 30 minutes; internal and external temperatures and humidities, temperatures of the thermal stores, internal air movement and solar irradiation.

Isolated measurements were also taken to check the accuracy of recorded data and to measure the ventilation rates by using tracer gas techniques and gas-spectrometry.

USER RESPONSE

Attendance ranges from 7000 to 10000 students per year, however, the user response is based on opinions of the teachers, who are there for the whole year.

The building is considered to be comfortable throughout the year, especially during the winter.

The users find the building aesthetically pleasing, and consider that it blends well with the traditional style of local architecture.

The client is also satisfied that the educational objectives of

CONTRIBUTION TO ANNUAL SPACE HEATING DEMAND

The total space heating load of 15 424kWh was entirely met by passive solar gains and internal gains.

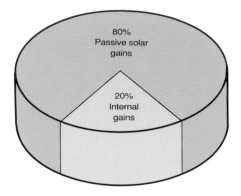

incorporating the passive solar systems have been completely fulfilled.

PERFORMANCE OF PASSIVE SOLAR DESIGN

● All the passive solar systems worked well, the traditional elements and the innovative Blanco wall.

● The building is considered comfortable throughout the year, despite the absence of an auxiliary heating system.

● Solar gains contributed 80% to the gross space heating load of 15424 kWh, and internal gains met the remaining 20%.

● The building is not occupied in the height of summer, but when it is occupied, it does not overheat (with the exception of the sunspace-corridor).

● Effective cooling is achieved through the provision of a sufficient number of shutters, and through operation of the Blanco wall as a solar chimney.

● Some form of solar shading device is required to be fitted in the sunspace corridor.

Blanco wall in north classroom on first floor.
Internal reflectors further increase solar gains to water drums.

COST OF BUILDING AND SOLAR ON-COST

The total building cost 25M Ptas in 1984.

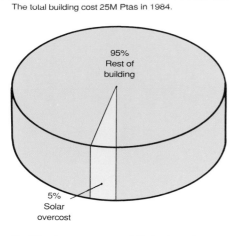

The 5% solar overcost was paid for by the savings resulting from the exclusion of an auxiliary space heating system.

During the period that the building was monitored, the winter was exceptionally mild (528 degree days, 17ºC base), thereby reducing the gross space heating load. Thus useful solar gains were less than predicted due to the reduced demand, but once adjustments have been made, the predictions agree well with the measured data.

COST EFFECTIVENESS

The overcost of the passive solar systems (glazing, thermal storage, reflecting panels and manual controls) totalled 1.2M Ptas in March 1984. This sum represented a 5% increase in the full project cost of 25M Ptas however, this increase was offset by the savings which resulted from the exclusion of a conventional heating system, eg, a gas fired boiler and radiators. Overall it is considered that passive solar heating and cooling systems, if integrated into the design, can result in a comfortable building throughout the year with no associated running costs and no additional construction cost.

MONTHLY SPACE HEATING LOAD

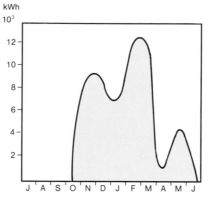

———— Net sp.htg load
　　　 Solar energy

MONTHLY AVERAGE TEMPERATURES

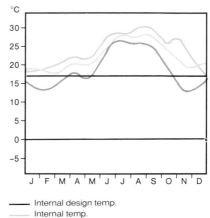

———— Internal design temp.
———— Internal temp.
———— Sunspace temp.
———— External temp.

Sunspace-corridor provides daylight and solar gains to classroom behind, and contains more water tanks for storing solar energy.

PROJECT DATA

BUILDING CHARACTERISTICS

Volume		1253	m³
Floor area		330.4	m²
Roof area		263.1	m²
External wall area		470.9	m²
Windows:	total area	120.2	m²
	south	111.9	m² 93%
	east	8.3	m² 7%

Thermal Characteristics

U value:	roof	0.615	W/m²K
	floor	1.4	W/m²K
	external walls	0.61	W/m²K
Windows:	double glazed	3.0	W/m²K
	single glazed	6.4	W/m²K
Sunspace glazing:	double glazed	3.0	W/m²K
	single glazed	6.4	W/m²K
Global heat loss coefficient (without ventilation)		1002	W/K
Infiltration rate		0.5	ach
Heated floor area		330.4	m²
Heated volume		1253	m³
Net heat load		0.135	GJ/m²
		37.4	(kWh/m²)

Site and Climate

Altitude		300	m
Latitude		38º15'	N
Longditude		0º50'	W
Average ambient temp:	Jan	10	ºC
	July	24	ºC
Degree days(base 15.5ºC)		576	days
Global irradiation on horiz.		16.48	MJ/m²/day
		4.58	(kWh/m²/day)
Sunshine hours		3068	hr/yr

Sunspace-Corridor

Volume		187.3	m³
Floor area		35	m²
Glass area:	wall	49.3	m²

Costs

Building:	25 000 000	Ptas	ECU 189 394
Solar features	1 143 252	Ptas	ECU 8 661 (4.6%)

SMAKKEBO PROJECT CREDITS

Client
Boligfonden SDS
Meldahlsgade 32
Vesterport
1613 Copenhagen K

Architect
Jorgen Andersen
Mordrupvej 99
3060 Espergaerde

Energy Consultants
Ove Morck & Peder Vejsig-Pedersen
Cenergia ApS
Walgerholm 17
3500 Vaerlose

Services Engineer
E Troelsgaards Tegnestue
Overgaden N Vandet 49 B
1414 Copenhagen K

Building and Services Contractor
Hoffman & Sonner A/S
Maltegardsvej 24
2820 Gentofte

Monitoring Organisation
Thermal Insulation Laboratory
Building 118
Technical University of Denmark
2800 Lyngby

Commission of the European Communities

● Large estate of 55, single storey, one to three bedroom houses, combines high levels of insulation with passive solar measures.

● 26% solar contribution to the gross space heating load contributes to an overall energy saving of 57% compared to conventional houses in Denmark.

● Large sloping windows with moveable insulation, and sunspaces, combined with a heat recovery ventilation system, maximise the use of solar gains.

● Innovative, thermosyphon solar water heating system, complete with collectors and storage tank, provides 60% of hot water but has overheating problems.

SMAKKEBO
SNEKKERSTEN
DENMARK

Project Background

The Smakkebo Building Project is a development of solar, low energy dwellings designed and built as part of the Danish participation in the IEA Solar Heating and Cooling Programme. The project comprises the construction of 55 dwellings, with the same solar and energy saving features. There are four sizes of dwelling, the smallest being a 1 bedroom house and the largest a 3 bedroom house. The houses are designed as direct gain solar houses with high levels of insulation and a passive solar water heating system.

OBJECTIVES

The primary objective of the Smakkebo project was to demonstrate that passive solar and low energy measures can be successfully implemented in the Danish housing industry in a cost-effective way without any limitations on the quality of the architectural design. A second objective was to verify the effectiveness of these techniques by carrying out a detailed monitoring programme. The brief required the design and construction of single family, detached or semi-detached dwellings, of various sizes from 62 to 97 m², and a community centre. The project was administered by Boligfonden SDS and built and financed according to the specific Danish governmental regulations relating to this type of housing. These imply fairly severe restrictions on size and costs.

ENERGY SAVING FEATURES

● Houses are orientated south ±15º, and spaced to avoid overshading.

● 62% of glazing is on the south side, including some sloping windows.

● Roller shutters on the sloping windows provide night time insulation and daytime protection against overheating.

● Thermal mass is provided in the internal walls.

● Small sunspaces are attached to the kitchens on the south side.

● High levels of insulation. including triple glazing, and effective draughtstripping have been incorporated.

● There is a heat recovery ventilation system.

● An innovative thermosyphon solar system provides domestic hot water.

SITE AND CLIMATE

The Smakkebo project was built on a 3.5ha site in Snekkersten, on the outskirts of Elsinore in the northern part of Zealand. It is surrounded by one and two storey houses and, being relatively high for the area, is fairly exposed to wind and sunshine. There is no shelter from trees or the adjacent houses since they are placed more than the minimum distance apart in order to avoid mutual shading.
The climate, which varies little throughout Denmark, is a

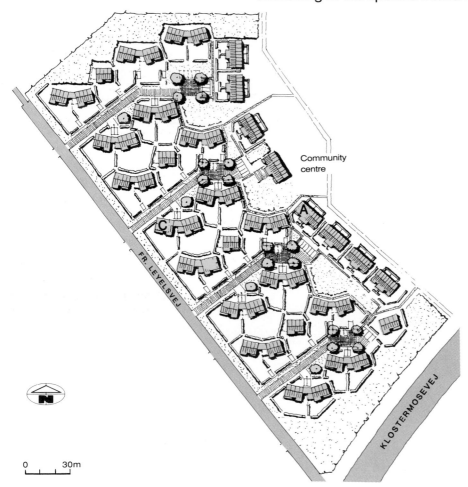

The site was laid out so that most of the houses faced south and there was no overshadowing.

Design Details

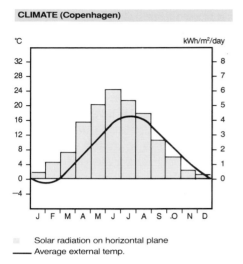

Solar radiation on horizontal plane
—— Average external temp.

coastal one with mild winters and relatively cool summers. The average temperatures are -1°C in January and +16°C in July. There are 1500 hours of sunshine each year, but only 10% of these are in the four months of November to February. Of the 2909 annual degree days,1889 are from November to February.

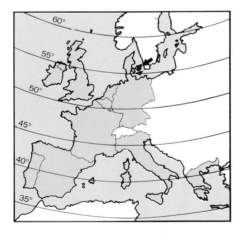

CONCLUSIONS

The passive solar and energy conservation techniques applied in the Smakkebo project have been shown to give a reasonable payback and required only 43% of the auxiliary energy used for space heating in similar houses built to the Danish Building Regulations. The heating load during the first year of monitoring was 2000 kWh higher than predicted due to significantly worse weather

conditions and because internal gains were somewhat lower than expected. The user acceptance of the houses was very high and enquiries showed general satisfaction with the thermal comfort within the houses. The heating load varied considerably among houses of the same type; a consequence of user effect. The solar hot water systems have proved to be very successful with a system efficiency of 49%, providing 57% of the hot water load.

On the south facade are the sunspace, the sloping window to the living room and the solar panels of the hot water system.

PLANNING

The site layout was designed so that most of the houses face within 15° of south. All are single storey, detached or semi-detached houses located to minimise overshading. Access to houses is via four cul-de-sacs off the main road running along the south-west of the site.

CONSTRUCTION

The houses are well insulated in all respects. The concrete floor slab rests on 220mm of insulating "leca nuts" (expanded clay clinker) and is covered by 75mm of rigid mineral fibre and a parquet floor. The load-bearing walls are of prefabricated construction with either brick or timber outer leaf, 180mm of mineral fibre filled cavity and a concrete inner leaf. Internal walls are also prefabricated. Roofs are black corrugated fibrous-cement sheets, on a timber frame with 250mm of mineral fibre insulation. The external roof slopes are 20° and the internal ceilings reflect this but at a reduced slope.

Windows are triple glazed, with the exception of the south facing sloping windows which are double glazed. Special attention was paid to draughtstripping and this has resulted in a natural ventilation rate as low as 0.06 airchanges per hour. The mechanical ventilation system provides the necessary air quality.

Design Details

SOUTH ELEVATION

`0    3m`

PASSIVE SOLAR DESIGN

The passive solar design comprises direct gain (with moveable insulation), attached sunspaces and thermosyphon solar domestic water heating. House orientation north-south, adequate spacing between the houses and 62% of glazing on the south side maximise direct gain. One large window ($3.4m^2$) in the living room, slopes at

The sloping living room window has an external roller blind.

approximately 60° to the horizontal to maximise entry of solar radiation during the heating season. This window is equipped with an external roller shutter which has two functions. During the winter it can be used at night time as an insulating shutter, and in summer it can be used to prevent overheating in

the house. The shutter is operated by an electric motor. The thermal mass of the internal walls and the inside leaf of the outer walls helps to store heat and maximise the use of the solar gain.

Small sunspaces ($6m^2$) are attached to the south facades at one end of the house adjacent to the kitchen area. These are double glazed with concrete sidewalls, one of which contains a double glazed door. Windows and doors from the house open directly into the sunspace and ventilation of the sunspace is by opening two of the roof panels or two of the front panels.

An innovative solar domestic water heating system has been integrated in the south facade, next to the sloping windows. The absorber and the storage tank of this thermosyphon system have been combined into one unit. This unit, comprising $3.5m^2$ of collector area and a 150 litre storage tank, is simply built in as an element of the wall. The system is completely passive, with the pressurised fluid in the collector circulating through a heat exchanger where it transfers heat to the water in the thin water storage tank behind. A one-way valve prohibits reverse circulation at night.

AUXILIARY HEATING SYSTEM

The houses are equipped with electric heaters in all rooms except for the entrance hall and the bathroom, where there is an electrically heated floor. It is also possible to install an electrical heating element in the inlet of the ventilation systems and a number of tenants have

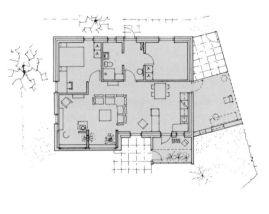

`0    3m`

This 2 bedroom, $97m^2$ house was fully monitored.

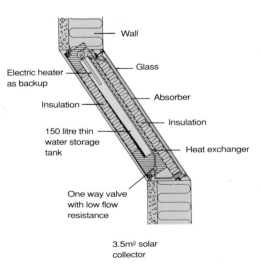

The thermosyphon solar hot water system.

done so. These heaters are all controlled by on/off thermostatic controllers with a sensitivity band of 1-2°C. A central night set-back device or intermittent heating controller, which allows all temperature setpoints to be lowered by 5°C, is provided in each house.

The ventilation system has a high efficiency, counterflow heat-exchanger which recovers heat from the exhaust air. It can be manually controlled to three different rates according to the needs of the occupants. The lowest rate is the basic ventilation level required by the Building Code, the next rate provides somewhat increased ventilation and the highest rate is intended for use while cooking.

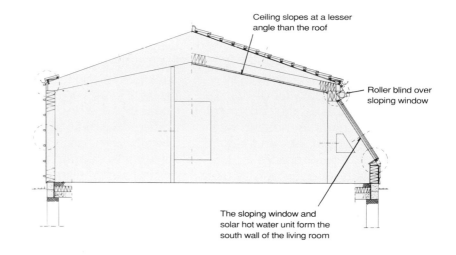

Ceiling slopes at a lesser angle than the roof

Roller blind over sloping window

The sloping window and solar hot water unit form the south wall of the living room

The innovative solar hot water system includes a 150 litre tank behind the collector.

An electrical heating element is provided in the top of the domestic hot water storage in the solar collector system and is controlled by a thermostat.

OPERATING MODES

In the heating season, solar radiation enters directly through the large sloping window into the living room and the mechanical ventilation system distributes the heat round the house. The door and windows from the sunspace to the kitchen area can be opened so that the warmed air passes into the house. At night, the roller shutter on the sloping window is closed to insulate the glazing. In summer, the roller shutter can be drawn to prevent the sun entering the house. There are no shading devices in the sunspace, although it can be ventilated by opening the door to the garden, and the windows. The solar water heating system operates automatically when the fluid in the collector circuit is hotter than the water in the storage tank behind. Thermosyphoning takes place in the primary circuit and heat is transferred to the water in the tank until it is at the same temperature as the fluid at the top of the collector. A one-way valve in the primary circuit stops reverse circulation when the storage tank is at a higher temperature than the fluid in the collector circuit, eg, at night.

The sunspace has no shading devices but panels of the roof and walls, and the door, can be opened for ventilation.

Performance Evaluation

MONITORING

Monitoring took place over the 1985/86 heating season. It included a combination of continuous, detailed performance measurements for one house and gross energy consumption data for all houses. In all the houses, the amount of electricity used for heating was recorded, together with the total electricity consumption.

A simple hour-counter was used in each house to count the number of hours in which the heating element in the hot water storage was in use.

The kitchen opens directly into the sunspace.

The readings (other than for the house with the detailed monitoring) were taken by the tenants themselves, using proformas on which comments on the use of the house, indoor temperatures, vacations and other matters could be recorded. This procedure worked remarkably well.

The 1985/86 winter was unfortunately much colder than average (1.5ºC lower) giving 10% more "degree days" than normal, and there was only 76% of the sunshine of a normal Danish winter.

USER RESPONSE

Generally the tenants responded positively to the heating and temperature levels within the houses. The natural lighting levels were seen as very satisfactory and the air quality thought to be very good, if on occasions too dry. There were some complaints about noise from the ventilation systems. All tenants claimed to use the control mechanism in the house, the night temperature set-backs on the electric heaters, the shutters over the sloping windows and the variable volume ventilation system. The doors between the sunspace and the house were well used to allow warmed air into the house and it appears that the sunspaces themselves were warm enough to be used as an extension to the houses from February onwards on sunny days. Overall, the tenants were very happy with their houses.

PERFORMANCE OF THE PASSIVE SOLAR DESIGN

● Solar gains contributed 25.5% to the gross space heating demand for 1985/86, despite an unusually cold and sunless winter.

● For a typical year, solar gains are estimated at 28% of gross space heating demand.

● The fully monitored Smakkebo house saved 57% of the energy used for space heating in a conventionally designed house.

● The rest of the Smakkebo houses achieved between 35% and 65% savings.

● The solar hot water system proved more effective than expected with an efficiency of 49%.

COMPARISON WITH CONVENTIONAL DESIGN

12 600kWh would be required to heat a similar house built to a conventional design.

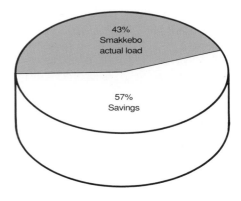

The fully monitored house in the Smakkebo project used only 5 400kWh of auxiliary heat over the 1985-86 heating season.

CONTRIBUTIONS TO ANNUAL SPACE HEATING DEMAND

The total annual space heating demand is 13 154kWh.

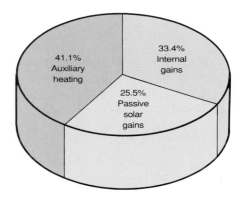

Solar gains provided 25.5% of the load during an unusually cold and overcast winter. In a typical winter, solar gains would provide 28% of the load.

● The auxiliary fuel used for hot water production (average of 3 houses) was 43% of the total hot water load in the houses.

However, there were two problems; with the shutters and the solar water heaters.
The shutters have to be cleared of snow and ice in severe weather conditions before being operated, otherwise they may become damaged. The problem is exacerbated by the use of the electric motors for moving the shutters, since if the shutters were operated by hand it could be felt if they were stuck half way and appropriate action could be taken.

TOTAL HOT WATER DEMAND

The total annual hot water demand was 2800kWh (average for three houses).

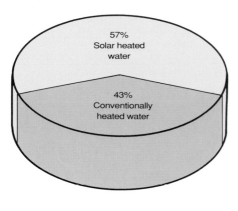

57%
Solar heated water

43%
Conventionally heated water

Solar heated water contributed 57% to this total demand.

AUXILIARY FUEL USED

The auxiliary fuel used was 9 900kWh.

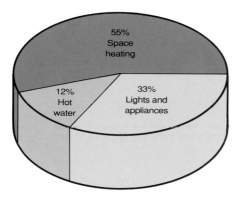

55%
Space heating

12%
Hot water

33%
Lights and appliances

The solar collectors have been more efficient than expected resulting in high temperatures in the collector circuit, up to about 115ºC. This, in combination with a gradual loss of pressure from the pressurised expansion vessels, has resulted in boiling in several of the collector circuits. This, in turn, results in loss of circulation and even higher temperatures which damage the insulation and vapour barriers around the pipes. Apparently, the pressure of the expansion vessels should be tested and maintained every year to avoid this.

NET MONTHLY SPACE HEATING LOAD

For the fully monitored house.

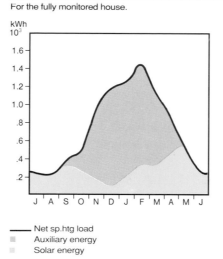

— Net sp.htg load
▪ Auxiliary energy
▪ Solar energy

SUNNY WINTER DAY

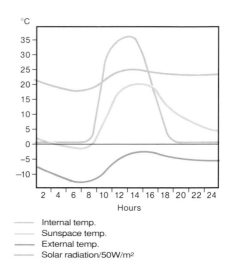

— Internal temp.
— Sunspace temp.
— External temp.
— Solar radiation/50W/m²

COST EFFECTIVENESS

As the houses were built according to special Danish regulations for cooperative building projects, total building costs had to be kept within given limits. These limits were only slightly extended because of the energy saving nature of this project. The project received standard Danish energy saving subsidies which amounted to approximtely Kr 15 000 per house. The actual overcost of the passive solar and energy saving measures, including the solar water heating system, is estimated at between Kr 50 000 and Kr 70 000. The value of the energy savings for both heating and hot water, for the house with detailed monitoring, was approximately Kr 6 600 per annum, giving a simple payback period of between 7.5 and 10.5 years. The project demonstrates that if energy conservation and passive solar features are built into the design from the beginning, reasonable payback times are possible.

PROJECT DATA

House Type C				Thermal Characteristics		
Volume		265 m³		U-values:	roof	0.18 W/m²K
Floor Area		85 m²			external walls	0.19 W/m²K
Window area:	total	8.2 m²			floor	0.17 W/m²K
	south:	5.8 m²	71%		windows	2.0 W/m²K
	vertical	0.8 m²			sloped window	3.0 W/m²K
	sloped	3.4 m²			with shutter closed	2.0 W/m²K
	onto sunspace	1.6 m²			sunspace glazing	3.0 W/m²K
	north	1.7 m²	21%	Heated floor area		85 m²
	east/west	0.7 m²	8%	Heated volume		265 m³
				Net heat load		37 kWh/m²
Sunspace				Infiltration rate		<0.1 ach
Volume		14 m³		Global heat loss coefficient		93 W/K
Floor area		6 m²		External Design Temperature		-12 ºC
Glass area:	roof	3 m²				
	walls	5 m²		Cost (1985 prices)		
Wall area: solid		7 m²		Building	Kr 650 000	ECU 82 000
				Passive Solar and		
Site and Climate				Energy Saving Features	Kr 50 000 -70 000	
Altitude		0 m				
Latitude		56º N				
Longitude		12º E				
Average ambient temp:	January	-1 ºC				
	July	16 ºC				
Degree days (17 ºC base)		2909 days				
Global irradiation on horiz		1015 kWh/m²				
Sunshine Hours		1500 hrs/yr				

ORBASSANO CREDITS

Client
UPSE (Unione Piemontese Sviluppo Edilizio)
Via Cristoforo Colombo 17
10129 Torino

Impresa Maciotta SpA
Corso G Ferraris 120
10129 Torino

Architects
R Gabetti & A Isola
Via Sacchi 22
10128 Torina

Project Management
Ufficio Tecnico Impresa Maciotta
Corso G Ferraris 120
10129 Torino

Building Contractor
Impresa Maciotta SpA
Corso G Ferraris 120
10129 Torino

Services Engineer and Contractor
C Ferrari srl   now:
Via Tunisi 37   Corso Matteotti 0
10134 Torino   10121 Torino

Energy Consultant
Softech srl
Via Cernaia 1
10121 Torino

Dipartimento Scienze e Tecniche per i Processi di
Insediamento
Facolta di Architettura - Politecnico di Torino
Viale Mattioli 39
10125 Torino

Monitoring Organisation
UPSE with consultancy from
Hi-tek srl
Via Cernaia 1
10121 Torino

Funding Support
CER (Comitato Edilizia Residenziale)
presso Ministero Lavori Pubblici
(Ministry of Public Works)
Piazzale Porta Pia
00198 Roma

CEC (Commission of the European Communities)
DG XII
Wetstraat 200
1049 Brussels
Belgium

Commission of the European Communities

- Innovative 10-storey apartment block of triangular design, provides maximum exposure to the south, with two fully glazed sides facing south-east and south-west.

- All 40 apartments have full width sunspaces on south-east or south-west sides adjacent to the main living room.

- Passive solar gain contributes 36% to the heating load, with overall savings of 51% compared to a similar block built to Italian Building Standards.

- Active air-heating solar panels on south splay provide 43% of the annual hot water demand, plus a 7% contribution to the space heating demand.

ORBASSANO

TORINO
ITALY

Project Background

Orbassano is a 10-storey tower block with forty dwellings, the majority of which are owner occupied. Triangular in plan, the block has sunspaces covering the complete south-east and south-west sides and a large active solar system on the splay between the two southerly sides.
Construction was completed in December 1984.

OBJECTIVES

The building was commissioned by UPSE (Unione Piemontese Sviluppo Edilizio), who have carried out an extensive Demonstration Programme which includes many passive solar and low-energy housing schemes in Piedmont. The client required multifamily accommodation, offering a mix of different dwelling sizes and wanted to test the effectiveness of a package of energy saving and solar measures under Po Valley climatic conditions. The UPSE consortium of builders mainly operates in this area and is therefore particularly interested in comparing innovative solutions, such as Orbassano, with more traditional ways of building.

ENERGY SAVING FEATURES

● Orientation of the block so that two of the three sides face south-east and south-west.

● Fully glazed south east and south west facades, with integral sunspaces, maximise solar gain to main living rooms.

● 195 m² of active solar air-heating collectors provide domestic hot water and contribute to space heating.

● High levels of insulation, including ground floor and roof slab, and double glazing, minimise heat loss.

● Thermostats and heat meters for individual flats, optimise the use of the communal auxiliary heating system.

SITE AND CLIMATE

The site is located on the edge of Torino at the bottom of the Chisone Valley, in an area of rapid urban growth, not far from a major access route to the centre of Orbassano. The plot is located at the centre of a proposed urban development comprising several tower blocks, though at present it is still partially surrounded by green fields.
The area around Torino is characterised by low winds, and mists which occur between October and January for a third of the days. The average

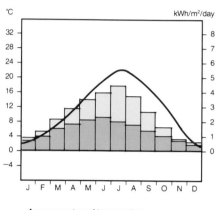

CLIMATE (Orbassano)

— Average external temperature
▨ Diffuse solar radiation
▨ Direct solar radiation

outside temperature is 11.2ºC (Jan: 2.4ºC, July: 21.6ºC). The site microclimate was carefully studied as part of the UPSE programme, and the location for the block chosen to minimise overshadowing. Only

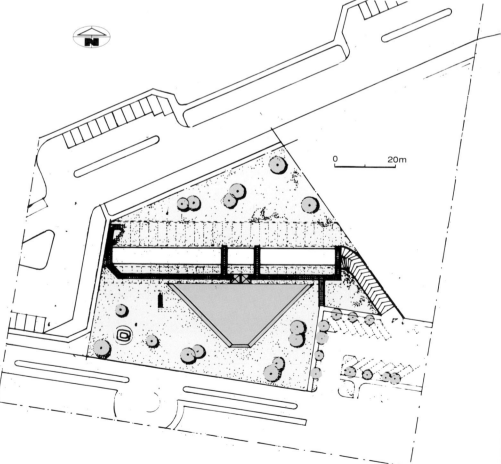

The block will eventually have several other tower blocks built in the surroundings.

the lower floors suffer significant shading and overall, the shading of the sunspace facade never exceeds 13%.

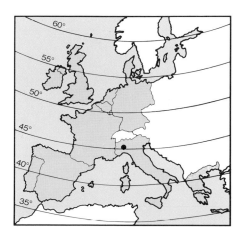

CONCLUSIONS

At present, the block rises alone out of the half completed development around, presenting a strange contrast to the rural backdrop of the Po Valley. This isolation will be reduced when similar planned blocks in the neighbourhood are built.

The building is successful in energy terms, saving 51% of the primary energy required to heat a similar block built to Italian Building Standards. The passive solar contribution to the net space heating load was on average 36%.

The Orbassano tower is in many ways an experimental "tour de force", a unique and unrepeatable example within the panorama of Italian solar housing.

PLANNING

In plan, the tower is a right angled triangle with the right angle trimmed off at 45°. It therefore has four elevations:- the hypotenuse faces north and becomes a high wall punctured by small square windows; the sunspaces, on the south-east and south-west symmetrical facades, display a full-height curtain-wall screen; and on the

chamfered front, facing due south, is the active solar system of vertical air collectors. A ramp serves a double row of garages located in the basement together with individual cellars and the heating plant room. There are four apartments per floor, ranging in size from one to three bedrooms. The entrance, staircase and elevators are on the north side of the building, and access galleries to the flats overlook a narrow skylight passage in the centre of the floor plan. All living rooms are connected to the sunspaces. The original decision to use a "system built" construction, determined an internal layout which is not ideal, giving a narrow frontage and a large depth to some rooms, long party walls and some poorly located kitchens.

The sunspaces are rather narrow in some places but do

The originality of the building is in the sharp contrast between the masonry north wall and the light, transparent south curtain walling.

CONSTRUCTION

Although planned to be constructed by an industrialised "tunnel system", the final construction was an insitu reinforced concrete frame, with solid concrete floors.

The north facing external wall is traditionally built from a double skin of hollow pot bricks with 50mm polystyrene cavity insulation. The south-east and south-west walls, overlooking the sunspaces, consist of prevarnished steel panels, with 40mm of insulation and with integral window frames. The sunspace cladding is a purpose-made product, designed and manufactured for this project. All

The north facade is a tall blank wall perforated by small windows. The main entrance is a light structure supporting two translucent cupolas.

provide space for use as extra living area. Unfortunately the central collector panels block the south view from parts of the central flats.

A transparent overhang surrounds the two south facades at roof level, providing weather protection to the glazing.

components of the continuous facade are also in prevarnished steel (mullions, frames, anchorage brackets, bolts, opaque panels). Security glass has been used.

The floor was insulated with 50mm of polystyrene and the roof with 50mm of mineral wool.

Design Details

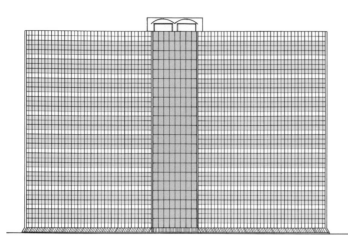

SOUTH FACADE

NORTH FACADE

The sunspaces and solar panels cover the entire south facades while entrances, stairs and lifts are on the north side.

0   15m

The only problems occurred when some solar air heating panels needed replacement, and this required a crane to be brought to the site.

blinds are placed behind the sunspace glazing.

The sunspace curtain-wall is subdivided into modular squares, 720mm x 720mm.

Direct cross-ventilation is possible only in the living/dining areas of the apartments. All bathrooms are internal and some kitchens only have windows overlooking the skylight passage, although others, at the outer ends of the plan, overlook sunspaces. The active air-heating panels on the splay between the sunspace walls total 195m² and are orientated due south. In the heating season between a third and a half of the air flow is used for pre-heating the ventilation air and the remainder for domestic water heating. In summer, the air is used only to provide the domestic hot water.

The sunspaces are the principal passive components with a total of 1136m² of glazing.

PASSIVE SOLAR DESIGN

The sunspaces cover the entire south-east and south-west frontages of the block, with a total floor area 820m². They are single glazed and have concrete floors to provide thermal mass. Between the sunspaces and the adjacent rooms there are large openings with double glazed doors fitted with PVC roller blinds. White canvas roller

The elevation is defined vertically, every fifth module, by a course of alternate blue and green panels. Between these courses, the third and fourth modules are entirely openable double windows, while the second module, which acts as a parapet, is of fixed glass and steel panels. Out of a total surface area of 1576m², 72% is glazed, of which 70% is openable.

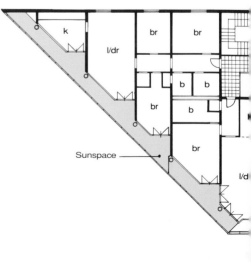

TYPICAL FLOOR PLAN

AUXILIARY HEATING SYSTEM

The auxiliary system is based on a gas-fired furnace, of some 200 kW nominal capacity, with two circuits serving the cast iron radiators of kitchens and bathrooms and the fan coils of the other rooms. Ventilation in winter is mechanically controlled; air is pre-heated by the solar air collectors, mixed with recirculated air and, when necessary, further heated by the fan coils as it enters the rooms. Part of the air heated in the collectors is utilised for hot water production, the water temperature can be further raised by an electric immersion heater in each apartment as necessary.

Individual thermostats in each apartment control the internal temperature and the system is adjusted via three-way valves on the two heating loops (serving radiators and fan-coils). The auxiliary energy consumption for space heating is metered for each apartment. The use of the solar heated air to heat the domestic hot water is controlled by a differential temperature sensor which compares the temperature levels of the hot water cylinder

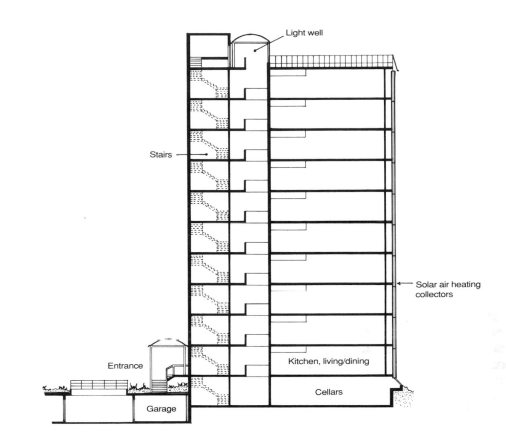

North-south section through centre of building.

and of the air from the collectors, so that when solar heat is available, the domestic water is pumped through an air to water heat exchanger.

OPERATING MODES AND CONTROLS

The depth of the sunspace allows the penetration of winter sunshine into the living spaces, but reduces solar penetration in summer. In winter, roller blinds are lowered at night for insulation, whereas in summer, if correctly positioned, they can improve comfort in the daytime. During mid-season and particularly in summer, the white canvas roller blinds are used as shading devices to prevent overheating and to control glare inside the sunspaces. Ventilation in summer is controlled by opening and closing the windows of the

sunspaces and the doors between the rooms and sunspaces. All these operations are manual.

There is a sharp contrast between the solid north wall and the transparent south curtain walling.

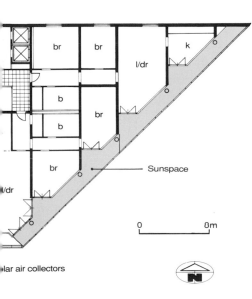

Performance Evaluation

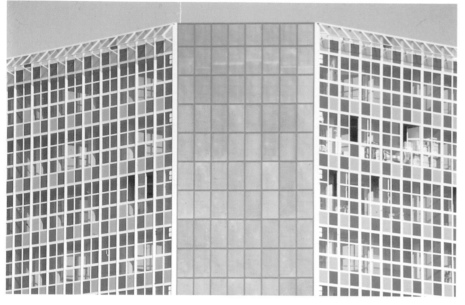
The active solar air heating panels occupy the splay between the main south elevations.

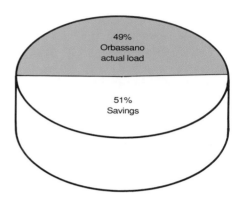

49%
Orbassano
actual load

51%
Savings

333 900 kWh (1202GJ) of primary energy would be required to heat the block if it were built to conventional Italian Building Bodes.

AUXILIARY FUEL USED (Primary energy)
The total primary energy used was 553 300kWh (1992GJ).

MONITORING

The building has been monitored over three years (1985-1988), though the first year was used mainly to optimise the system and tune the monitoring system. Two apartments were monitored, with measurments made of temperatures in the sunspaces, adjacent rooms and rooms on the north side. The auxiliary fuel consumption and the active solar contributions, were also measured.

USER RESPONSE

No general survey of occupants has been carried out. There is evidence that the sunspaces are well liked, though they cannot be used throughout the whole year. The monitoring data indicates that there is summer overheating but no complaints have been received. It is assumed that occupants have solved the problem by opening all windows to generate cross ventilation, when necessary. The energy awareness of the occupants has undoubtedly been raised by the use of individual thermostats and energy meters.

PERFORMANCE OF PASSIVE SOLAR DESIGN

● The passive solar contribution to the annual net space heating load was 36%, and the active system contributed a further 7%.

● Overall the block saved 51% of the primary energy needed to heat a similar block built to Italian Building Standards.

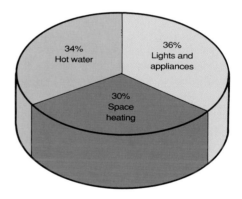

34% Hot water

36% Lights and appliances

30% Space heating

A transparent overhang surrounds the building at roof level.

● Summer temperatures in the sunspaces as high as 37ºC were recorded, though temperatures in the adjacent south rooms did not rise above the maximum external temperatures (31ºC). Temperatures in the northern rooms did not rise above 27ºC.

● The active system contributed 43% to the annual domestic hot water demand. Even over the heating period, the active system provided 21% of the hot water demand.

CONTRIBUTIONS TO TOTAL SPACE HEATING DEMAND

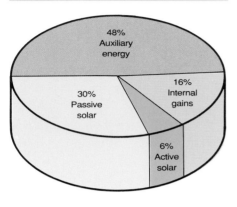

The total annual space heating demand for the whole building was 268 600Wh (967GJ).

COST OF BUILDING AND ON-COSTS

The total project cost was L4 350M.

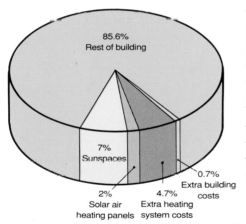

Compared to a conventional bulding of the same size the overcost of the layout and insulation measures was 0.7% of the total cost. Sunspaces cost nearly 7% of the total , solar panels 2% and modifications to, and controls for, the heating system, another 4.7%

"This strange triangular object, ironically baptised by its designers the radiator".

NET MONTHLY SPACE HEATING DEMAND AND SUPPLY

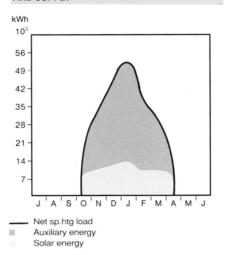

— Net sp.htg load
■ Auxiliary energy
▫ Solar energy

COST EFFECTIVENESS

The total project cost was L4 350M. The simple payback period for the package of energy saving and passive solar measures is estimated to be between 15 and 20 years. This does not take into account the value of the sunspaces in terms of the extra living space they provide for much of the year.

PROJECT DATA

Building		
Total volume of housing scheme	13 483	m³
(incl. cellars, excl garages)		
No. of floors (excl cellars and garages)	10	
No. of flats	40	
Total floor area (excl garages)	4 708	m²
Total roof area	428	m²
Windows: total area	582	m²
north area	140	m²
south-east area*	221	m²
south-west area*	221	m²
(* glazed doors overlooking sunspaces)		

Sunspaces		
Volume	2 229	m³
Floor area	819	m²
Total wall area	1 576	m²
Glass area	1 136	m²
Opaque area	440	m²

Active solar collector area	195	m²

Thermal			
U value:	roof	0.68	W/m²K
	floor	0.68	W/m²K
	north perimeter wall	0.67	W/m²K
	south-east &		
	south-west walls		
	(overlooking sunspace)	0.80	W/m²K
	sunspace glazing	5.0	W/m²K
	windows (double glazed)	2.5	W/m²K
	windows with		
	night insulation	1.7	W/m²K

Mean U value:	0.68	W/m²K
Global heat loss coefficient	4800	W/K
Infiltration rate	0.5	ach
Heated volume	8730	m³
Heated floor area	3413	m²
Heat loss surface / volume	approx 0.4	m²/m³
Net heat load/heated area	66.4	kWh/m²
External design temperature	- 8	ºC

Site and Climate		
Altitude	302	m
Latitude	45º01'	N
Longitude	7º33'	E
Average ambient temperature:		
annual	11.2º	C
January	2.4º	C
July	21.6º	C
Degree days (base 19 ºC)	2570	days
Global irradiation on horiz.	1372	kWh/m²
Sunshine hours: annual	1979	hrs
Oct - April	908	hrs

Costs (1984 prices)		
Total cost of scheme	4 350M	It Liras
	(3.1M	ECU)
Building extra cost	30M	It Liras
	(21 428	ECU)
Sunspaces	300M	It Liras
	(214 285	ECU)
Solar collectors	87M	It Liras
	(62 142	ECU)
Heating system extra cost	207M	It Liras
	(147 857	ECU)

TEMPERATURES ON A TYPICAL WINTER'S DAY

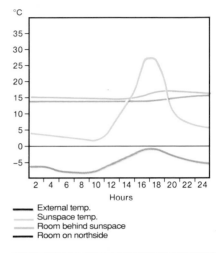

— External temp.
— Sunspace temp.
— Room behind sunspace
— Room on northside

TEMPERATURES ON A TYPICAL SUMMER'S DAY

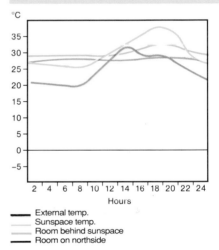

— External temp.
— Sunspace temp.
— Room behind sunspace
— Room on northside

LES COCHEVIS CREDITS

Clients
Societe anonyme d'HLM du Val d'Oise
Le Forum
Allee Maurice Ravel
95310 Saint-Gratien

Cergy Ville nouvelle (E.P.A.)
Establisement public d'amenagement
BP 47
95012 Cergy

Architect
S.C.P.A. Boschetti-Quin
169 rue du Chateau
75014 PARIS

Energy Consultant and Services Engineer
SODACO
(no longer trading)

Building Contractor
Enterprise General e du Limousin
(no longer trading)

Monitoring Organisation
Le CETIAT
Plateau du Moulon
BP No 19
91402 Orsay Cedex

Commission of the European Communities

- 21 houses designed on solar principles built for sale near Paris.

- Solar gain provides 22% of gross heating load, with overall energy savings of 45% compared to a conventional design.

- Solar features include sunspaces, fan assisted Trombe walls, rock stores and solar water heating collectors.

- Solar features are considered to improve the resale value of the properties. Owners have organised an "energy consumption competition".

LES COCHEVIS
CERGY PONTOISE
FRANCE

Project Background

There are two basic house designs. with two small sunspaces (left) and with one large sunspace (right). The air-heating wall collector can be seen between the two sunspaces.

This development built in 1983 was the first climate respecting housing built for sale near Paris. Of the 39 houses built, 21 were designed on solar principles, 10 being purely passive and 11 including active systems.
The project was the winning entry by a team of young architects in a competition called "Habitat Original Par la Thermique (HOT)", and was built by the Public Construction Office of the new town of Cergy-Pontoise.

DESIGN OBJECTIVES

The architects wanted to incorporate the latest materials into contemporary housing, and utilise solar gain to minimise the heating load. A basic restraint was the cost limit fixed by the Government.

ENERGY SAVING FEATURES

● Sunspaces and large south facing windows capture passive solar gains.

● Main living rooms are located on the south side with service areas and buffer spaces on the north side.

● Solar air-heating wall collectors (Trombe walls) provide warm air directly to living rooms and store some heat.

● $5m^3$ pebble stores in some houses store heat from the solar wall collectors - the active solar system for space heating.

● Solar water-heating roof collectors provide water heating in some houses - the active solar system for domestic hot water.

● The houses are built to a compact plan with high levels of insulation and a mechanical ventilation system.

SITE AND CLIMATE

The new town of Cergy-Pontoise is located 50km north west of the centre of Paris on the Paris-Dieppe highway. Access to Paris is easy with a choice of motorway, trains, tubes and buses.

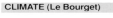

CLIMATE (Le Bourget)

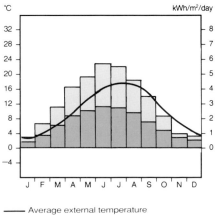

——— Average external temperature
■ Diffuse solar radiation
■ Direct solar radiation

The site is in the Z.A.C. (an area designated for a full development of housing and services) of Jouy le Moutier and enjoys a **privileged** position facing the Hautil Forest on a south facing slope. Most

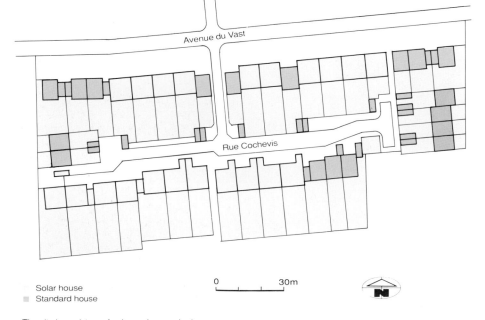

Avenue du Vast

Rue Cochevis

0   30m

■ Solar house
■ Standard house

The site is a mixture of solar and non-solar houses.

Design Details

facilites are available within easy reach.

The climate is typical for central northern France with average annual rainfall (57cm per year) and 1700 hours of sunshine. The average annual temperature is 10.7°C, ranging from a monthly average of 2°C in January to 17.5°C in July.

There is little to modify the microclimate except that the area around the site is fairly flat and so gives rise to relatively high winds.

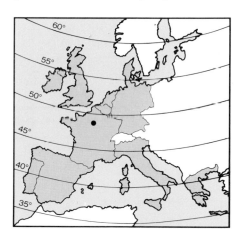

CONCLUSIONS

The homes are liked by the inhabitants, where fuel bills for heating are reduced on average by one quarter compared to conventional housing.

However, the pebble store did not work well and there are some problems with overheating, particularly in the bedrooms.

PLANNING

33 of the 39 two storey houses are laid out in two terraces across the site facing south, with the remaining 6 facing east- west. The whole forms a small estate with a central access road. The houses have 3 or 4 bedrooms, with an open plan living area on the ground floor.

21 of the houses are "solar" houses and the remaining 18 are of conventional design. The south facing houses have large gardens on the south sides and small ones on the north.

CONSTRUCTION

The external walls are constructed of 200mm hollow breeze blocks with 80mm of internal insulation. Party walls are double thickness with one hollow block and one solid block. The floors are a polystyrene block system with a ventilated cavity beneath. The pitched roofs are insulated with 150 mm of glass fibre and covered with concrete tiles. All windows are double glazed.

The solar houses have fully glazed south facades on the ground floors with small roof lights for the first floor and central raised roof sections containing one window and solar water-heating panels. There are two different house designs, one with two small sunspaces and a central solar wall collector and the other with a larger central sunspace and an internal Trombe wall.

A variety of colours is used on the houses; red, blue and green for the joinery; pink, grey and stone for the walls; brown, black and yellow for the roof tiles.

Some constructional difficulties were experienced with the solar features, primarily because of the lack of ready-made products.

PASSIVE SOLAR DESIGN

The solar house layout is designed to maximise the usefulness of gains by locating the principal living rooms and bedrooms on the south side, with garages, cellars and entrance halls acting as a buffer zone on

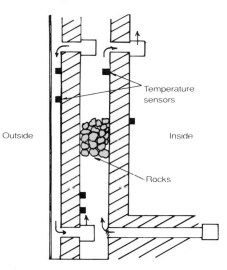

The use of the rock store is controlled by two fans and several thermostats.

the north side.

The south facades are completely glazed on the ground floor, including the solar wall collectors, and there are attached sunspaces. The houses are in two designs the "single-sunspace" and the "double-sunspace".

On the north elevation, garages and entrance halls provide a buffer space to the main living rooms.

Design Details

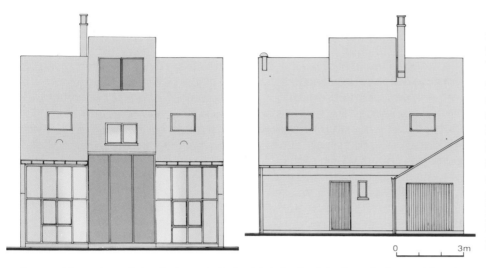

The ground floor on the south elevation is completely glazed, including the air-heating wall collectors, while on the north side there is practically no glazing on the ground floor.

The single-sunspace design has a large single storey central sunspace (11m² floor area) with a Trombe wall forming the back of the sunspace. In 5 of the houses the warm air in the cavity of the Trombe wall circulates by convection into the room when heating is needed. The back wall also stores heat which later radiates into the room. In the other 5 houses with single sunspaces, the wall is insulated on the inside with 100mm of polystyrene and the movement of the warm air from the cavity to the adjacent room is assisted by a thermostatically controlled fan. The storage effect of the wall can thus be utilised more efficiently with the use of the fan system. There are central double doors from the living room into the sunspace and internal metallised roller and venetian blinds are provided for summer shading. Much of the glazed area of the sunspaces can be opened for summer ventilation.

The double-sunspace design has two smaller sunspaces (6m² each) on either side of the central solar collector and storage unit. The sunspaces have doors opening into the living and breakfast rooms, and the same blinds and opening facilities as the "single" design sunspaces. The central solar unit combines a solar collector, a thermal store and a fan system. The 12m² vertical air collector consists of plastic ribbed sheeting in front of the insulated 5m³ pebble store. There are high and low level ducts between the collector and the store, and the store and the adjacent living rooms. The pebble store is a 600mm deep by 2.6m by 3.2m high concrete box surrounded by 60mm of polystyrene.

Depending on the size of house, the active solar domestic hot water systems comprise one or two roof mounted collector panels of either 3 or 4 m², with 200 or 300 litre storage tanks.

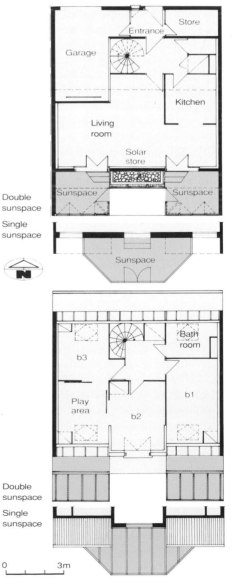

There are several variations in internal layout, though all have an open plan ground floor.

A Trombe wall forms the back of the sunspace in the single sunspace designs.

AUXILIARY HEATING SYSTEMS

Traditional electric convector heaters with central thermostatic control provide the auxiliary heating, and electricity also provides the hot water. In addition an open fire is provided towards the rear of the living room.

There is a ducted mechanical ventilation system with heat recovery. Ventilation air drawn from outside at roof level passes through heat exchangers in the roof space where it is preheated in winter by the exhaust air drawn from the kitchens and bathrooms. In summer the extract air is exhausted without passing through the heat exchanger.

On the double sunspace designs the vertical collector between the sunspaces is part of the solar storage system. On the raised central part of the roof are mounted the active solar water heating collectors.

OPERATING MODES AND CONTROLS

The sunspaces provide warm air to the adjacent living rooms, when available and required, directly through adjoining windows. Openings in the walls and roofs of the sunspaces provide ventilation of unwanted warm air in summer and the roller and venetian blinds are pulled down to reduce solar gain as necessary.

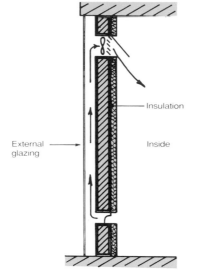

INSULATED WALL   UNINSULATED WALL

The uninsulated Trombe walls operate by convection while the insulated walls are fan assisted. The uninsulated design warms the room by direct radiation, while the insulated design provides better storage control.

In the single sunspace houses the Trombe wall inside the sunspace stores heat during sunny days and air is circulated by a fan to the adjacent room through the space between the wall and the glazing as required. The fan is controlled by a thermostatic probe which delivers air when the temperature in the wall is above 25°C. In summer the ventilation slots between the wall and the rooms are closed.

In the double-sunspace homes

The central solar system uses two fan systems. Hot air from the collector when above 25°C is circulated into the rock store by a low or high speed fan depending on the temperature. When heat is needed in the house another fan circulates room air through the rock store. The temperature of this air can be increased with a 1/2kW electric heater if required. Control of both fan systems is by thermostats in the collector, the store and the room.

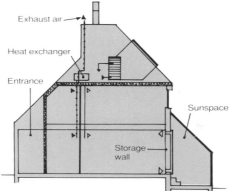

In the heating season, warm air from the sunspaces passes directly into the main living rooms, and the Trombe wall provides storage and additional warmed air as required.

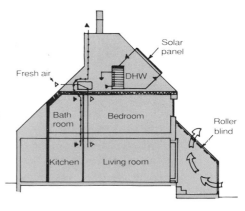

In the summer blinds and large opening areas prevent overheating of the sunspaces.

Performance Evaluation

MONITORING

Monitoring of one double-sunspace house was carried out for two years. Room temperatures were measured with platinum probes and heat meters were used to monitor the mechanical ventilation system and the solar collection and storage system. Daily electricity consumptions of the convector heaters, the mechanical ventilation system and the hot water system were also measured. To collect the required meteorological data, a solarimeter and a temperature probe were installed on the roof of the sunspace.

interest in the solar aspects. One year an "energy consumption competition" was organised by the residents. The solar aspects are also considered to be good in terms of the resale value of the houses.

This is reinforced by the owner of one house who, after it was destroyed by fire, rebuilt it to exactly the same design including all the solar features.

when reclaiming heat from the store and a poor control system which meant that at times air from the house was heating the store!

The energy consumption of the two house types is thought to be very similar.

The performance of the heat recovery/ventilation system is considered to be good, 545 kWh of useful heat being provided during the heating season.

High temperatures were recorded in summer with a maximum of 36°C in the south facing bedroom. Average daily summer temperatures were as high as 29°C in the bedrooms and 25°C in the living rooms. The latter was considered high but acceptable.

The 12m² solar collector between the sunspaces consists of a plastic ribbed sheeting in front of the insulated store.

USER RESPONSE

The inhabitants like the house layout with its buffer spaces on the north side and the living room and kitchen opening onto the sunspaces on the south side. The operation of the active solar system seems to cause some problems and its use is not maximised because of this. There is some overheating in summer, particularly in the bedrooms, but the inhabitants seem to be successful in using the blinds and have not complained about overheating. On the estate in general there seems to be considerable

PERFORMANCE OF THE PASSIVE SOLAR FEATURES

Overall the monitored house used only 55% of the energy used for space heating in a conventional house, a cost saving of 26%. Solar gains contributed 22% to the gross space heating demand and most of this was passive solar gain.

The active solar system is estimated to have contributed only 169 kWh of energy (1.5% of the gross demand) over the heating period. Problems with this system include excessive heat losses, insufficient air flow

COMPARISON WITH CONVENTIONAL DESIGN

(Double sunspace house)
The net auxiliary energy used in a similar house of conventional design would be 13 000kWh.

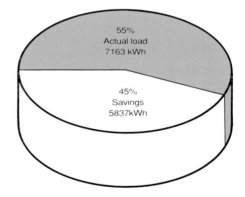

55%
Actual load
7163 kWh

45%
Savings
5837kWh

CONTRIBUTIONS TO SPACE HEATING DEMAND

(Double sunspace house)
The gross heating load for the house was 12 439kWh.

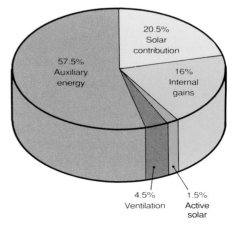

57.5%
Auxiliary
energy

20.5%
Solar
contribution

16%
Internal
gains

4.5%
Ventilation

1.5%
Active
solar

COST EFFECTIVENESS

Both the layout of the development and the solar features made this a relatively high cost scheme. The individual overcost is around 11% on the cost of a conventional house, varying from 9% for the single-sunspace houses to 13% for the double-sunspace. Taking the average annual fuel cost savings of 5000 FF, gives payback periods of between 11.5 years and 16 years, taking no account of the value of the increased space and amenity provided by the sunspaces.

NET MONTHLY SPACE HEATING DEMAND AND SUPPLY

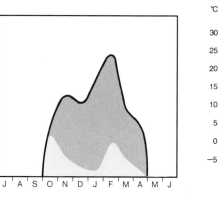

— Net sp.htg load
▪ Auxiliary energy
▫ Solar energy

AVERAGE TEMPERATURES

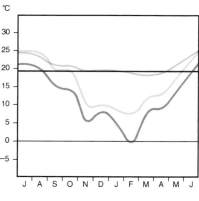

— Internal design temp.
— Internal temp.
— Sunspace temp.
— External temp.

AUXILIARY FUEL USED ANNUALLY

(Double sunspace house)
The total auxiliary fuel used was 11 954kWh.

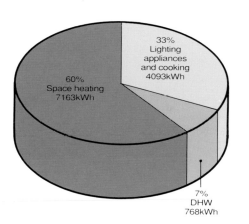

- 33% Lighting appliances and cooking 4093kWh
- 60% Space heating 7163kWh
- 7% DHW 768kWh

COST OF FUEL USED ANNUALLY

(Double sunspace house)
The total cost of fuel used was 8 250FF (1 184ECU).

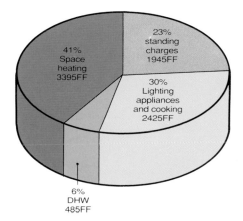

- 23% standing charges 1945FF
- 41% Space heating 3395FF
- 30% Lighting appliances and cooking 2425FF
- 6% DHW 485FF

COST OF BUILDING

(Double sunspace house)
The total cost of the house was 680 000FF (1983 prices).

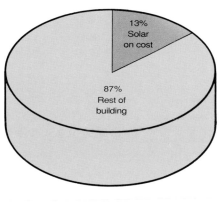

- 13% Solar on cost
- 87% Rest of building

The room on the south side opens onto the sunspaces.

PROJECT DATA

Double-Sunspace House

Volume	240	m³
Floor area	88-98	m²
Roof area	126	m²
External wall area (inc gable end)	73	m²
Windows: total area	12.9 m²	100%
south	10.2 m²	80%
north	2.6 m²	20%

Thermal Characteristics

U value: roof	0.27	W/m²K
floor	0.80	W/m²K
external wall	0.42	W/m²K
windows	2.60	W/m²K
skylights	2.85	W/m²K
sunspace glazing	5.0	W/m²K
Mean U value	1.9	W/m²K
Global heat loss coefficient	228	W/K
Infiltration rate	(not known)	
External design temperature	-7	°C
Heated floor area	88	m²
Heated volume	240	m³
Net heat load	33	kWh/m²

Site and Climate

Altitude	66	m
Latitude	48.58	°N
Longitude	2.27	°E
Average ambient temp: Jan	3	°C
July	17.5	°C
Degree days (base 18°C)	2758	days
Global irradiation on horiz	1127	kWh/m²
Sunshine hours	1707	hr/yr

Costs (1983 prices)

Building	FF 680 000	ECU 97	662
Solar features	FF 81 000	ECU 11	690

Sunspace (double-sunspace)

Volume	22.4	m³
Floor area	6.8	m²
Glass area: roof	6.0	m²
wall	9.2	m²
Wall area: solid	3.2	m²

SCUOLA ELEMENTARE CREDITS

Client
Comune di Finale Emilia (MO)
Piazza Verdi 1
Finale Emilia

Architects
Prof. arch G. Cuppini, ing. G. Cicognani,
arch. S. Piazzi, ing. L. Tundo
Studio Tecnico Cuppini e Associati
Piazza S. Giovanni in Monte 6
Bologna

Services Engineers
Prof. ing. G. Raffellini
Via Bellombra 2
Bologna

p.i. C. Zambonelli
Via Croara 4
S. Lazzaro di Savena (BO)

Energy Consultant
Solar arch. Stephen Hole
Boston,
Mass. (U.S.A.)

Project Management
Ing. G. Cicognani

Ing. A. Pedrazzi
Via Roma 1
41038 San Felice sul Panaro (MO)

Prof. ing. G. Raffellini

Building Contractor
A.C.E.A. Costruzioni S.p.A.
Via Statale Nord 12 no 18/c
41037 Mirandola (MO)

Services Contractor
Berni Cavallini s.n.c.
Via Di Mezzo 15
41037 Mirandola (MO)

Monitoring Organisation
AGIP Petroli
Via Laurentina 437
00144 Roma

Commission of the European Communities

- Primary school incorporates direct gain and thermal storage systems, to produce a 17% passive solar contribution to the gross space heating load.

SCUOLA ELEMENTARE
MASSA FINALESE
ITALY

- Classrooms have south-facing bay window extensions each fitted with a concrete "brise-soleil", to provide both shade and storage of solar gains.

- School hall has an indirect gain system, which stores solar gains for later use.

- Clever use of natural lighting creates different effects in the various zones of the school.

Project Background

The school hall and the two-storey classroom blocks viewed from the south-west.

This energy efficient primary school combines passive solar design using both direct and indirect gain systems, with fabric insulation. There are eighteen classrooms, a dining room, and a school hall (which is used in the evenings for other purposes). The school does not have its own sports hall, instead it shares one with a nearby secondary school.
Construction was completed in Autumn 1984, and the school was monitored over the 1985/86 heating season.

The primary school is in Massa Finalese, 50km from Modena.

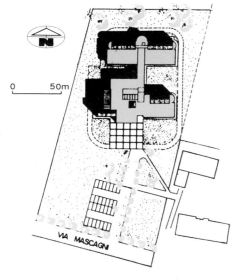

OBJECTIVES

The local and regional authorities were keen to have a successful example of solar technologies applied to a public building to encourage the construction of more energy efficient buildings in the area. Solar energy consultants advised on the design so that the solar features were integrated with the overall architectural style.
The designers sought a building scale appropriate for young children and were careful to balance the needs of the solar technologies with those of a teaching environment.

ENERGY SAVING FEATURES

● The school faces south, with a 15° offset to the west, and the two classroom blocks, along an east-west axis, are spaced apart to avoid overshading.

● South-facing bay window extensions attached to the classrooms receive direct solar gains, provide thermal storage and act as shading devices.

● Rooflights provide light and solar gains to the circulation spaces, and the school hall has an indirect gain system.

● An atrium also provides light and solar gains to the centre of the service area, and in particular to the surrounding dining room.

● Walls have insulation externally applied to eliminate thermal bridges, the floor slab and roof are also insulated and all windows are double glazed.

● The mechanical ventilation system incorporates an air-to-air heat exchanger.

● The kitchen and ancillary spaces are located on the north side of the service area, to act as a buffer zone.

● 14m² of roof mounted active solar collectors provide hot water for the kitchen.

SITE AND CLIMATE

Massa Finalese is a small agricultural town, in the eastern part of the Po Valley, 50km from Modena. The site is in a part of the town which is currently being developed, although the immediate surroundings are still largely agricultural. Overall, the site has good solar access with limited shading from the surrounding buildings and vegetation.
The primary school will be part of an education park, with the facilities also open to the community at large.
The annual average outside temperature is 14.7°C (Jan: 3°C, July: 27°C), with 2170 degree days (base 19°C).

Design Details

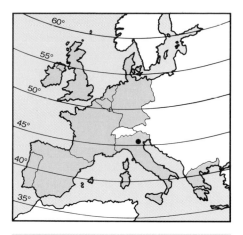

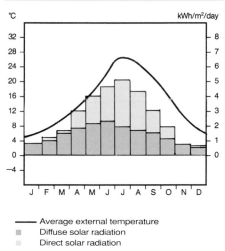

CLIMATE (Modena)

——— Average external temperature
▪ Diffuse solar radiation
▪ Direct solar radiation

CONCLUSIONS

The energy saving measures, together with the passive solar systems have led to a reduction of over 18% in the primary energy used for space heating, compared to a conventional Italian school of the same volume, and assuming it also has an air-to-air heat exchanger.

PLANNING

The overall design uses both direct solar gain and stored solar energy to heat the building, each area having its own passive solar system. The building faces south with a slight offset to the west (15°) so that it can take full advantage of the late morning sun, after the early fog and mists,

characteristic of the Po Valley, have disappeared.

The designers deliberately avoided a linear layout along an east-west axis, which is typical of "solar architecture". Two parallel rows of classrooms are linked together by a perpendicular corridor. These blocks are carefully positioned to avoid shadows falling onto the glazed south facades.

The classrooms are located on the ground and first floor. The wing to the north also has a basement.

On the west part of the front block there are deep, single storey spaces; immediately off the entrance, the offices and dining room are grouped around an atrium, whilst the school hall is further to the west. The hall has its own entrance, as it has a separate use in the evenings.

up the principal load-bearing structure. The walls, 250mm thick, are placed at 6m intervals, thereby defining the width of the classroom unit. The outer walls are insulated with an external layer of 50mm extruded polystyrene. The prefabricated intermediate floor slabs and the flat roof sections measure 1.2m x 6.0m and run east-west. These modules, called "predalle", are of reinforced concrete and hollow pot blocks.

The roof is insulated with 50mm of extruded polystyrene, under bituminous felt and gravel.

The ground floor slab is reinforced concrete with 50mm insulation beneath, thus providing internal thermal mass.

All windows have pre-varnished aluminium frames and are double glazed. On the ground

The bay window extensions of the classrooms and offices, and the atrium produce an attractive south facade.

The resulting layout has created partially enclosed areas, protected by the buildings, which are suitable for outdoor school activities.

CONSTRUCTION

The building is a combination of prefabricated elements and in-situ construction. The overall structure is designed to have considerable thermal inertia. The concrete walls (running north-south) and floors make

floor, security glass has been used. The inclined rooflights above the corridors and in the hall are of polycarbonate, with sheet metal sandwich panels insulated with expanded polyurethane forming the opaque roof slopes.

Apart from the hall which has a brickwork outer leaf, the exterior of the building is plaster finished, using a yellow ochre colour typical of the area. In contrast, the window frames are red.

Design Details

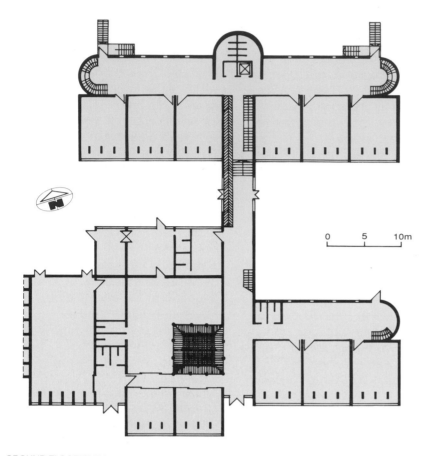

GROUND FLOOR PLAN

The different parts of the school are carefully spaced to avoid overshadowing.

PASSIVE SOLAR DESIGN

Each south elevation has 305m^2 of vertical glazing and 135m^2 of inclined glazing (45°) forming the bay window extensions. The north facade consists of a blank wall with only narrow windows, all equally spaced apart.

All the classrooms have bay window extensions on the south side with a glazed surface nearly 3m high, consisting of openable vertical windows at the top and bottom, with a central inclined non-openable window. Between the classroom walls, and immediately behind the glazed surface, there is a concrete brise-soleil made from vertical pilasters positioned parallel to the classroom walls, which carry a horizontal corbel. On top of this, there are three small walls oriented south west. These produce a screen through which solar gains can pass in the early morning, but which traps and stores solar gains later in the day. Behind the internal brise-soleil there are thick cotton curtains.

External awnings are placed in front of the glazed extensions and are used to prevent overheating and to control glare. In addition, on the upper floor, the bay windows are profiled in such a way as to provide a fixed overhang for those on the lower floor, giving summer shading.

Rooflights in corridors and circulation spaces provide these areas with daylighting, and indirectly light the north sides of the classrooms as well. These south-facing rooflights (inclined at 30°) admit light and solar radiation. The light is reflected off the external north wall, whilst solar energy is stored in it (the external insulation maintains thermal mass inside the building).

The hall is used after school by the local community, so an indirect gain system has been employed to store and release heat later in the day. An inclined concrete surface collects and stores solar radiation entering through the rooflights, releasing it later in the day. In this way the surface behaves like a Trombe Wall. Indirect lighting is also introduced through the south-facing rooflights and from a row of recessed tilted windows on the west side. The inclined surface deflects the light so that it enters the hall at low level between a row of pilasters.

A colonnaded atrium provides light and solar gains to the dining room. As the dining room is only used for short periods it was not thought necessary for it to face south. Narrow rooflights have been cut into the flat roof above the dining room to admit daylight. The kitchen and ancillary spaces are located on the north side of this large service area, and act as a buffer zone.

The concrete brise-soleil behind the bay windows has three small walls on top of a corbel, which admit or store solar gains. The supply air duct is also visible.

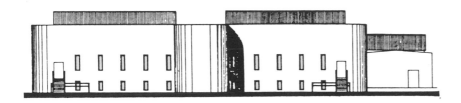

SOUTH FACADE

The south facade consists mainly of bay window extensions, both on the ground and first floors, however the hall only has south-facing rooflights.

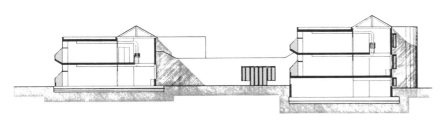

NORTH FACADE

The north facade is austere, with only narrow windows spaced equally apart. A liftshaft and emergency stairs are housed in the centre, whilst at each end there are spiral staircases.

SECTION THROUGH THE SCHOOL

0   10m

Each major part of the building has its own light quality: classrooms are very luminous and have good views; along the corridors the rooflights capture the sunlight; in the hall the hidden sources of light create quite a dramatic effect, and in the atrium the overhead light source and columns produce a varying pattern of light and shade.

When the heating and mechanical ventilation system is not in operation, natural ventilation is provided by opening windows in the classrooms and along the corridors. In the lower part of the classroom doors, there are grilles to assist cross ventilation. Roof-mounted active solar water heating collectors (14m²) supply hot water for the kitchen.

AUXILIARY SYSTEMS

A gas-fired boiler supplies both heated ventilation air and a conventional wet heating system.

The air-based system provides the required air changes to the various parts of the school (1.5 to 2.5 ac/hr) at a temperature dependent upon external conditions, but never exceeding 25°C.

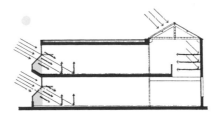

Direct and indirect solar gains in the classrooms and corridors.

A steel-foil air-to-air heat exchanger recovers heat from the exhaust air, with an efficiency of around 55%. The air-handling plant can operate on recirculated air only, when fresh air is not needed, or on both fresh and recirculated air during school hours.

The water-based system feeds heating coils placed in the air outlets in each classroom. These coils allow the temperature of the supply air to be finely adjusted. There are radiators in service areas and corridors, since warm air heating is not permitted in these zones.

CONTROLS

The passive controls are very simple; the users open or close windows, lift or lower external awnings and draw or open the curtains. The external awnings are electrically operated.

OPERATING MODES

Winter days - solar gains enter through the south-facing windows and rooflights, once the early morning fog has lifted. The walls above the brise-soleil in each classroom store some solar energy, and the inclined surface in the school hall collects and stores solar gains, corresponding to the extended use of the hall. If glare becomes a problem in the classrooms, the curtains behind the brise-soleil can be drawn. Spring, early summer and

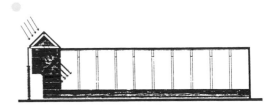

Indirect solar gains and lighting in the school hall.

Performance Evaluation

The school hall receives natural daylight through inclined windows and at low level between pilasters.

autumn days - the external awnings have to be correctly positioned to avoid glare and overheating. The horizontal platform of the brise-soleil shades the classroom, and the upper bay window extensions offer shading to the lower level, by providing a fixed overhang. In addition, the curtains can be drawn. Opening the windows promotes cross ventilation. The school is not occupied in the height of the summer.

MONITORING

The school was monitored over the 1985/86 heating season. Measurements were taken of the internal temperatures in a few classrooms, the entrance hall and the main hall, at intervals over the winter. Gas consumption was recorded each month. The solar water heaters were a very standard system and therefore were not monitored.

USER RESPONSE

The teachers and pupils enjoy the functional and spatial qualities of the school, even though they do not thoroughly understand the thermal behaviour of the building or the operation of the systems, particularly the individual thermostats in the classrooms. Glare was a problem at the beginning, before the curtains were installed, and overheating problems, especially in spring and autumn, have given rise to many complaints.

PERFORMANCE OF PASSIVE SOLAR DESIGN

● Passive solar gains contributed 17% to the gross space heating load, and the heat recovery system contributed a further 12%.

● Overall, the design saved 18% when compared to the primary energy used for space heating in a conventional school, assuming the reference school also has heat recovery.

● The solar water heaters had no operating problems, and produced about 40% of the hot water needs of the kitchen.

● Temperature regulation within each classroom has a marked effect on overall energy savings. A 4-5°C increase in the set point temperature, above 19°C, can double gas consumption.

● There were overheating problems for the first 2 years.

The classrooms became considerably more comfortable once external awnings were fitted. These are electrically operated from the inside. Nevertheless, the corridors still suffer from overheating as there are no vents at the top. Extract fans and fixed louvres in front of the polycarbonate rooflights will be fitted to alleviate the problems of both high temperatures and glare.

COST EFFECTIVENESS

The passive solar measures cost L126M, nearly 5% of the total building cost, resulting in a simple payback period of 24-25 years. This is long, however the increased available space in the classrooms, due to the attached sunspaces, and the high quality of the environment created generally, should also be taken into account when evaluating the resulting benefits.

The south-facing rooflights provide daylight and solar gains to the corridors, where coloured air ducts become a feature.

COMPARISON WITH CONVENTIONAL DESIGN

391 111kWh (1408 GJ) of primary energy would be required to heat the school if it were built to a conventional design (assuming heat recovery were still included).

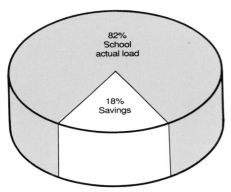

82%
School
actual load

18%
Savings

321 944kWh (1159 GJ) was the primary energy used for space heating over the 1985/86 heating season.

CONTRIBUTIONS TO ANNUAL SPACE HEATING DEMAND

The total annual space heating demand was 398 611kWh (1435 GJ).

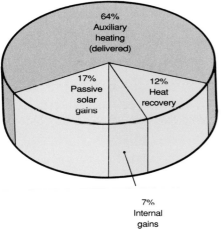

64%
Auxiliary
heating
(delivered)

17%
Passive
solar
gains

12%
Heat
recovery

7%
Internal
gains

AUXILIARY FUEL USED (PRIMARY ENERGY)

Over the whole year 404 116kWh (1455 GJ) of auxiliary energy were used.

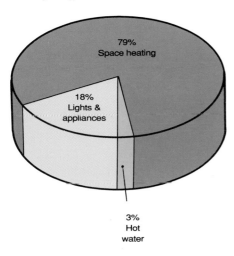

79%
Space heating

18%
Lights &
appliances

3%
Hot
water

NET MONTHLY SPACE HEATING LOAD

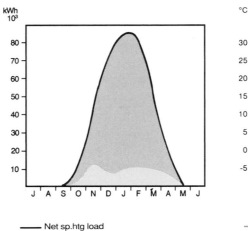

kWh
10³

J A S O N D J F M A M J

— Net sp.htg load
Auxiliary energy
Solar energy

MONTHLY AVERAGE TEMPERATURES

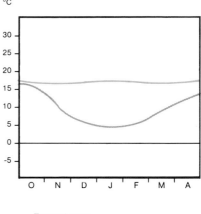

°C

O N D J F M A

External temp.
Internal temp.

Bay windows on the upper level provide a fixed overhang for those on the lower level, reducing summer overheating.

PROJECT DATA

Building		
Volume	9600	m³
Floor area	3110	m²
No. of floors	2	+basement
Flat roof area	1650	m²
Windows: total area	1184.6	m²
south area	1145.0	m²
east & west area	19.2	m²

Solar Collectors		
Area	14.0	m²

Thermal Characteristics		
U value: flat roof	0.43	W/m²K
pitched roof	0.53	W/m²K
perimeter walls	0.57	W/m²K
windows	3.7	W/m²K
Mean U value approx.	0.98	W/m²K
Global heat loss coefficient	7420	W/K
Infiltration rate: winter	2.2	ach
summer		natural
Heated volume	9120	m³
Heated floor area	2268	m²
Surface/Volume ratio	0.6	m²/m³
Net heat load	164.2	kWh/m²
External design temperature	-6	°C

Site and Climate		
Altitude	20	m
Latitude	44° 38'	N
Longitude	10° 56'	E
Average ambient temp.: annual	14.7	°C
January	3	°C
July	27	°C
Degree days (base 19 °C)	2170	days

Global irradiation on horiz:
annual	3624 MJ/m²	(1007 kWh/m²)
Oct - April	1274 MJ/m²	(354 kWh/m²)

Sunshine hours:
annual	2279	hrs/yr
Oct - April	891	hrs

Costs (1985 prices)		
Building *	2 316 M Liras	1 597 000 ECU
Active system	12 M Liras	8 200 ECU
Passive system	126 M Liras	86 900 ECU
Building on-cost	68 M Liras	46 900 ECU
Heating system on-cost	70 M Liras	48 200 ECU

* active, passive and auxiliary systems are included.

VIELHA HOSPITAL CREDITS

Client
Generalitat de Catalunya (regional government)

Architects & Energy Consultants
Servei d'Arquitectura i Enginyeria
Institut Catala de la Salut
Head of the team: Joaquim Prats (arch)
Gran Via de les Corts Catalanes, 587
08007 Barcelona

Project Management
Jose I Galan (arch)
Joaquim Baquer (tech arch)
Granduxer, 5-15, despatx 8
08021 Barcelona

Joaquim Prats (arch)
Servei d'Arquitectura i Enginyeria

Building Contractor
Cubiertas y MZOV, SA
Placa Gala Placidia, 20
08012 Barcelona

Monitoring Organisation
Direccio General d'Energia
Departament d'Industria i Energia
Generalitat de Catalunya
Av Diagonal, 449, 7th floor
08036 Barcelona

Commission of the European Communities

VIELHA HOSPITAL

CATALONIA
SPAIN

● Careful facade design with a large area of south facing glazing and shading, optimises useful solar gains and controls summer overheating.

● Overall heating requirements reduced by 62% compared to a conventional hospital design.

● Passive solar gains contribute 33% to the gross space heating load.

● Zoning control systems maximise the use of solar gains and minimise consumption of auxiliary fuel.

● Energy savings result in additional capital costs being paid back in less than five years.

Project Background

On the north side of the hospital there is a ramp to provide access for ambulances.

The hospital is in Vielha, the principal town in the Aran Valley region, 270km to the north of Barcelona. The building is part of the public health network, and belongs to the "Institut Catala de la Salut". It is occupied on a 24 hour basis and caters for 100 out-patient appointments a day, in addition to having 29 beds.

OBJECTIVES

The aim of this project is to demonstrate the advantages of using solar gains and energy saving measures combined with efficient energy management strategies, in a public sector building with demanding thermal comfort requirements.
The building also demonstrates the energy savings achievable by measures tailored specifically to an area with an alpine climate, using traditional materials, within planning constraints.

ENERGY SAVING FEATURES

● Large south-facing windows collect solar gains, and massive walls and floors provide efficient heat storage.

● Clerestory windows at the top of the south facade supply the north side of the top storey with natural daylight.

● A compact shape, resulting in a low surface to volume ratio, high levels of insulation and a draught lobby, minimise heat loss.

● Natural ventilation in summer, achieved by opening windows in the north and south facades, provides the necessary cooling in most areas, reducing the need for air conditioning except in specific areas.

SITE AND CLIMATE

Vielha has a population of only 6000 inhabitants but, being located in a beautiful valley in the Pyrenees mountains, it attracts many tourists. 924m above sea level, the climate is typically alpine, with cold winters and warm summers. The average external temperature in January is 2.6ºC, and in July, this average rises to 17.8ºC. There are 3226 degree days (18ºC base) per year.
The hospital is sheltered from local winds by the surrounding mountains which are 2000m high . The neighbouring buildings do not restrict solar access, however the mountains cast shadows at the beginning and end of the day.

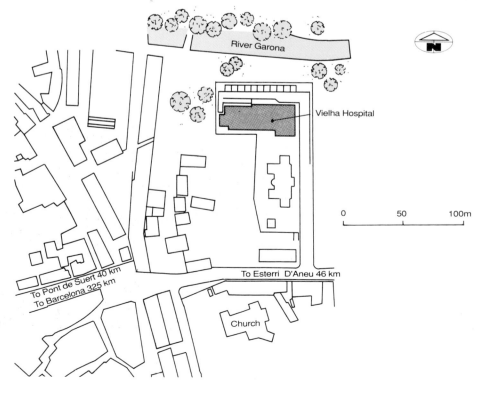

Design Details

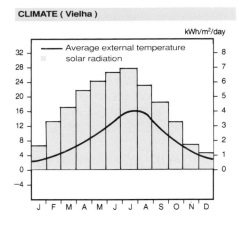

CLIMATE (Vielha)

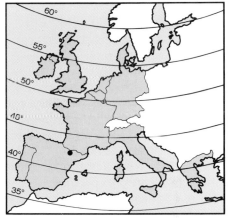

View of the double height waiting area. The first floor is visible on the right hand side.

PLANNING

The building has a compact rectangular shape, and comprises a basement for the building services and the staff, and three floors above which house the main hospital facilities. The clinics, X-ray room and operating theatre are on the ground and first floors, whilst the wards are separate, on the second floor.

DESIGN DETAILS

The ground, first and second storeys receive solar gains through the highly glazed south facade. The waiting area is double height, open to the first floor. This produces good heat flows to distribute the solar gains.

Jun 21st

Dec 21st

CONSTRUCTION

The heavyweight design, in accordance with local construction techniques where stone is in general use, provides sufficient solar storage capacity and thermal inertia for the building without the need for additional thermal mass. External walls are constructed from 250mm local stone, 50mm expanded polystyrene, 50mm

0   50m

Design Details

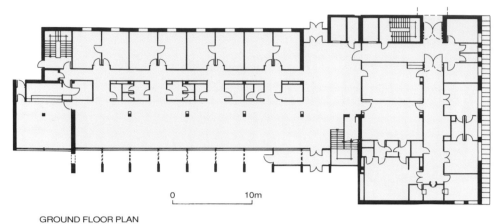

GROUND FLOOR PLAN
The clinics, x-ray room and operating theatre are arranged on the ground floor and first floors.

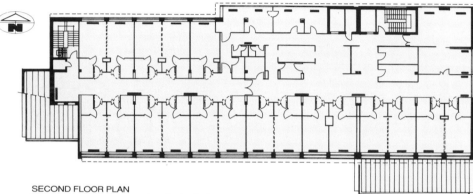

SECOND FLOOR PLAN
On the second floor there are twenty nine beds.

Clerestory windows in the corridor of the second floor.

cavity,100mm brick and plaster.The half-buried walls of the basement are 150mm stone and 250mm concrete also insulated with 50mm polystyrene.

The roof is a timber structure insulated with 50mm expanded polystyrene, and with a zinc covering.Expanded polystyrene has also been used to insulate the edges of the floor slab. All the windows and doors in the south facade are double glazed, and all other windows have secondary glazing with 100-200mm spacing. The west facade is almost windowless. Good quality workmanship has resulted in a low air change rate.

PASSIVE SOLAR DESIGN

Double glazed windows cover the major part of the south facade, a width of 58m. In front there are horizontal supports, and canvas awnings can be suspended between these and the wall, thereby providing shading.
The solar gains are distributed inside the building through the corridors. The double height waiting area provides a direct connection between the ground and first floors.
Concrete and dark coloured ceramics are used for internal surfaces and the massive floors store some of the solar radiation incident upon them, providing about 40m³ of direct storage.
Venetian blinds are fitted on the top floor, to regulate the amount of daylight and to reduce excess solar gain when necessary.

AUXILIARY HEATING AND COOLING SYSTEM

A gas-oil boiler and conventional radiator system are used to provide auxiliary space heating for the hospital, and the boiler also supplies the hot water requirements.
On the north side of the hospital there is a ramp to provide access for ambulances, and this is heated from underneath to prevent it freezing in winter.
An air conditioning system is

There is insulation in the walls , roof and perimeter foundations

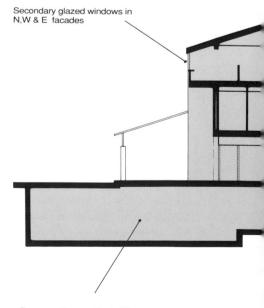

Secondary glazed windows in N,W & E facades

Basement houses the building services

0   10m

fitted in some of the more specialised rooms, for example the X-ray room.

CONTROLS

The south facade integrates permanent solar controls, such as the cantilevered overhang adapted from classical Mediterranean architecture, with moveable shading devices. External canvas awnings can be pulled out in front of the south facade, to reduce solar penetration to the ground floor. On the second floor, the venetian blinds are used to control incoming solar radiation. The thermal mass of the building also helps to moderate temperature swings.

The auxiliary heating system supplies five separate zones in the building, which are independently controlled according to the occupancy pattern; for example consulting rooms are only used in the mornings, whereas the in-

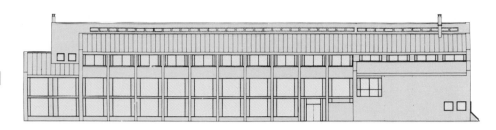

SOUTH ELEVATION

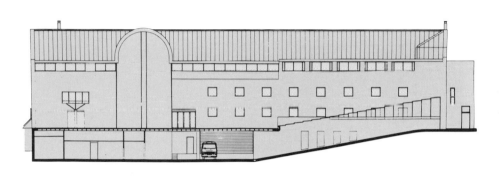

NORTH ELEVATION

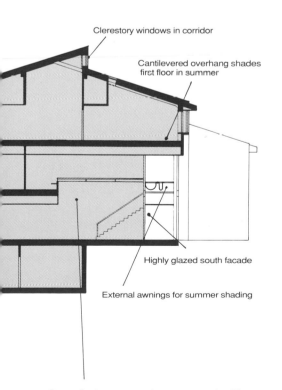

Clerestory windows in corridor

Cantilevered overhang shades first floor in summer

Highly glazed south facade

External awnings for summer shading

Convective loop operates between ground and first floors

patients on the second floor require comfortable conditions 24 hours a day.

OPERATING MODES

On sunny days in winter, solar gains enter through the highly glazed south facade, where blinds have been raised, heating the air and thermal mass. The heating systems are automatically switched off in zones where solar gains are sufficient.

At night, the blinds are closed to reduce heat losses especially on the second floor, which is still occupied. Different parts of the building are isolated and the heating system supplies only those zones in use.

In summer during the day, the blinds on the second floor are lowered, whilst most of the windows are opened, especially those on the east facade.

At night, the windows are opened or closed depending on the need for cooling and ventilation.

The heating system is turned off from early June to the end of September.

External awnings positioned to reduce solar gains to the ground floor.

Performance Evaluation

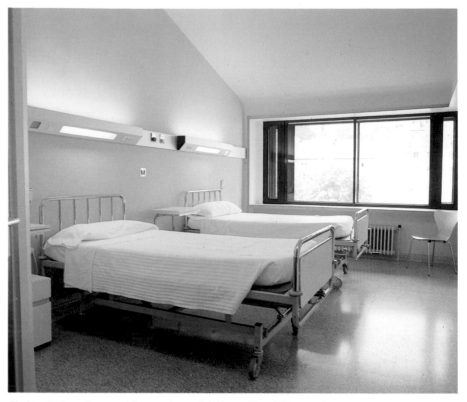

The in-patients, on the second floor, require comfortable conditions 24 hours a day.

The auxiliary fuel used for space heating in a similar conventionally designed hospital would be 583 050 kWh, assuming the same useful gains and a 10% passive solar contribution.

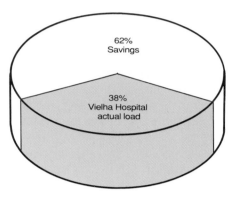

The total space heating demand is 505 000kWh.

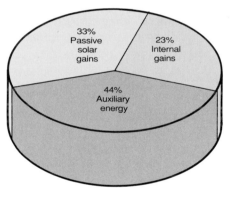

Auxiliary heating is provided by a gas-oil boiler with radiators.

MONITORING

The building has been monitored for a year from March 1987, with some preliminary tests being conducted between January and March 1987.
Hospital technical staff assisted in the monitoring task. They took readings of the auxiliary energy consumption in each zone and recorded the number of out-patients attending the hospital.
An automatic data acquisition system recorded temperature fluctuations in several parts of the building and took measurements of the external air temperature. Other variables measured were:-
total daily solar irradiation; electricity consumption for lights and medical services; and in summer, times when the windows were open.
During the year in which the building was monitored, the winter temperatures were, on average, 2-3°C higher than those normally experienced.

USER RESPONSE

Medical and ancillary staff at Vielha hospital are satisfied with the building's performance compared to other similar hospitals, especially considering the way it makes use of solar gains and natural lighting. They comment favourably on the attractive spaces created by the designers; especially the highly glazed double height waiting room, and the amount of natural light entering the hospital generally.

PERFORMANCE OF PASSIVE SOLAR FEATURES

● The auxiliary energy required for space heating has been reduced by 62% compared with a similar building built to a conventional design, with the same internal gains and assuming a 10% solar contribution.
Bearing in mind its large volume, the high standard of thermal comfort required and the climate in which the building is situated, this is a significant saving.

● Passive solar gains contributed 33% to the gross space heating load, another 44% was supplied by auxiliary energy and internal gains met the rest of the demand.

● Due to 24 hour occupancy, there is a heating requirement even in the summer. In July, August and September the solar gains provided 100% of this.

AUXILIARY FUEL USED ANNUALLY

AUXILIARY FUEL USED ANNUALLY

Total annual fuel and electricity used is 385 187kWh

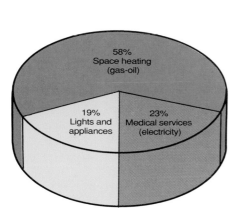

MONTHLY SPACE HEATING LOAD

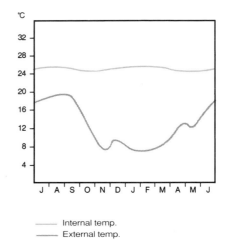

——— Net sp.htg load
■   Auxiliary energy
■   Solar energy

MONTHLY AVERAGE TEMPERATURES

——— Internal temp.
——— External temp.

COST OF FUEL ANNUALLY

Total annual cost of fuel plus electricity is 3 511 824 Ptas, at 1988 prices.

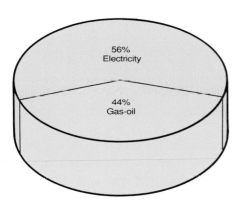

because some of the passive solar features are an integral part of the building or are required by the local planning regulations.

The main extra costs were the result of using double or secondary glazing for all windows, and a control system for the auxiliary heating which could control five zones individually. These two measures only represent 1% of the total building cost of 400 M Ptas (1985 prices).

The space heating cost averages out at 30 000 Ptas a week over the whole year, and this gives a simple payback period of less than five years.

Heatmeters on the different heating circuits.

● The zone control system was adequate and temperature fluctuations over the heating season were only ±4°C around the internal set point temperature of 24°C.

● It is hoped that performance may be further improved by better regulation strategies and control of the direct gain /auxiliary energy balance.

COST EFFECTIVENESS

Assessment of cost-effectiveness is difficult

PROJECT DATA

Building			Site and Climate		
Volume	7557	m³	Altitude	924	m
Floor area	2883.6	m²	Latitude	42.5°N	
Roof area	751	m²	Longitude	0°	
External wall area	1651	m²	Average ambient temp: Jan	2.6	°C
Windows: Total area	398	m²	July	17.8	°C
South:	324.7	m²	Degree days (18°C base):	3226	days
Others:	73.3	m²	Global irradiation on horiz:	1460	kWh/m²
			Sunshine hours:	1788	hr/yr
Thermal Characteristics					
U value Roof:	0.47	W/m²K	**Costs** (1985 prices)		
Floor:	1.1	W/m²K	Building:	400 M Ptas	(2 920 000 ECU)
External walls:	0.51	W/m²K	Solar features:	3.05 M Ptas	(22 300 ECU)
Windows:	2.6	W/m²K	Extra wall insulation:	0.65 M Ptas	(4 700 ECU)
Global Heat Loss Coefficient:	4433.4	W/K	Controls for heating		
Infiltration rate:	0.5	ac/h	system:	1.0 M Ptas	(7 300 ECU)
External design temperature:	- 4	°C			
Heated floor area:	2883.6	m²			
Heated volume area:	7557	m³			
Net heat load:	135	kWh/m²			

HAUS WALDMOHR CREDITS

Client
Dipl.Ing. (FH) Anton Büdel
Saar-Pfalz-Str. 83
D-6797 Waldmohr

Architects
Prof. Dr. Thomas Herzog
Imhofstr. 8
D-8000 München

Prof. Otto Steidle
Genter Str. 13
D-8000 München 40

Supporting Government Agency
Bundesministerium für Forschung und Technologie
(BMFT)
Stresemannstr 2
D-5300 Bonn 2

Supervision
Projektleitung für das Biologie-, Oekologie- und
Energieforschungsprogramm (PBE)
Kernforschungsanlage Jülich GmbH
Postfach 19 13
D-5170 Jülich

Monitoring Organisation
Fraunhofer-Institut für Bauphysik (IBP)
Bereich Wärme/Klima
(Institutsleiter: Prof. Dr. -Ing habil. K.A. Gertis)
Nobelstr. 12
D-7000 Stuttgart 80
(Project Management: Dipl.-Ing. Hans Erhorn)

Social Research
Fraunhofer-Institut für Systemtechnik
und Innovationsforschung(ISI)
Institutsleiter: Prof. Dr. H. Krupp)
Breslauer Str. 48
D-7500 Karlsruhe
(Project Management Dr. rer.pol.Thomas Meyer)

Subcontractor
Solarbüro Landstuhl
(Leitung: Dipl.-Ing.Thomas Krötz)
Postfach 18 05
D-7400 Tübingen

Commission of the European Communities

HAUS WALDMOHR

LANDSTUHL
GERMANY

- Large single family house has extensive south-facing glazing, including an integrated sunspace, and an earth sourced heat pump.

- Passive solar gains provided nearly 36% of the energy entering the house, although the actual solar contribution was lower.

- Sunspace used as a winter garden and circulation space, also provides an effective buffer space.

- High levels of insulation and a compact form, balance heat losses from the large areas of glazing.

- Roller blinds provide both insulation at night and protection from the sun in summer.

Project Background

The Solar House Waldmohr, part of the demonstration project Landstuhl, is a large single family house of a lightweight timber design, constructed mainly by the owner and his family.
The Landstuhl Project, which includes 25 single family solar houses equipped with both active and passive systems and monitored for two years, is funded by the German Ministry for Research and Technology.

OBJECTIVES

The objectives of the Landstuhl project are:
- to demonstrate designs of houses with low space heating demands;
- to demonstrate the working, effectiveness and economics of new technologies and new building designs;
- to explore technical problems and suggest ways of overcoming and avoiding them;
- to examine the economic, legal and social barriers to the implementation of low energy housing.

The trees surrounding the house do not obstruct solar gains in winter, but do provide useful shading in summer.

ENERGY SAVING FEATURES

● Heat losses minimised by high levels of insulation, including some windows with low emissivity glazing, together with a compact shape and the use of buffer zones.

● Large, two storey sunspace/winter garden and highly glazed second floor studio collect solar gains.

● Moveable internal insulation over sunspace and studio windows, reduces heat loss at night.

● Auxiliary heating is from an electric heat pump which extracts heat from the ground via heat exchanger pipes.

SITE AND CLIMATE

The house is built on the eastern outskirts of Waldmohr, a village near Homburg/Saar, in the western part of West Germany. The Mannheim - Saarbruecken autobahn runs between Waldmohr and Homburg. To the east is the area, formerly marsh, of "Landstuhler Bruch" which runs between Kaiserslautern and Homburg.
The site is 310m above sea level and is surrounded by older houses and tall trees. The climate is typical for Germany with over 3600 degree days per year and an external design temperature of -12ºC. Maximum summer temperatures are around 31ºC.

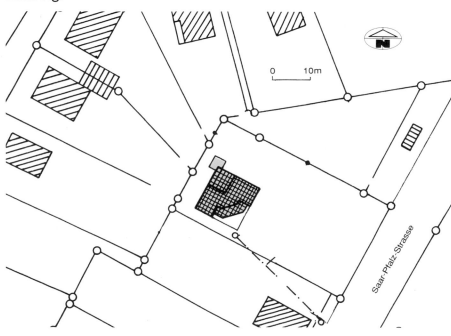

Haus Waldmohr is built in the north-west corner of the plot, and has a large garden to the south-east.

Design Details

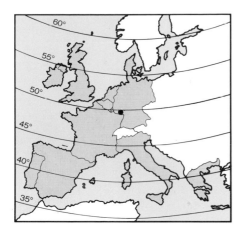

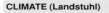
CLIMATE (Landstuhl)

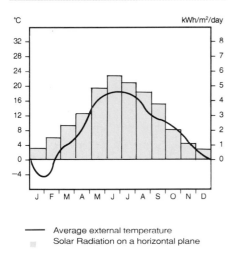

°C | kWh/m²/day

32 — 8
28 — 7
24 — 6
20 — 5
16 — 4
12 — 3
8 — 2
4 — 1
0 — 0
−4

J F M A M J J A S O N D

— Average external temperature
■ Solar Radiation on a horizontal plane

PLANNING

The house is built in the north-west corner of the site and has a large garden to the south-east. The surrounding trees provide useful shading in the summer, without obstructing solar gain to the house in winter.

The house plan is symmetrical about a diagonal axis running north - south. The main staircase is located in the northern corner giving access to the first floor and the smaller second floor studio/office. Across the southern corner there is the two storey sunspace, which acts as a circulation and buffer space, as well as being used as a winter garden. Single glazed partitions provide access to the living rooms

from the sunspace. Additional light and ventilation to the rooms is provided by small windows on the other sides.

CONSTRUCTION

The ground floor slab and the small cellar to the north are constructed in concrete. The main structure is a concrete post and beam construction with timber internal and external cladding and timber intermediate floors. There are high levels of insulation:- 100mm of fibreglass in the ground floor under 60mm of screed, 110mm of fibreglass in the walls and 120mm of foamed glass behind a timber lining in the roof. The upper floors are finished in timber while the ground floor has 7mm limestone slab flooring. There are small ventilation windows on the northern sides of the house and these use low emissivity glazing. Apart from the upper studio/office, all other windows are single glazed but open onto the sunspace, which is double glazed. The studio has a mixture of double glazed south-facing windows and low emissivity coated double glazed northern windows (U value 1.4W/m²K).

The north-west facade is timber clad with very few windows. The north-east facade is similar.

Apart from the concrete flooring and framing, the whole house was constructed by the owner and his family over a period of three years.

PASSIVE SOLAR DESIGN

The house plan is rectangular with the sides facing SE and SW and NW and NE, but with the south corner cut off to give the two storey sunspace a direct south aspect. All rooms (except the bathroom) are arranged to have main windows onto the sunspace. Circulation spaces are in the sunspace and the northern corner, so that both act as

The house plan is symmetrical about a diagonal axis running north-south. Across the southern corner the two storey sunspace has a direct south aspect.

Design Details

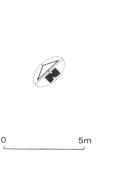

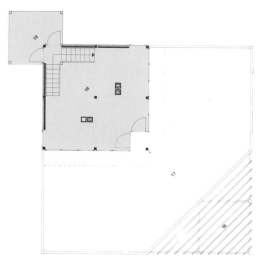

GROUND FLOOR PLAN
All principal rooms have main windows onto the two storey sunspace.

SECOND FLOOR PLAN
The studio/office occupies the north corner, separated from the rest of the house.

buffer zones to the main habitable rooms.

The sunspace is a two-storey, double glazed timber structure with a floor area of nearly 31m² and with 54m² of

by the trees that surround the house.

The studio/office on the top floor occupies a small area at the north corner of the plan and thus operates as a

In the highly glazed studio, roller blinds provide night-time insulation and, assisted by the glass overhangs, protection from the summer sun.

glazing. It has a solid roof. Roller blinds inside the sunspace provide insulation for the glazing at night. These blinds also control summer overheating assisted by the solid roof of the sunspace, which reduces the penetration of the high summer sun, and

separate unit. It is completely glazed on the south-east and south-west sides with double glazing. There are insulating roller blinds, as in the sunspace, and external glass shading devices have been installed above the southern windows to reduce summer solar gain.

AUXILIARY HEATING SYSTEMS

There are two auxiliary heating systems in the house. The main system is an electric heat pump which uses three 40m heat exchanger pipes buried in the garden, as the heat source. The system is rated at 5.2kW electric input and 17.5kW output. The distribution system consists of radiators in the bedrooms and children's room, and underfloor heating elsewhere.

North-facing balcony/gallery

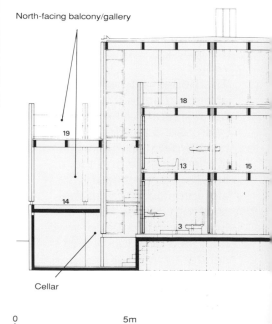

Cellar

Performance Evaluation

SOUTH-EAST ELEVATION

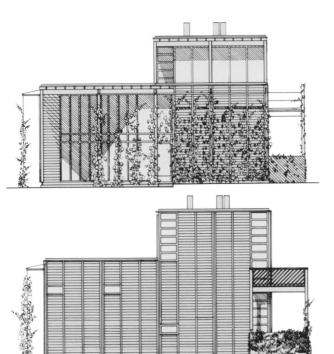

NORTH-EAST ELEVATION

The other heating system is a wood burning stove in the living room which is designed to provide 15% of its output directly to the room and 85% to a buffer store from where it is passed to other rooms via the underfloor heating system. The sunspace can be heated if required, though this was not necessary during the monitoring period.

The heat pump also provides the domestic hot water, via a separate storage tank.

OPERATING MODES AND CONTROLS

In the heating season, the roller blinds are raised during the daytime to allow light and solar radiation into the sunspace, the living rooms and the studio. At night, the blinds are lowered to reduce heat loss. The windows between the living rooms and the sunspace can be opened and closed according to the temperature difference between the two areas.

In the summer, the sunspace is automatically protected from the sun by the foliage of the adjacent trees and by the solid roof. The roller blinds can be used for further shading, though this reduces daylight inside the house. The sunspace provides a buffer space to external temperatures in summer, in the same way as it reduces heat loss in winter.

The studio is partially sheltered from summer sun by the fixed glazed screen over the southern windows, and the blinds can also be used for shading.

All control of the solar systems is manual.

MONITORING

The house was extensively monitored over one heating season and one summer period from May 1986 to May 1987. The following information was collected from a total of 71 measuring points at 15 minute intervals:-
- the opening of all doors and windows;
- internal temperatures;
- electricity consumption for heating, hot water and cooking;
- lighting and appliance consumptions;
- the input and output of the heat pump;
- hot water usage;
- external temperatures;
- global irradiation;
- external humidity;
- wind direction and speed;
- output of the wood burning stove to the heating system;
- the differential temperatures in the buried heat exchanger pipes.

The amount of wood used in the stove was recorded by the owner and an efficiency of 70% assumed. In addition, tracer gas methods were used to assess the airchange rates in the house and sunspace. The occupants were interviewed every six months.

On the first floor, a gallery looks out onto the sunspace which is used for growing plants.

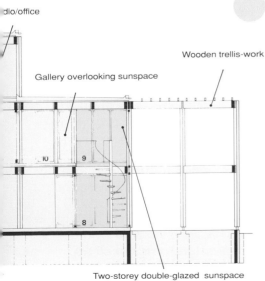

dio/office

Gallery overlooking sunspace

Wooden trellis-work

10   9

8

Two-storey double-glazed sunspace

NORTH -SOUTH SECTION

Performance Evaluation

USER RESPONSE

The occupants are very happy with the quality of life in the house and particularly with the indoor climate. The house warms up rapidly with the sun and yet retains heat well. The sunspace is used only for growing plants but serves well as a buffer space, protecting the living rooms from temperature extremes.
The insulating blinds are used every evening in winter and in general the occupants have learned through experience to control the ventilation and shading in summer.

PERFORMANCE OF PASSIVE SOLAR DESIGN

● The energy used for space heating (excluding the solar contribution) was 55% lower than the average for the housing stock in West Germany.

● Solar gains provided nearly 36% of the energy entering the house , although some of these gains were lost due to "surplus ventilation" by the occupants.

The sunspace protects the living rooms from temperature extremes making the indoor climate very pleasant.

● Internal gains provided nearly 12% of the energy entering the house.

● In summer the temperatures in the sunspace and living room remained below the external temperatures, suggesting the success of the shading from trees and blinds, an important aspect in solar design.

● Occupant behaviour was considered to have a greater effect on auxiliary fuel consumption than any of the energy saving features included.

The overall heat loss from the house, as indicated by the mean U value (0.64W/m^{2}K), is only 3% better than regulations despite the highly insulated structure. This is due to the large areas of glazing, particularly in the studio/office. It is suggested that extending the use of low emissivity glass to all the studio glazing, and the sunspace, would have significantly reduced energy consumption.
The coefficient of performance of the heat pump, which used brine as the heat carrying medium, was lower than expected, 2.5 rather than 3.4. 54% of the auxiliary energy used for space heating came from the ground, while the electricity to drive the heat pump provided 37%. The wood burning stove supplied the remainder.
The house performs in different ways according to external conditions. On overcast winter days, with external temperatures between 1°C and -1°C, living room temperatures were as high as 24°C, dropping to 21°C at night when the heating was turned down.

COMPARISON WITH CONVENTIONAL DESIGN

Based on the average for W. German housing stock, a typical house of this size would require 66 782kWh for space heating.

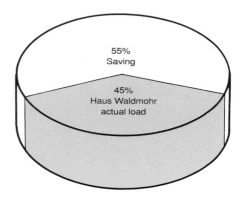

55%
Saving

45%
Haus Waldmohr
actual load

For Haus Waldmohr the actual load includes auxiliary heating and internal gains.

TOTAL ENERGY LOSSES

Surplus ventilation by the occupants increased the heat losses of the house above the predicted value of 33 725kWh, to 38 949kWh.

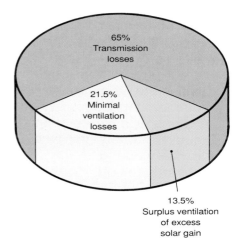

65%
Transmission
losses

21.5%
Minimal
ventilation
losses

13.5%
Surplus ventilation
of excess
solar gain

Temperatures in the sunspace averaged 10°C less. There was no solar contribution to the maintenance of internal temperatures.
On clear, sunny winter days, with external temperatures between 0°C and - 4°C, there were significant solar gains to the living rooms and therefore a significant reduction in the auxiliary heating requirement.
On hot summer days, with external temperatures as high as 31°C, the internal temperatures did not climb above 24°C due to the effective shading.

TOTAL ENERGY INPUTS

The total energy entering the house rooms was 38 949kWh.

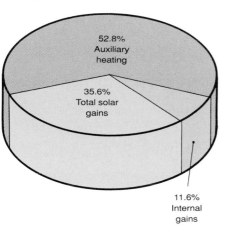

SOURCES OF AUXILIARY ENERGY FOR SPACE HEATING AND HOT WATER

The total auxiliary heating was 23 838kWh.

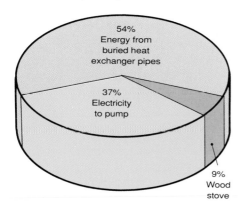

COST EFFECTIVENESS

A lot of the construction work of the house was performed by the owner himself. Due to the architectural quality of the design and its construction, the house belongs to an upper price category. It is very difficult to compare the total cost with a conventional design or to separate out passive components: for example, it makes no sense to simulate the integrated sunspace as a separate component. Such a modification would have meant a total alteration to the design.
The increased insulation of the house certainly proved to be cost effective.

NET MONTHLY SPACE HEATING DEMAND AND SUPPLY

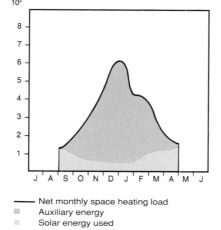

— Net monthly space heating load
▪ Auxiliary energy
▪ Solar energy used

MONTHLY AVERAGE TEMPERATURES

— Internal temp
····· External temp
— Winter garden /Sunspace temp

THREE SUNNY DAYS IN WINTER

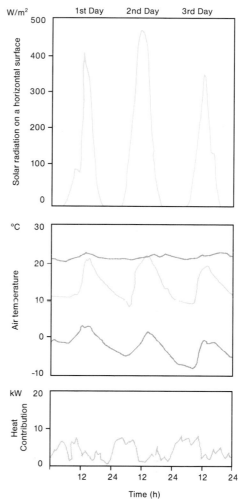

– Living room temp.
– Sunspace temp.
– External temp.
– Auxiliary heat contribution to the house.

PROJECT DATA

House (excl sunspace)

Volume (heated)	739.0	m³
Floor area	238.3	m²
Roof area	109.0	m²
External wall area	233.0	m²
Window area: total	104.1	m²
single glazed	51.4	m²
double glazed	37.3	m²
low emissivity	15.4	m²

Sunspace/Winter garden

Floor area	30.8	m²
Glazed area	54.3	m²

Thermal Characteristics

U Value roof	0.25	W/m²K
floor	0.36	W/m²K
external walls	0.33	W/m²K
windows	5.2; 2.6; 1.4	W/m²K
Mean U value	0.64	W/m²K
External design temperature	- 12°C	
Infiltration rate (at windspeed 0.3m/s)	0.3	ach
Heated floor area	238.3	m²
Heated volume	739.0	m³
Net heat load	105.0	kWh/m²

Site and Climate

Altitude	310 m
Latitude	49° 20' N
Longitude	7° 30' E
Measured degree days (HP Sept-May)	
1986/87	3688 (base 18.7°C)
Mean global irradiation: (HP Sept-May)	
horizontal 1986/87	2.2 kWh/m²/day
vertical (south) 1986/87	2.1 kWh/m²/day

REFERENCES

1. Reiss, J; Erhorn, H; Kuhl, W; Oswald, D and Steinborn, F; 'Passive Solarenergienutzung in bewohnten Eigenheimen. Messergebnisse und energetische Analyse für das Solarhaus in Waldmohr' Report WB 24/88 of Fraunhofer-Institut für Bauphysik, Stuttgart (1988).

2. Fraunhofer-Institut für Bauphysik und Fraunhofer-Institut für Systemtechnik und Innovationsforschung (Eds) 'Abschlussbericht zum Demonstrationsprojekt Landstuhl'. Stuttgart/Karlsruhe (forthcoming).

LES GARENNES CREDITS

Client
SA d'HLM "LES TROIS VALLEES"
8, rue Charles Pathe
94300 VINCENNES

Architects
L. Bouat, Y. Draussin, J Guillaume, J. Massip
Altelier De Site
17 rue Mordillat
92260 FONTENAY-AUX-ROSES

J. Auzolle
36 rue des petits Hotels
75010 PARIS

Energy Consultant
Get Ingenierie
28 boulevard de la Bastille
75012 PARIS

Services Engineer
Bet de Bouygues Entreprise
dcmi Challenger
2 rue Stephenson
Saint-Quentin-en-Yvelines
MONTIGNY LE BRETONNEUX

Building Contractor
Societe Bouygues Challenger
1 avenue Eugine Freyssinet
78061 SAINT-QUENTIN-EN-YVELINES CEDEX

Services Contractor
Sunspaces
Societe Frametac
55 boulevard de Stalingrad
94400 VITRY-SUR-SEINE

Windows
Societe Ballimann
6 rue d'Estienne d'Orves
92110 CLICHY

Solar system
(Solar collectors)
SOLEFIL -
(no longer trading)

(Installation)
Societe Zell
7 rue Nicolas Robert
93600 AULNAY-SOUS-BOIS

Monitoring Organisation
Le Cetiat
Plateau du Moulon
BP No. 19
91402 ORSAY CEDEX

Commission of the European Communities

● Major town centre, multi-storey housing development, features passive solar design.

● Full-height sunspace structures give individual sunspaces, varying in size, to each of the larger flats.

● Thermostatically-controlled fan systems transfer warm air from sunspaces to living rooms as required.

● An average solar contribution of 33% to the space heating load was recorded, with a maximum solar contribution of 41% .

LES GARENNES
SAINT-QUENTIN-EN-YVELINES
FRANCE

Project Background

This project comprises 148 apartments in six blocks built in the centre of the Garennes area, within a new town. The six blocks are a mixture of three, four and five storeys, some with shops at ground level and three or four floors of flats above. They were designed along passive solar principles to take advantage of the large south facades dictated by the road layout. The project was completed in 1985 and attracted extra subsidies for the solar features from the "Plan Construction", a programme whereby some money is available for innovative developments.

The site is in an area of 1. 100 dwellings located along the "Vallée de la Bièvre".

OBJECTIVES

The client was the Public Construction Office for Moderate Rent Housing which is responsible for much new town construction. The initiative for the passive solar design came from the architect who had previous experience in similar apartment blocks. The principal objective of the scheme was to achieve a high standard of architecture with a coherent image for a public sector development. A secondary objective was the promotional value of the sunspaces and solar panels.

ENERGY SAVING FEATURES

● All the blocks are well insulated and have double-glazed windows.

● The larger flats have main living rooms on the south side with stairs and service rooms on the north.

● Full-height sunspace structures provide each of the larger flats with an individual sunspace.

● Each sunspace has a thermostatically-controlled fan to supply solar heated air to the living room.

● Roof mounted active solar panels preheat the domestic hot water.

CONCLUSIONS

The project is a success in that the flats are pleasant and comfortable to live in and fuel bills are low. Payback periods of between 8 and 12 years are achieved, depending upon the living-room thermostat set point.

SITE AND CLIMATE

The project is located in the new town of Saint-Quentin-en-Yvelines, near Versailles, 25km south-east of Paris. The district of Les Garennes is to the south of Saint-Cyr-l'Ecole, near the Bois de la Garennes, with the village of Guyancourt to the east.
The climate is generally "Parisienne Regional" and there is little that moderates the microclimate. The minimum

0   20   40m

monthly average temperature is 3.8°C and the maximum is 17.5°C, with an average of 2700 degree days per annum (18°C base). The predominant winds are from the south-west and north-west, and fog is common.

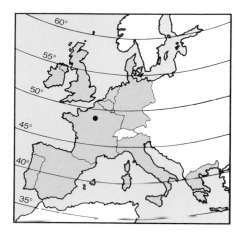

CLIMATE (Trappas)

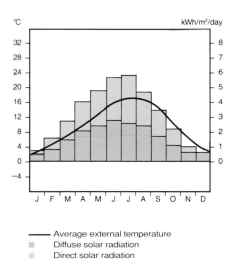

— Average external temperature
■ Diffuse solar radiation
■ Direct solar radiation

The site is at the junction of four roads in the centre of the district. These roads which divide up the site are the main links to adjacent districts, and the area is well served by public transport.

PLANNING

The site layout was largely determined by its location at the road junction. The main road, the Boulevard Ludwig Van Beethoven, runs nearly due east/west and thus encouraged a north/south orientation of the buildings. To mark this important cross roads it was decided to make the central buildings five storeys high so they would stand out above the adjacent three and four storey buildings. The ground floors of the five storey blocks contain shops and communal facilities such as a day nursery and creche, with three storeys of apartments above, and services (including the active solar systems) at the top. Gardens, children's play areas and car parking are located adjacent to the buildings. 116 of the apartments have 3-5 rooms and have double exposure, giving both south and north aspects. The remaining 32 apartments have only 1 or 2 rooms and are located at the intersection of the blocks, with east or west aspects.

DESIGN DETAILS

The buildings present a dramatic appearance particularly from the south, due to the full-height sunspaces forming large glass and metal "cascades" down the facades. The roof mounted active solar collectors continue the angle of the sunspaces projecting up above the fifth floor. North facades are characterised by the multi-level metal structures of the entrance halls and staircases.

CONSTRUCTION

Apart from the unusual sunspace structures, each building is of standard construction. There is a reinforced concrete frame with 160mm structural partition walls. The south facade is 160mm in-situ concrete and

The triangular windows of the kitchens add character to the north facade.

Design Details

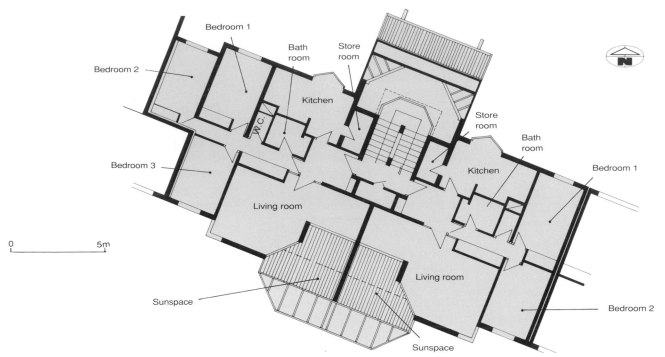

First floor plan showing double sunspace on the south side and entrance on the north.

the north facade is constructed in prefabricated sections; behind these walls 80-90mm of polyurethane insulation has been applied internally. The main roof is 160mm reinforced concrete insulated with 60mm polyurethane, whilst above the full-height sunspace the roof is 160mm reinforced concrete and 30mm polyurethane with an internal plaster finish.

The sunspaces vary in size from 13m² on the ground floor to 6m² on the third floor.

Floors are also constructed from 160mm reinforced concrete, with 60mm insulation.

The sunspace structure is stainless steel with single glazing. The seal between the in-situ concrete and the sunspace was effected with a built in durable double silicon seal. All windows are double glazed.

PASSIVE SOLAR DESIGN

The main blocks face south and 70% of the window area is located on the south side. Living rooms and some bedrooms in the larger apartments are on the south side, with stairs, kitchens and other bedrooms on the north. The large full-height sunspace constructions give individual sunspaces to each of the larger flats. These vary in size from 13m² floor area on the ground floor to 6m² on the third floor due to the tapering shape of the structures. In these flats, the living room opens directly off the sunspace and in addition there is a fan which blows warm air into the living room if required. The fan can be set to operate automatically

when the living room temperature is below 20ºC and that in the sunspace is above 20ºC.

The light metal structure of the sunspace and the single glazing allow maximum penetration of sunlight into both the sunspace and

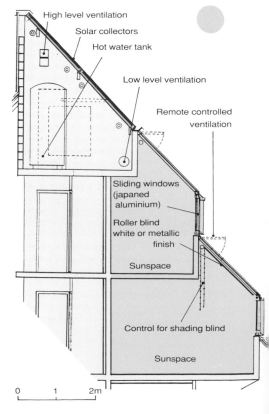

Section of upper storeys

adjacent rooms. To prevent overheating in summer, the individual sunspaces have large openable windows and white internal roller blinds.

AUXILIARY HEATING SYSTEMS

Auxiliary space heating is by a thermostatically-controlled electric convector heater in each room. A mechanical ventilation system extracts air from the kitchen and bathroom, new air being drawn in through the bedrooms.

Domestic hot water is provided by the 235m^2 of roof mounted solar water-heating panels. A group of panels preheats water for six to eight dwellings in a storage tank and supplementary heating is provided by immersion heaters at night in a second tank.

OPERATING MODES AND CONTROLS

In the heating season the blinds are raised, and solar gains enter the sunspace, and the south-facing rooms. When the sunspace temperature rises above 20ºC the fan operates to draw warm air into the living room, as long as the living room is below 20ºC. When these conditions apply, the room convector heater is automatically turned off.

In summer, when heating is not required, the sunspace blinds can be lowered and the windows opened for ventilation.

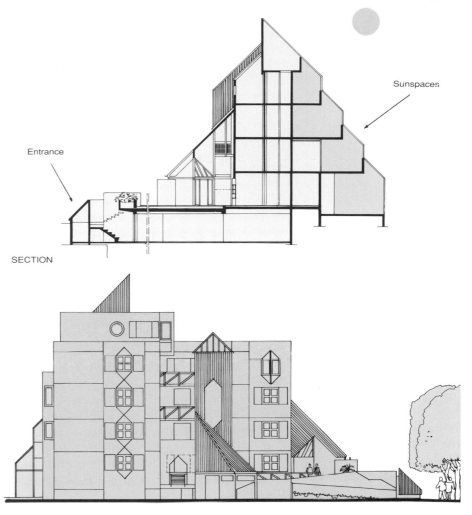

Entrance

Sunspaces

SECTION

END ELEVATION

SOUTH ELEVATION

NORTH ELEVATION

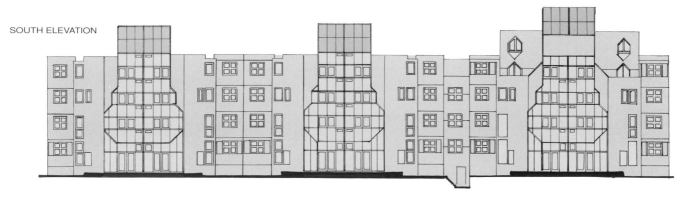

Performance Evaluation

The sunspaces have white roller blinds and vents at high level.

MONITORING

Two full years of monitoring data are available, 1985-1987, for 10 dwellings with different sunspace arrangements. Measurements were made of:- meteorological conditions; electricity consumption for space heating, water heating and appliances; exhaust air from kitchens and bathrooms; air movement from sunspaces to living rooms; and temperatures in sunspaces and living rooms. The solar water heating systems were also monitored.

USER RESPONSE

The sunspaces are well liked and are used for a variety of purposes including growing plants, storing possessions and drying clothes.
However, despite the information provided to the occupants by the architect, the sunspaces and the solar water systems were not used to best advantage in energy terms. The sunspace windows were left open at times when the sunspaces could have provided useful heat to the houses, and thermostat settings on the living room fans and heaters were altered from optimal. Neither did the occupants in all cases

manage the solar shading of the sunspaces to best advantage, so temperatures as high as 45°C were recorded, compared to 32°C where blinds and windows were correctly operated.
The effect of providing "free" solar heated water appears to have been that occupants used three times the typical amount.

PERFORMANCE OF PASSIVE SOLAR FEATURES

● The average solar contribution to the space heating load for 10 apartments was 33%.

● For a typical four room apartment (type T4) the solar contribution was 41% leading to a saving in auxiliary fuel use of 55% compared to a conventional design.

● There was a large variation in annual electricity consumption for identically sized apartments, from 2 263kWh to 9 214kWh in the case of type T4.

● The fan systems for moving solar warmed air from the sunspaces to the living rooms were not very effective due to the difficulty of regulating their use and the air leakage of the sunspaces, combined with the absence of effective return air vents from the living rooms to the sunspaces.

Although the blinds and ventilation arrangements in the sunspaces were adequate to control temperatures in summer, high temperatures were recorded where occupants did not operate the systems effectively.
The active solar systems did not produce large energy savings and there has been one system failure.

COST EFFECTIVENESS

The solar features cost 12% of the total building cost, ie 39 000FF in 1982. The sunspaces and fan systems cost 36 000FF of this, and the remainder was for the active solar water heaters.
A payback period of 12 years is achieved for the solar measures as the flats were operated, ie with the living room thermostats set at 19°C. However in dwellings where the set point temperature is 17°C instead, the payback period is reduced to 8 years. In addition to the energy savings they produce, the sunspaces have a value because they provide extra living space to the apartments for some of the year.

COMPARISON WITH CONVENTIONAL DESIGN
(4 room apartment)

10 328kWh would be required to heat a similar house built to conventional design.

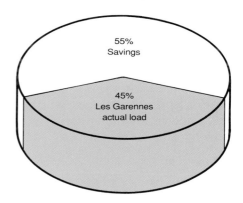

CONTRIBUTIONS TO ANNUAL SPACE HEATING DEMAND
(10 Monitored dwellings)

The total annual space heating demand for 10 dwellings was 102 129 kWh.

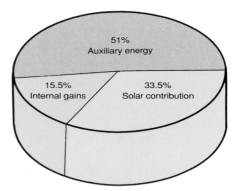

NET MONTHLY SPACE HEATING DEMAND AND SUPPLY

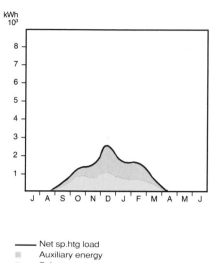

kWh
10³

- —— Net sp.htg load
- ▨ Auxiliary energy
- ▨ Solar energy

MONTHLY AVERAGE TEMPERATURES

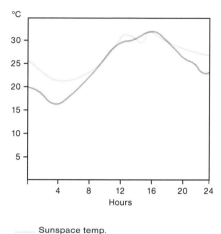

°C

- —— Internal design temp.
- ‑‑‑ External temp

EXTERNAL AND SUNSPACE TEMPERATURES, JULY 1985

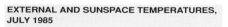

°C

- —— Sunspace temp.
- ‑‑‑ External temp.

CONTRIBUTIONS TO ANNUAL SPACE HEATING DEMAND
(4 room apartment)

The total annual space heating demand was 10 821 kWh.

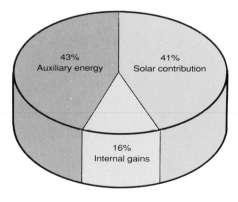

- 43% Auxiliary energy
- 41% Solar contribution
- 16% Internal gains

The north elevations are characterised by the metal structure of the entrance halls and stairs.

AUXILIARY FUEL USED ANNUALLY
(4 room apartment)

The total auxiliary fuel used was 7 881kWh.

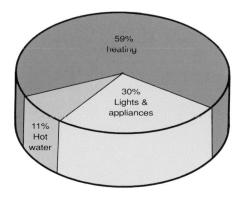

- 59% heating
- 30% Lights & appliances
- 11% Hot water

PROJECT DATA

Building (Type T4)

Volume	227.0	m³
Floor area	91.0	m²
Roof area	80.0	m²
External wall area	33.5	m²
Windows: total area	21.5	m² 100%
south	15.0	m² 70%
north	6.5	m² 30%

Sunspace

Volume	27.0	m³
Floor area	11.0	m²
Glass area:roof	8.7	m²
wall	5.3	m²
Wall area: solid	8.0	m²
Effective aperture	4.0	m²

Thermal Characteristics

U Value: roof	0.40	W/m²K
ground floor	0.55	W/m²K
external walls	0.40	W/m²K
windows	2.9	W/m²K

sunspace glazing	5.0	W/m²K
Mean U value	1.54	W/m²K
Global heat loss coefficient	182	W/K
External design temperature	-7	°C
Heated floor area	80.0	m²
Heated volume	200.0	m³
Net heat load	100	kWh/m²

Site and Climate

Altitude	168.0	m
Latitude	48° 46' N	
Longitude	2° 1' E	
Average ambient temp: Jan	3.8	°C
July	17.5	°C
Degree days (base 18°C)	2 709	days
Global irradiation on horiz	1 127	kWh/m²/yr
Sunshine hours	1 707	hr/yr

Costs (1982 prices)

Building total	329 000FF	46 532	ECU
Solar features	39 000FF	5 516	ECU

ISTITUTO TECNICO COMMERCIALE CREDITS

Client
Amministrazione Provinciale di Viterbo
Via A. Sassi, 49
Viterbo

Architects
Coop. Citta e Territorio s.r.l.
N. Ceccarelli, E. de Santis, R. Meli, A. Meloni
now:
I.P.R. s.r.l.
Palazzo Gardini
Viale Trento
01100 Viterbo

Structural Engineer
Ing. M. Alessi
Via San Bonaventura
Viterbo

Services and Energy Consultant
Ing. M. Arduini (I.P.R.s.r.l.)
Ing. P. de Santis (I.P.R.s.r.l.)

Building Contractor
Franco Governatori Costruzioni s.r.l.
Strada Statale Cassia Nord, 86 300
Montefiascone

Services Contractor
S.I.T. Societa Impianti Termotecnica
(no longer trading)

Monitoring Organisation
Ing. M. Romanazzo of ENEA (Comitato Nazionale
per lo Sviluppo dell Energia Nucleare e delle
Energie Alternative)
ENEA CRE Casaccia
Via Anguillarese, 301
00060 Santa Maria di Galeria (Roma)
with consultant Ing. M. Arduini of I.P.R. s.r.l.

Commission of the European Communities

● Prize winning school design incorporates energy conservation and active and passive solar technologies to give a 51% saving in the primary energy used for space heating compared to a conventional design.

ISTITUTO TECNICO COMMERCIALE

MONTEFIASCONE
ITALY

● Fan-assisted solar air-heating panels provide 25% of the net space heating demand.

● Direct solar gain from south-facing windows and a large sunspace contribute 22% to the net space heating demand.

Project Background

The technical high school for commercial studies is the result of a national competition launched in 1979 by the Province of Viterbo; this design won first prize. Construction was completed by 1982 and the school was monitored over the 1984/85 school year.

OBJECTIVES

The public administration of Viterbo wanted to test the effectiveness of a package of energy saving and solar measures when applied to an educational building in relatively favourable climatic conditions.

The competition brief explicitly required the use of passive and active solar technologies to be integrated into the overall architectural image of the school. As well as the experimental energy features, the school was planned to have facilities for use by both the students (aged between 14 and 18) and the local community, to provide the surrounding area with a focus of interest.

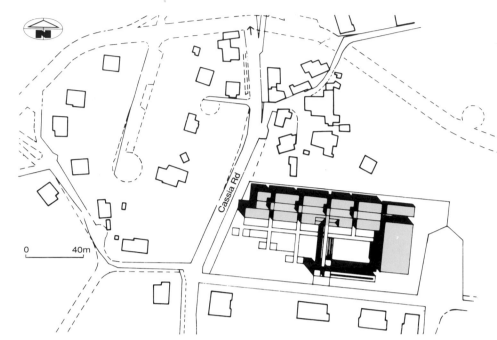

The technical high school for commercial studies is in the outskirts of Montefiascone.

ENERGY SAVING FEATURES

● The long, narrow floor plan is oriented east/west to maximise the collection and use of solar gains.

● Large areas of glazing with external shading devices and fan-assisted vertical air-heating collectors cover the south facade.

● A multi-level sunspace acts as an entrance hall and provides a buffer zone between inside and outside.

● High levels of insulation, the elimination of cold bridges and double glazing throughout, minimise heat losses.

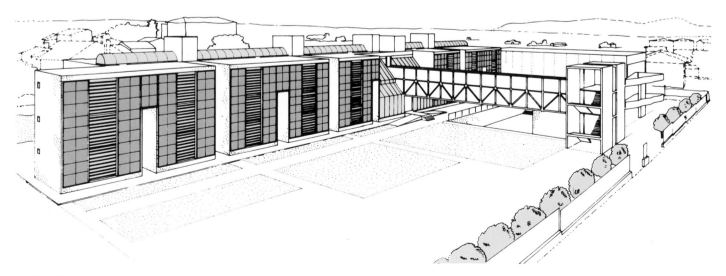

View from the Cassia Road.

The main building has recesses to emphasise the split into five teaching units. A dual deck footbridge provides access, via the sunspace, on the first and second floors.

Design Details

SITE AND CLIMATE

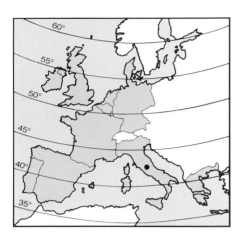

20km from Viterbo, Montefiascone is in a hilly area 590m above sea level, at the foothills of the Apennines. The town overlooks Lake Bolsena, 5 km away, which is surrounded by vineyards and olive groves.

The school itself is on Cassia Road, the ancient Roman road linking the capital to the north-west of the peninsula, in the outskirts of Montefiascone, and very close to the lake. The site is surrounded by low density urban development.

Overall, the site enjoys a good position with little noise disturbance or atmospheric pollution. The surrounding vegetation and buildings do not obstruct the site and the open space in front is a pleasant sunny area.

Trees to the north of the site provide the school with windshielding from the "tramontana", a cold northerly wind.

The average external temperature in January is 6.5°C, rising to 21°C in July. The heating season lasts from mid-October to mid-April, and there are 2190 degree days (19°C base).

CLIMATE (Montefiascone)

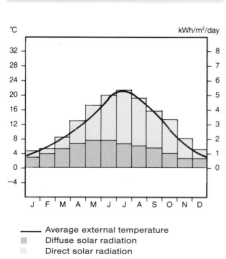

Average external temperature
Diffuse solar radiation
Direct solar radiation

DESIGN DETAILS

The project attempts to integrate the school and the town, by providing facilities that can be used by both. The ground floors of the school buildings are devoted to mixed-use areas (the library, assembly hall, sports hall, open-air theatre, etc) and the upper floors are reserved for those spaces used only by the school.

Internally, the building conveys

The impressive multi-level sunspace acts as an entrance hall.

a strong "high tech" image with the exposed air-ducts and water pipes in "pop-art" colours, and with different sources of natural lighting.

PLANNING

The main building, excluding the sports hall, is 94m long, 20m wide and three storeys high, with recesses which emphasise the split into five teaching units. A wide central corridor runs the full length of the school, connecting the three-storey units, and providing a link to the sports hall.

CONCLUSIONS

The energy saving measures, together with the passive and hybrid solar systems, have led to a reduction of over 50% in the primary energy used for space heating compared to a conventional Italian school of the same volume. Solar gains contributed 47% to the net space heating load.

The solar air-heating panels, which provide make-up ventilation air, are particularly well suited to use in schools where high air change rates (2.5ach to 3ach) are required in occupied classrooms.

Design Details

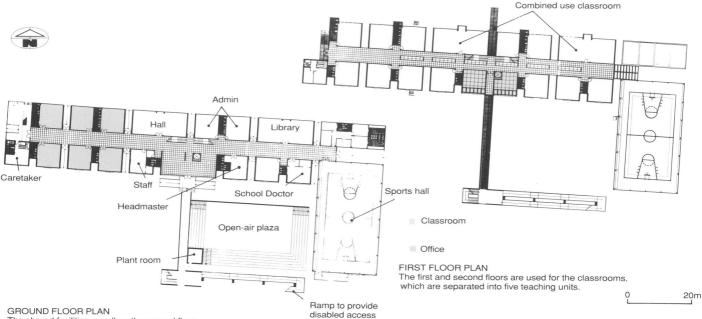

Combined use classroom

Admin

Hall

Library

Caretaker

Staff

Headmaster

School Doctor

Sports hall

Open-air plaza

Plant room

☐ Classroom

◼ Office

FIRST FLOOR PLAN
The first and second floors are used for the classrooms, which are separated into five teaching units.

0   20m

Ramp to provide
disabled access

GROUND FLOOR PLAN
The shared facilities are all on the ground floor.

On the first and second floors, each unit has two classrooms with their associated service rooms plus a combined use classroom. On the ground floors, there are the offices, the shared facilities and the caretaker's flat.

An external staircase and a ramp lead to the dual deck footbridge, which enters the main building on the first and second floors, through the sunspace. A lift in the sunspace provides access to other floors. The open-air theatre is located in a sunken plaza, protected on all sides by the buildings and by the pedestrian walkways, thus making it particularly good for outside activities.

CONSTRUCTION

Load-bearing concrete walls run north-south, at 7.2m intervals, and are internally insulated with 70mm mineral wool. The north facade is constructed from sheet metal sandwich panels each 1m by 10m, insulated with 60mm foamed polyurethane. The panels are fixed externally to the concrete floors to prevent cold bridging through the horizontal slabs.

Two thirds of the south facade is covered with solar air-heating panels. Behind them there are insulated panels of the same type as those used on the north facade.

The concrete ground floor and the roof are insulated with aerated clay to thicknesses of 100mm and 150mm respectively.

All the windows are double glazed and those on the south facade are fitted with external blinds.

A steel structure, attached to the side walls, supports the sunspace glazing; both this and the barrel vault above the central corridor are made from polycarbonate sheets.

The sports hall is entirely prefabricated, with a perimeter load-bearing steel frame and horizontal tubular trusses. The footbridge, which spans the school grounds, is also a steel structure.

The two main constructional problems which have occurred are peeling of the black selective coating on the air-heating panels, and clouding of the polycarbonate sheets of the sunspace. The panels therefore require recoating with a more durable material, whilst eventually all the polycarbonate sheets of the sunspace will need replacing. However, the decreased transparency of the polycarbonate glazing has had a positive benefit in that glare is reduced. Otherwise this

The dual deck footbridge and ramps help to form the plaza.

might have been a problem, as the sunspace is not fitted with any form of shading device.

PASSIVE SOLAR DESIGN

The south facade is a regular pattern of vertical air collectors, and windows protected by moveable, horizontal, aluminium louvres. Each teaching unit has a south facade made up of two identical modules, each 7.2m by 9.6m. The modules are three storeys high and consist of two columns of solar air-heating panels with a row of windows in between.

The collectors, which cover 389m^2, are the main solar feature of the school. They are made from 6mm single glazing, covering corrugated iron sheet which has a black selective surface, with insulated panels behind.

In the bottom of the collectors there are air inlet dampers, and at the top, behind the corrugated iron, the warmed air is ducted out into the supplementary heating system. Fans at the top of the panels assist the air circulation.

The 200m^2 of double-glazed south-facing windows are covered with horizontal "brise-soleils", manually operated from the inside to control daylight and sunlight

penetration. These metal louvres are 2.4m long at 300mm centres.

The central corridor, which runs the whole length of the main school building, has a barrel vault roof to introduce daylight to the centre of the building, thus reducing the electric lighting load. None of the polycarbonate glazing is openable, nor are there any shading devices.

The impressive multi-level

desired temperature and humidity levels. The warm air is then ducted to the classrooms etc.

Individual classrooms have room thermostats and any supplementary heating needed is provided by fan coils, fed by the boiler.

Since warm air heating is not allowed in service areas, radiators provide the necessary heating in these zones.

The north facade has small openings and projecting structures which contain the service rooms.

sunspace, which acts as an entrance hall, is a focal point along the length of the teaching block, with its full-height stepped glazed surface (100m^2 of vertical polycarbonate glazing and 50m^2 of 45° inclined glazing) providing a view inside the building. It is not fitted with shading devices and there is no ventilation at the top.

AUXILIARY HEATING SYSTEMS

Auxiliary space heating is provided by a gas-oil boiler. The entire building is sub-divided into four zones, each served by its own air-treatment unit. In the unit, fresh air from the air-heating collectors and recirculated air from the classrooms are brought together, and taken to the

76m^2 of active solar water-heating collectors are fitted vertically on to the south perimeter wall of the sports hall and provide hot water via a 2 500 litre storage tank.

OPERATING MODES AND CONTROLS

In winter, windows are closed and the adjustable louvres are positioned to allow penetration of the sun deep into the classrooms. Mechanical ventilation provides the necessary air changes.

During autumn, spring and early summer, the aluminium sunscreens have to be correctly positioned to prevent glare and overheating. Natural ventilation is provided by opening windows in the classrooms and along the corridors.

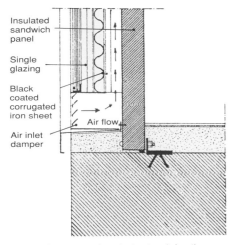

Insulated sandwich panel

Single glazing

Black coated corrugated iron sheet

Air flow

Air inlet damper

Detail of lower part of vertical solar air-heating panels.

Performance Evaluation

The central corridor has a polycarbonate barrel vault roof to admit light. Half way along, the sunspace joins on the right.

The passive controls are extremely simple, the users open or close the windows, and manually adjust the externally fitted louvres.

MONITORING

The monitoring of the school, over the 1984/85 heating season, was to the Class C standard . Hourly readings were taken of internal temperatures in three classrooms and in the sunspace, and crude measurements were made of the air velocity from the collectors. Measurements were also taken to determine the efficiency of the heat recovery on the mechanical ventilation system and the efficiency of the water-to-air heat exchangers. Finally, fuel consumption was metered. The monitoring lasted for only three months, and the data were then extrapolated with the aid of degree days, for the remainder of the period. Inevitably, this method cannot fully assess the contribution of solar gains.

USER RESPONSE

Generally, there have been no complaints about the thermal comfort within the school. The occupants have complained much more about the poor standard of maintenance within the school. The only design problems have been the reduced transparency of the polycarbonate sheets, and, in summer, some overheating of the sunspace which does not have any shading or ventilation openings.

PERFORMANCE OF PASSIVE SOLAR DESIGN

● The fan-assisted solar air-heating panels contributed 25% to the net space heating load, and a further 22% was provided by direct solar gains through the south-facing windows and the sunspace.

● The school saves 51% of the primary energy used for space heating in a conventional design of school.

● There is a substantial difference between the classrooms facing south and those facing north both in terms of temperatures maintained, up to 3°C when the heating system is off, and in the amount of daylighting.

● Monitoring data indicate summer overheating in the top floor classrooms.

● 40% of the hot water demands were met by the active solar water-heating panels fitted to the side of the sports hall.

● The fans in the solar air-heating panels used 12% of the total electricity demand of the school.

The fan coils are only used to improve classroom temperatures for a few weeks of the year, during very cold weather, for the rest of the time the warm air heating is sufficient.

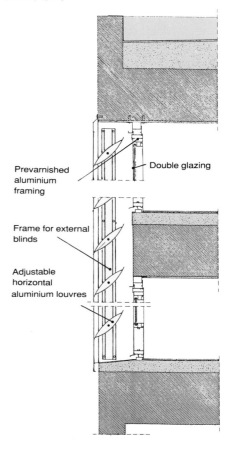

Prevarnished aluminium framing

Double glazing

Frame for external blinds

Adjustable horizontal aluminium louvres

Vertical section of south-facing window with external horizontal louvres.

COMPARISON WITH CONVENTIONAL DESIGN

A conventionally designed school would require 591 400kWh of primary auxiliary energy for space heating for a year.

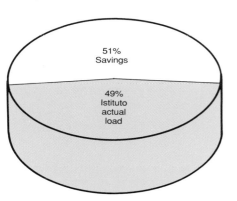

51% Savings

49% Istituto actual load

CONTRIBUTIONS TO ANNUAL SPACE HEATING DEMAND

The total annual space heating demand is 735 560kWh of delivered energy.

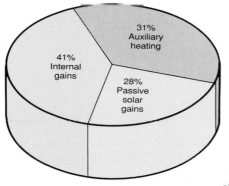

31% Auxiliary heating

41% Internal gains

28% Passive solar gains

The fan-assisted solar air-heating panels provided 15% of the gross space heating demand, and direct solar gains provided another 13%.

NET MONTHLY SPACE HEATING DEMAND AND SUPPLY

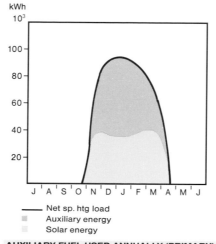

kWh
10³

J A S O N D J F M A M J

——— Net sp. htg load
▪ Auxiliary energy
▫ Solar energy

AUXILIARY FUEL USED ANNUALLY (PRIMARY)

The primary auxiliary fuel used annually is 1 151 390kWh.

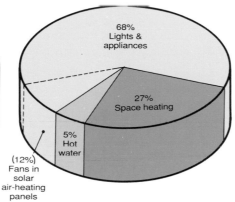

68% Lights & appliances

27% Space heating

5% Hot water

(12%) Fans in solar air-heating panels

40% of the hot water demand was supplied by the active solar water-heating panels.

MONTHLY AVERAGE TEMPERATURES

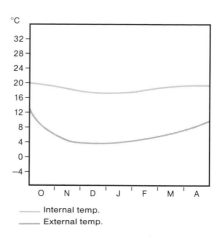

°C

O N D J F M A

——— Internal temp.
——— External temp.

Internal view of the sunspace, with the footbridge continuing into it at first floor level.

COST EFFECTIVENESS

The full package of solar measures: the passive, hybrid and active features, cost L237M in 1982, ie 13% of the total building cost. Based on the first year's energy savings, this gives a simple payback period of 18-19 years. This figure does not ascribe a value to the high quality spaces created throughout the school. Overall the total cost of the school, at L 1800M, appears relatively low when compared to other schools. This is because building costs in central and southern Italy are slightly lower than those in northern Italy and because the school has been constructed to a lower standard, generally.

PROJECT DATA

Building (main school block)

Total volume	18 300	m³
Floor area	5 000	m²
No of floors	3	
Roof area	1 600	m²

Bdg (sports hall & service block)

Total area	6 000	m²
Floor area	760	m²
Roof area: sports hall	643	m²
Windows:Total area	852	m²
South	200	m²
North	50	m²
East and west	150	m²
Barrel vault in school building	320	m²
Roof light in sports hall	132	m²

Sunspace

Vertical glazing	100	m²
45° glazing	50	m²

Fan assisted air-heating panels

Area	389	m²

Active solar water-heating collectors

Area	76	m²

Thermal Characteristics
U-value:

South perimeter wall		0.45 W/m²K

North perimeter wall	0.40	W/m²K
East-west walls	0.71	W/m²K
Floor	0.69	W/m²K
Roof	0.71	W/m²K
Windows	3.4	W/m²K
Mean U value	0.67	W/m²K
Global heat loss coefficient	6340	W/K
Infiltration rate: winter	1 (mean) ac/hr	
summer	natural	
Heated volume (inc sports hall)	21 650	m³
Heated floor area(")	6 250	m²
Heat loss surface/volume approx	0.45	m⁻¹
Net heat load/heated area	305	kWh/m²
External design temperature	- 3	°C

Site and Climate

Altitude	590	m
Latitudo	42° 25'N	
Longitude	12° 05'E	
Average ambient temp: annual	13	°C
Jan	6.5	°C
July	21	°C
Degree days (base 19°C)	2190	days
Global irradiation of horiz	1640	kWh/m²
Sunshine hours	2545	hrs/yr

Costs (1982 prices)

Building	1 800M Liras
Active solar measures	180M Liras
Passive solar measures	
-sunspace	52M Liras
-window sunscreens	5M Liras

OVERBOS 8 CREDITS

Authority
Municipality Haarlemmermeer
PO Box 250
2130 AG HOOFDDORP

Client

Private Property	Rented Property
Van Groeningen	Gemeentelijk
Makelaardij	Woningbedrijf
716, Hoofdweg	PO Box 250
2132 BV HOOFDDORP	2130 AG HOOFDDORP

Urban Design
Dienst Onderzoek and Ruimtelijke
Ordening (DORO)
PO Box 147
2130 AC HOOFDDORP

Architect
Bakker & Boots B V
Postbus 141
1742 GR SCHAGEN

Project Management
Bouw Technische Dienst
PO Box 58
2130 AB HOOFDDORP

Energy Consultant
Ketel Raadgevende Ingenieurs
PO Box 2886
2601 CW DELFT

Funding Organisation
Nederlandse Maatschappij
Voor Energie En Milieu B.V. (NOVEM)
PO Box 8242
3503 RE URECHT

Participation
Werkgroep 2000
PO Box 2000
3800 DA AMERSFOORT

Building Contractor
Cooperatief Bouwbedrijf Moes va
PO Box 535
8000 AM ZWOLLE

Monitoring Organisation
Woon/Energie
38j Crabethstraat
2801 AN GOUDA

Project Advisor
Provinciaal Bureau Energie (PBE)
Houtplein 33
2012 DE HAARLEM

27

Commission of the European Communities
OVERBOS 8
HOOFDDORP
NETHERLANDS

Project Background

South elevation shows the large area of glazing.

In 1984, the municipality of Haarlemmermeer decided to abandon the idea of using district heating systems and instead to build according to the principles of passive solar energy use. Hence, after an experimental "Energy Park" of 56 solar houses in Hoofddorp, they developed the 275 houses at Overbos 8 as a field trial of the new passive solar guidelines they had set up. The houses, built between 1985 and 1987, include two

blocks of duplex apartments and five rows of houses for the elderly. More than half of all the houses are for private ownership and the rest are to be rented.

The Dutch national research programme on the rational use of energy in the built environment (REGO) and the Netherlands Agency for Energy and the Environment (NOVEM) have carried out the evaluation study of the scheme.

In all the new housing in Hoofddorp, the municipality has to comply with stringent cost limitations, set numbers of houses per finance category, and exact specifications regarding land use. The aim at Overbos 8 was to remain within these constraints, and at the same time to build housing along the passive solar guidelines; to explore the consequences of these guidelines on the urban designs; and to involve 60% of the prospective occupants in decision-making. None of the energy saving features were to be subsidised and only minor allowances could be made for the learning curve of the design process.
The new guidelines which were implemented require:

● the reduction of heat losses by insulation and ventilation control;

● the use of passive solar energy to meet as much of the space heating load as possible;

● good solar access to outdoor spaces;

● a good indoor climate.

ENERGY SAVING FEATURES

The houses, being the first to be designed to the guidelines, have the following energy saving features:

● three quarters of the dwellings face south, with entrances on the north and living rooms on the south;

● 83% of the glazing is on the south side;

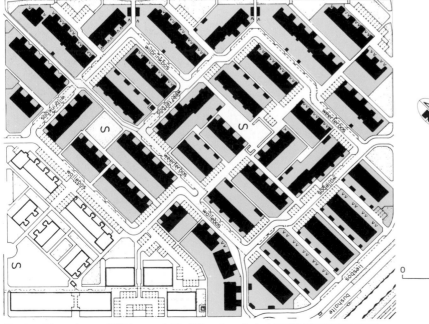

0   50m

Overbos 8 is a scheme of 275 houses in Hoofddorp, the principal town in Haarlemmermeer.

Design Details

- they are well insulated, and include double glazing of all windows and special insulating glazing in living rooms and kitchens;

- a mechanical ventilation system with heat recovery has been installed in each house.

SITE AND CLIMATE

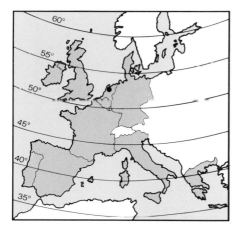

The municipality of Haarlemmermeer is situated 20km south-west of Amsterdam. A large number of new districts have been developed in the area since 1960. Schiphol, Amsterdam Airport and a growing number of related industries are situated in the polder of Haarlemmermeer, once Lake Haarlem . The polder is completely flat and 4m below sea level. Overbos 8 is close to the Hoofddorp Energy Park . Although the prevailing winds are south-westerly, most cold winds are north-easterly. The heating season runs from mid-September to mid-May.

CLIMATE (Schipol)

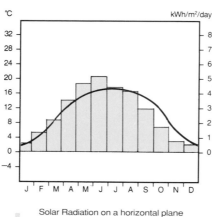

- Solar Radiation on a horizontal plane
- Average external temperature

CONCLUSIONS

The "solar" layout has not increased the plot size nor the length of the road network above normal, and the site layout is interesting with good views from the main windows. Compared to conventional designs, the south-facing Overbos 8 houses saved 63% of the fuel used for space heating, with a solar contribution of 37% to the net space heating load. In the west-facing houses the solar contribution was on average 21%.

The building costs did not exceed the norms for social housing and the occupants are reported to be very happy with their homes.

PLANNING

The layout and design of the 275 dwellings was established after extensive consultation. Sixteen public meetings took place at which the future inhabitants indicated priorities and made choices with regard to the layout (length of blocks, siting of the dwellings, parking, open spaces) and the dwellings (floor plan, width and depth of the houses). The architect was chosen by the inhabitants, from a shortlist provided by the municipality.

The site layout was designed to avoid overshadowing of south facades.

Design Details

Out-house

Parking space

W.C.

Hall

Kitchen

Living room

Terrace

GROUND FLOOR

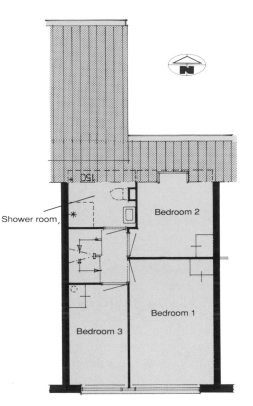

Shower room

Bedroom 2

Bedroom 3

Bedroom 1

FIRST FLOOR

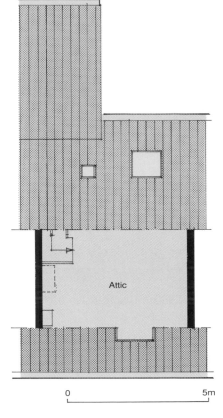

Attic

0   5m

SECOND FLOOR

Almost all the dwellings are single family houses of two or three storeys with pitched roofs. The layout is such that 75% of the houses face south with minimal overshadowing (the obstruction angle is less than 17º). This has been assisted by an asymmetrical cross section which gives a lower northern roof gutter. Careful planning of gardens, living rooms and attached out-houses gives a pleasant view from the houses. The density is 45 dwellings per 10 000m².

CONSTRUCTION

The houses are constructed with in-situ concrete floors and walls, and with an outer skin of brick or prefabricated panels. The roofs are finished in concrete tiles. 140mm of mineral fibre insulation is placed in the roofs and walls

and polystyrene of varying thicknesses is used to insulate the ground floors.
All windows are double glazed, with those in the living rooms

and kitchens having 15mm gas filled cavities and a selective coating on the glass, giving a U value of 1.3 W/m²K.

Entrances and out-houses are located on the north sides.

PASSIVE SOLAR DESIGN

The site layout and internal planning of the dwellings have been chosen to maximise passive solar gain. Three quarters of the houses have living rooms facing south and care has been taken to minimise overshadowing both by the spacing of the blocks and by lowering roof lines. $10m^2$ of glazing in each house is located on the south side, with only $2m^2$ on the north side.

Entrances are located on the north sides where possible and the "out-houses" are either attached on the north side or at the ends of the gardens on the south side.

AUXILIARY HEATING SYSTEM

Auxiliary heating is supplied by gas fired, fanned flue boilers, located in the roofspaces. There are radiators in all rooms and thermostats in the living rooms. The domestic hot water is also supplied by the boilers.

A mechanical ventilation system extracts air from the kitchen, bathroom and toilet at a rate of between 130 and 175 m^3/hour, and blows fresh air, heated by a heat exchanger, into each of the three bedrooms at a rate of $50m^3$/hour. The ventilation air finds its way via the circulation spaces to the living room ensuring a supply of fresh air throughout the house under all conditions of use.

OPERATING MODES AND CONTROLS

The Overbos 8 houses operate in much the same way as normal houses. Windows can be opened to promote ventilation when the mechanical system is not in

ASYMMETRIC CROSS SECTION

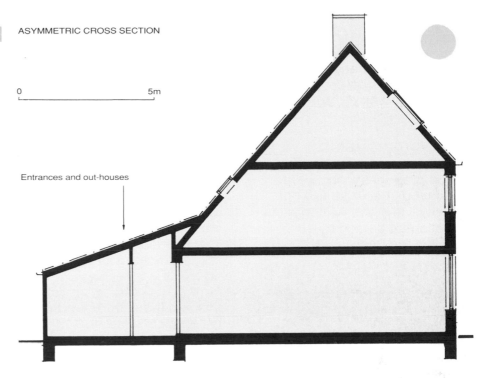

0 — 5m

Entrances and out-houses

use and curtains can be drawn to provide shading. The heating system controls are designed to respond to solar gains and hence the thermostats are positioned in the south-facing living rooms. The mechanical ventilation system distributes solar gains around the house by drawing air through the house and extracting it from the kitchen and bathroom. The heat

exchangers ensure that solar and internal heat gains are recycled.

MONITORING

Two of the houses were monitored for 1 month each, using a 60 channel data logger. Data collected included solar radiation and air and surface temperatures. Gas and electric meters were

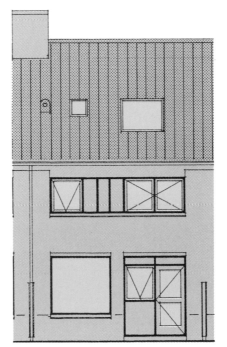

South elevation, 3 storey house

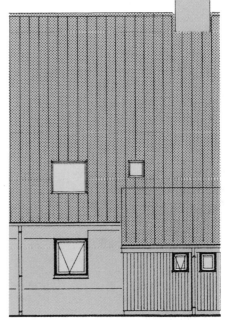

North elevation, 3 storey house

Performance Evaluation

read regularly and random tests were carried out to determine air change rates, rates of air extraction from kitchens and air density under different conditions.

USER RESPONSE

A comprehensive occupants' survey has been carried out both by means of written questionnaires and by some face to face interviews.
The survey dealt with:-

● general assessment of the dwellings, neighbourhood and facilities;

● use of heating system, ventilation and solar heating;

● assessment of the consultation process;

● gas consumptions.

68% of occupants completed their questionnaires.
The occupants were in general very content with the internal conditions, the house layouts and the solar orientation.
They appreciated being able to control the heating to maximise the use of solar

USER SURVEY RESULTS

	Percentage liking	Percentage disliking
House layout	84	4
South facing gardens	94	2
House privacy	80	8
Garden privacy	58	22
Winter solar heating	89	4
Summer solar heating	96	1
Sun entering living rooms	97	2
Air quality in the houses	81	7
Central heating system	82	7
Extraction from kitchen	35	49
Ventilation air in bedrooms	71	16

gains and there were hardly any complaints about overheating in summer (although overheating was predicted by the models). The only complaints about this came from occupants of west-facing dwellings.
There were some complaints about the ventilation systems, particularly the noise and the inability of the systems to extract adequately from the kitchens. The latter problem can be overcome by the addition of a cooker hood connected to the system. Those who participated in the consultation process generally appreciated this experience.

PERFORMANCE OF PASSIVE SOLAR DESIGN

The monitored results and the fuel meter readings taken by the occupants, confirmed the theoretical calculations on energy consumption.

● The houses which faced south had overall energy savings of 63% compared to houses built to conventional standards with no special solar design features.

● The solar contribution to the net space heating load was 37% for the south-facing houses.

● In comparison, the west-facing houses used 22% more energy for heating and their solar contribution was down to 21% of the net heating load.

COST EFFECTIVENESS

There were no additional costs involved either in the "solar layout" of the site or in the houses themselves. The overall cost of the houses, including the extra insulation measures, was within the limits of the available budget so no extra subsidies were needed.

The occupants are very contented with their houses and there were virtually no complaints about overheating.

COMPARISON WITH CONVENTIONAL DESIGN
(4/5 room south facing house)

The net auxiliary energy used in a similar house of conventional design would be 18 000kWh per year of primary energy.

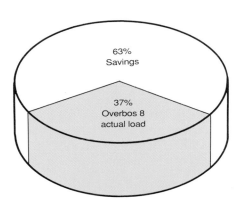

63%
Savings

37%
Overbos 8
actual load

NET MONTHLY SPACE HEATING DEMAND AND SUPPLY
(4/5 room south facing house)

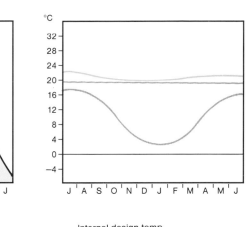

kWh
10³

—— Net sp. htg load
▓ Auxiliary energy
░ Solar energy

MONTHLY AVERAGE TEMPERATURES
(4/5 room south facing house)

°C

—— Internal design temp.
—— Internal temp.
—— External temp.

CONTRIBUTIONS TO ANNUAL SPACE HEATING DEMAND
(4/5 room south facing house)

The gross heating load for this house was 14 150kWh per year of primary energy.

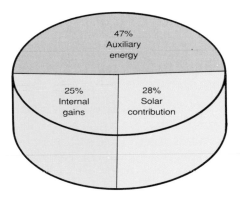

47%
Auxiliary
energy

25%
Internal
gains

28%
Solar
contribution

AUXILIARY FUEL USED ANNUALLY
(4/5 room south facing house)

The total primary auxiliary fuel used was 18 390kWh.

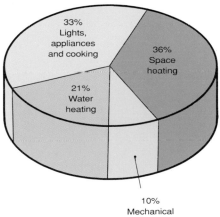

33%
Lights,
appliances
and cooking

36%
Space
heating

21%
Water
heating

10%
Mechanical
ventilation

PROJECT DATA

Building		
4 room dwelling, type 9		
Width	5.17	m
Depth	8.40	m
Volume	290.0	m³
Floor area	98.0	m²
Roof area (incl windows)	72.0	m²
External wall area (incl windows)	44.0	m²
Windows: total	12.7	m²
south	10.6	m²
north	2.1	m²
Thermal Characteristics		
U Value roof	0.26	W/m²K
floor	0.29	W/m²K
external walls	0.27	W/m²K
windows: kitchen & living room	1.3	W/m²K
other windows	3.1	W/m²K
Global heat loss coefficient	Not known	
Infiltration rate (incl HVAC)	0.7	ach
of which natural ventilation	0.3	ach

Infiltration rate (50 Pa)	3.1-3.8	ach
External design temperature	-10	°C
Heated floor area	83.0	m²
Heated volume	240.0	m³
Net heat load	79.0	kWh/m²
Site and Climate		
Altitude	-4	m
Latitude	52	°N
Longtitude	4	°E
Average ambient temp: annual	9.4	°C
Jan	2.3	°C
July	16.6	°C
Degree days (base 18.3°C)	3140	days
Global irradiation on horizontal	1167	kWh/m²
Sunshine hours	1549	hrs/yr
Costs (1988)		
Total per house	99 500 Dfl	42 785 ECU
Solar cost	0	
Extra Insulation	2 500 Dfl	1 075 ECU

CARRIGEEN PARK CREDITS

Client
Clonmel Corporation
Town Hall
Clonmel
Co. Tipperary

Architects
Delany MacVeigh and Pike
Owenstown House
Fosters Avenue
Blackrock
Co. Dublin

Energy Consultant
J. Owen Lewis
13, Mount Merrion Avenue
Blackrock
Co. Dublin

Building Contractor
Hally and Sons Ltd
Ardfinnan
Co. Waterford

Monitoring Organisation
Michael Finn
An Foras Forbartha
St Martin's House
Waterloo Road
Dublin 4

Funding Support
Directorate General XVII
Commission of the European Communities
Wetstraat 200
1049 Brussels
Belgium

Department of Energy
25 Clare Street
Dublin 1

Commission of the European Communities

● Large estate includes standard houses, highly insulated houses and passive solar houses also with high insulation levels.

● The 22 solar houses have 71% of the glazing on the south facade and incorporate two-storey sunspaces.

● Measured solar contributions average only 20%, compared to predicted values of 31%.

● High occupant satisfaction is demonstrated by lower occupant turnover.

CARRIGEEN PARK

CLONMEL
IRELAND

Project Background

The dominant feature of the south facades is the carefully designed sunspaces.

The design of the project was based on an entry which won joint second prize in the first CEC Passive Solar Competition in 1980. Clonmel Corporation commissioned the architects to develop the design to provide houses suitable for their own building programme.

The whole scheme comprises 63 three bedroomed houses, of which 22 are of standard design and construction, 19 are highly insulated and 22 are built with high standards of insulation, larger south facing windows and two-storey sunspaces. The estate was completed in 1984.

OBJECTIVES

● To develop an energy conscious house type, which could be used for the public housing programme, using passive solar techniques together with sophisticated conservation methods.

● To demonstrate the possible energy savings at National and European Community levels.

● To demonstrate how these house designs could be used in a medium density housing estate to create a good environment.

● To identify by monitoring the features which were most successful, and to establish the cost of these features and the likely pay-back periods, with a view to incorporation in future schemes.

ENERGY SAVING FEATURES

● High levels of insulation in walls and roofs are combined with a square house plan to minimise heat loss.

● The house terraces are generally along an east/west axis, with main living rooms located on the south side having large windows.

● Two-storey sunspaces are provided with openings onto the two living rooms and two of the bedrooms.

SITE AND CLIMATE

The 3.5ha site is part of development land owned by Clonmel Corporation at Carrigeen Park, in the south east of Ireland. The site is on a south facing slope (with a fall of about 1 in 20), sheltered to the north by a hill, and to the east by an existing wood. The prevailing winds are from the south-west, with cold easterly winds common in winter.

Average temperatures increase from 4ºC in January to 14.5ºC in July, with 3277 degree days per year (18.3ºC base).

Passive solar houses

Design Details

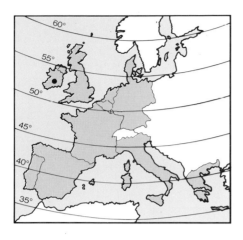

CLIMATE (Birr)

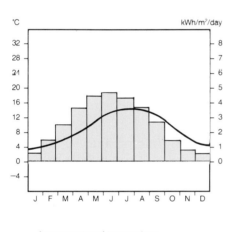

— Average external temperature

☐ Solar Radiation on a horizontal plane

CONCLUSIONS

In the solar houses, the solar contribution to the gross space heating load was 20%. Overall the passive solar houses were estimated to save 38% of the auxiliary fuel heating requirements of houses built to conventional standards. However, fuel bills in the solar houses were no lower than in the highly insulated houses.

The general level of occupant satisfaction with all three house types was very high. In addition, the householders in the passive solar houses considered the sunspaces to be worthwhile extensions to their houses.

PLANNING

The 63 houses are laid out mostly in east/west terraces which combine the advantages of an economical layout and maximised solar gain, whilst achieving fine views from all the houses. The density of the project is 24 houses per hectare.

The house types are developed from the standard "metric envelope" plans used on all local authority housing in Ireland.

CONSTRUCTION

The solar houses are constructed from 100mm concrete blocks with 100mm cavities fully filled with glass fibre insulation. The external face is cement rendered. The walls between the sunspaces and the living rooms are 215mm solid brickwork, to act as heat stores. The ground floors are solid concrete with 50mm of expanded polystyrene insulation. In the sunspaces 50mm of perimeter insulation is provided around the slabs. The roofs are insulated with 150mm of insulation under concrete roof tiles. The

windows are all double glazed in hardwood frames with draughtstripping, while the sunspaces are single glazed, again constructed in hardwood.

The standard houses incorporate the mandatory minimum standards of construction and insulation for houses permitted by the Department of the Environment. Single glazing in softwood frames with no draughtstripping, 40mm glass fibre cavity insulation, 100mm glass fibre roof insulation and 25mm of expanded polystyrene perimeter insulation, have been used. The highly insulated houses have the same insulation standards as the passive solar houses.

PASSIVE SOLAR DESIGN

The houses are arranged in terraces running east/west with living and dining rooms and two of the three bedrooms located on the south sides. Entrance halls and stairs cover a large proportion of the north sides. 71% of the glazing is on the south facade and double glazing is used throughout.

Only a quarter of the glazing is on the north side.

Design Details

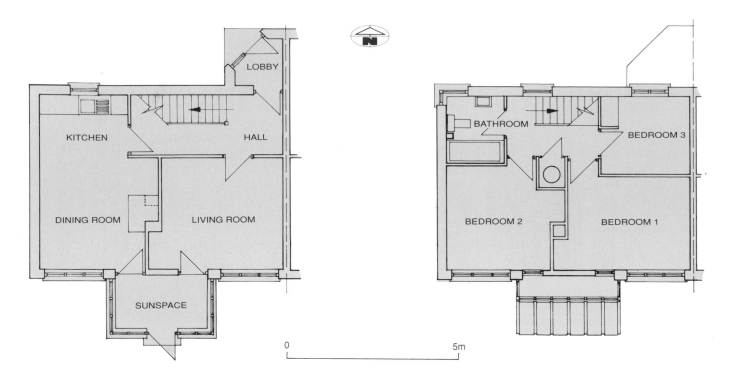

KITCHEN

LOBBY

HALL

DINING ROOM

LIVING ROOM

SUNSPACE

GROUND FLOOR PLAN

BATHROOM

BEDROOM 3

BEDROOM 2

BEDROOM 1

FIRST FLOOR PLAN

0   5m

The two-storey, single glazed sunspaces are constructed in hardwood and attached at the centre of the south facades. In each house, both the living and dining rooms have doors opening directly onto the sunspace and the two adjoining bedrooms on the first floor have windows opening onto the sunspace. The sunspaces reduce from 2m wide on the ground floor to 0.5m on the first floor. The roofs above the first floor sections of the sunspaces are opaque continuations of the main roof, and shade both the sunspaces and large south facing windows of the houses. The glazed sloping roofs above the ground floor sections of the sunspaces are provided with roller blinds for summer shading. Opening windows are provided at the sides of the sunspaces at high and low levels. The solid floors (with under slab insulation) and the solid walls between the sunspaces and the rooms provide thermal storage.

AUXILIARY HEATING SYSTEMS

A gas-fired wet central heating system, incorporating an 8.9kW balanced flue boiler, is installed in all three house types. Temperature control in the ground floor rooms is by thermostatic radiator valves. A roomstat/timeswitch linked to a motorised zone valve controls heating of upstairs rooms, and a second valve controls domestic water heating. These systems have been used for space heating since natural gas

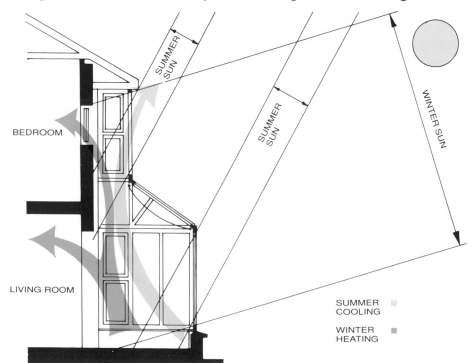

BEDROOM

LIVING ROOM

SUMMER SUN

SUMMER SUN

SUMMER SUN

WINTER SUN

SUMMER COOLING

WINTER HEATING

SECTION THROUGH SUNSPACE

Performance Evaluation

became available in the area, late in 1987. Prior to this, space heating was from a single solid fuel stove located in the kitchen/dining room, with an electric immersion heater providing the hot water.

OPERATING MODES AND CONTROLS

In the heating season, the low winter sun enters the houses directly through the south facing windows and through the sunspaces. The windows and doors onto the sunspaces can be opened to allow the warm air from the sunspaces into the houses. Sun falling onto the solid walls at the back of the sunspaces warms the houses later in the day. In summer, the opaque sunspace roofs and the overhanging main house roofs, shield the upper windows from direct sun. The roller blinds can be drawn over the central roofs of the sunspaces to shield both the sunspaces and the rooms behind. The sunspaces are ventilated by opening the low and high level windows. All control of these operations is manual.

Satisfaction with the houses was demonstrated by a user survey four years after completion, showing that 90% of tenants were still the original occupants.

MONITORING

Monitoring of the three house types with gas central heating was carried out from November 1987 to July 1988. Natural gas and electricity consumptions were measured for all houses, and internal temperatures were measured in two thirds of the houses. Ambient air temperatures, temperatures in the sunspaces, and temperature gradients across the solid sunspace walls were also measured. Thermal performance tests were carried out on the natural gas boiler and the solid fuel boiler in a separate pair of test houses.

Over the period January 1984 to summer 1985 solid fuel use in the kitchen/dining room stoves was measured for all houses, and temperature measurements were carried out in 12 houses. Pressurisation tests were conducted to assess air change rates, and some site assessment of window opening times was made.

USER RESPONSE

Based on a survey carried out some months after occupation (with the solid fuel heating in use), the general level of satisfaction with all three house types was found to be very high. Only three occupants expressed a general dissatisfaction with the houses. Comfort levels in winter and in summer were

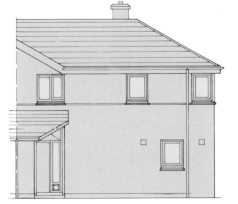

SOUTH ELEVATION

NORTH ELEVATION

Performance Evaluation

All the householders considered the sunspaces to be a worthwhile addition.

PERFORMANCE OF PASSIVE SOLAR DESIGN

The monitoring which took place with the gas fired central heating systems in use was the most informative. Compared to the control houses on site, the Carrigeen Park solar houses save 22% of the auxiliary contribution to the gross space heating load. However, the control houses had a lower energy consumption than predicted, probably due to reduced infiltration rates. Therefore, when compared to a theoretical conventional design, the solar houses show a better performance and save 38% of the auxiliary energy required for space heating.

A 20% solar contribution to the gross space heating load was achieved, though on average, the passive solar houses used the same amount of fuel for auxiliary heating as the well insulated houses.

Calculated solar contributions to the gross space heating load, based on standard weather data, gave 31% for the solar houses compared to 21% for the well insulated houses and 18% for the standard houses. The discrepancy between the measured and theoretical results is thought to be due in part to a lack of understanding and thus inefficient use of the heating systems, and to non-optimal operation of the sunspace openings. Also the calculations assumed light net curtains at all windows and the lower actual gains may well be due to heavier curtains being used.

Due to a number of difficulties with the earlier monitoring of the houses using the solid fuel heating systems, this

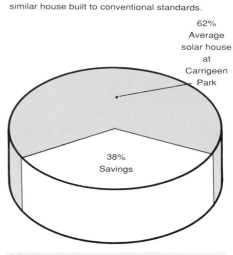

62% Average solar house at Carrigeen Park

38% Savings

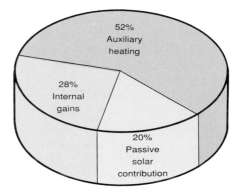

52% Auxiliary heating

28% Internal gains

20% Passive solar contribution

queried specifically in the survey, as were any perceived advantages and disadvantages of the sunspaces.

All the householders in the passive solar houses considered the sunspace a worthwhile addition to the houses. Just over half noted that the sunspace made the house warmer, and when asked specifically about this point the figure rose to just over three quarters. Other advantages noted were the use for clothes drying, the additional space provided, draught reduction and a place for the cultivation of indoor plants.

A second survey, carried out in May 1988 when the gas heating had been installed, also indicated a high level of satisfaction with the three house types. In particular there was a significant increase in the degree of satisfaction with house temperatures in winter.

analysis of the auxiliary fuel consumptions of the three different house types was inconclusive.

However the monitoring of the sunspace temperatures showed that average monthly temperatures were 1°C to 2°C higher than calculated, other than in April and May, indicating that solar gains in the sunspaces were greater than calculated.

Measurements of the wall temperatures between the sunspace and the house, show that net energy transfers through the walls are extremely small, less than 1kWh per day. The measurements also show that there was an outward energy flow from the house to the sunspace between November

COST OF BUILDING AND SOLAR ON COST

The total cost of building one solar house was IR £25 580 in 1986.

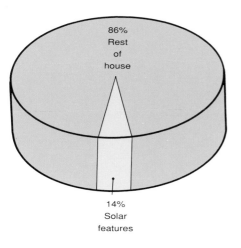

86% Rest of house

14% Solar features

NET MONTYLY SPACE HEATING DEMAND AND SUPPLY

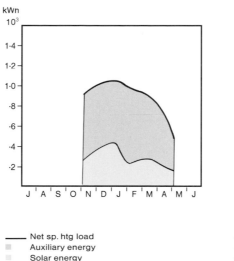

kWn

J A S O N D J F M A M J

— Net sp. htg load
▪ Auxiliary energy
▪ Solar energy

MONTHLY AVERAGE TEMPERATURES

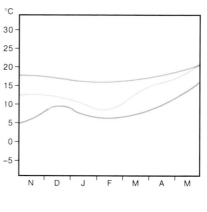

°C

N D J F M A M

— Internal temp.
— Sunspace temp.
— External temp.

and February and an inward flow at all other times of the year.

COST EFFECTIVENESS

The extra cost of the solar features was IR £3 120 per house or an on-cost of 14% compared to the well insulated house. However the additional elements of passive solar design employed in the solar houses did not result in any significant increased savings in average fuel bills. The measured gas consumption in both the well insulated and passive solar houses was 22% less than that for the standard houses.The glazed sunspaces of the passive solar houses did however provide the householders with the additional benefit of an extra living space. The perceived benefit of the sunspace may be reflected in the pattern of change of tenancy among the three house types. For the passive solar houses 90% of householders surveyed in 1988 had occupied their houses since construction, which compared with 52% and 65% for the standard and well insulated houses respectively.

The 'solar ' layout of the site also gave all the houses good views from the south-facing windows.

PROJECT DATA

Passive Solar House: End Terrace				Mean U value	0.66	W/m²K
Volume	209	m³		Global heat loss coefficient	175.9	W/K
Floor area	81.6	m²		Infiltration rate	1.0	ach
Roof area	40.8	m²		External design temp	-1.0	°C
External wall area	68.8	m²		Heated floor area	81.6	m²
Windows: total area	15.8	m²		Heated volume	209	m³
south	11.1	m²	71%	Net heat load	82.6	kWh/m²
north	4.1	m²	26%			
				Site and Climate		
Sunspace				Altitude	40	m
Volume	12.4	m³		Latitude	52° 30' N	
Floor area	4.3	m²		Longitude	7° 42' W	
Glass area	25.1	m²		Average ambient temp:		
Solid wall area	8.7	m²		Jan	4.0	°C
				July	14.5	°C
Thermal Characteristics				Degree days (base 18.3°C)	3277	days
U value: roof	0.23	W/m²K		Global irradiation on horiz	1010.0	kWh/m²
floor	0.35	W/m²K		Sunshine hours	1302	hr/yr
external walls	0.31	W/m²K				
windows	2.9	W/m²K		**Costs (Sept 1986)**		
sunspace glazing	4.7	W/m²K		Building:	IR £25 580	ECU 34 932
				Solar features:	IR £3 120	ECU 4 261

PEDRAJAS DE SAN ESTEBAN CREDITS

Clients
Junta de Castilla y León (Valladolid)
D.G Vivienda y Arquitectura
Francisco Suárez, 4
Valladolid

Ministerio de Obras
Públicas y Urbanismo
D.G de Arquitectura y Vivienda
Castellana, 67
28046 Madrid

Architects
Isaac Crespo
Gabilondo, 28, 10º 1
Valladolid

Fernando Bravo
Ramos Carrion, 11
28002 Madrid

Energy Consultants
R. Serra
E.T.S Arquitectura de Barcelona UPC
Diagonal, 649
08028 Barcelona

R. San José
Facultad de Ciencias
Universidad de Valladolid
Prado de la Magdalena s/n
47005 Valladolid

Consultant
S. Vega
E.T.S Arquitectura de Valladolid
Universidad de Valladolid
Cta. Salamanca s/n (Huerta del Rey)
47014 Valladolid

Monitoring Organisation
IER/CIEMAT
Avda. Complutense 22
28040 Madrid

Dpt de Construcciones Arquitectónicas y
Dpt de Fisica Aplicada III
Universidad de Valladolid

Funding
IER/CIEMAT

Commission of the European Communities

PEDRAJAS DE SAN ESTEBAN

VALLADOLID
SPAIN

● Public sector housing scheme, consisting of 60 apartments in three blocks, designed with extensive passive solar features.

● Each apartment has a large sunspace directly connected to the south-facing rooms, a thermal storage wall behind the sunspace and an air-heating solar panel giving heat to the north-facing bedroom.

● 68% solar contribution to the gross space heating load, results in a payback period of only 3 to 4 years.

Project Background

The bottom part of the sunspace glazing is in wired glass for safety reasons. There are openings in the upper part to provide ventilation.

This project consists of three blocks of flats, sixty in total, built according to passive solar principles for the Direccion General de Arquitectura y Vivienda (MOPU, Madrid) and the Junta de Castilla y León (Valladolid). Completed in 1987, the flats were monitored from May 1987 for 12 months.

OBJECTIVES

The client wanted three blocks of flats, arranged around a communal area. The aim was to build low cost housing, utilising passive solar design techniques, to give significant energy cost savings for the lowest possible capital investment, in a typical rural area with a continental climate. Construction and maintenance costs had to be kept to a minimum as the housing was for the public sector. Despite this, due to the climate, it was necessary to install an auxiliary heating system in each flat.

ENERGY SAVING FEATURES

Each flat incorporates the following energy saving measures:

● an internal layout which ensures that the living room and two bedrooms face south, with service areas to the north;

● most glazing located on the south side with only small openings on the north side;

● a sunspace directly connected to the three south-facing rooms;

● a mass wall to the rear of the sunspace, which stores solar gains;

● an air-heating solar panel, fan and duct system which provides warm air to the northern bedroom;

● a compact shape combined with a highly insulated structure, to minimise heat losses.

SITE AND CLIMATE

The project is located in the village of Pedrajas de San Esteban, which has just over 3 000 inhabitants. Valladolid, which is the capital of the region with 400 000 inhabitants, is 40km away. The 2 000m^2 site is on the outskirts of the village. It has a favourable orientation and is open to the south, although the other three sides are bounded by roads. To the west there is a

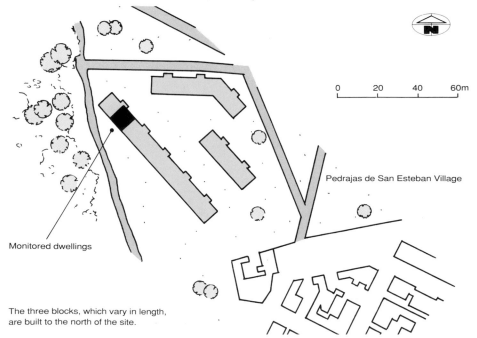

Monitored dwellings

The three blocks, which vary in length, are built to the north of the site.

Pedrajas de San Esteban Village

0   20   40   60m

small pine forest, and to the east is the main village. Pedrajas de San Esteban is 850m above sea level and experiences a continental climate with cold, dry winters and hot summers. The average temperature in January is 3.3°C, and in July it is 21.3°C.

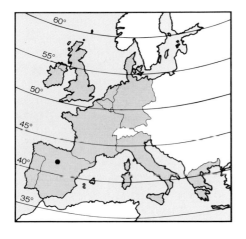

CLIMATE (Valladolid)

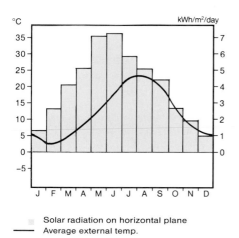

Solar radiation on horizontal plane
— Average external temp.

There are 2 333 degree days per year (18°C base). Fog is relatively common and reduces the available direct solar radiation.

CONCLUSIONS

Passive solar design principles have been well applied to this estate at Pedrajas de San Esteban. There is a 68% solar contribution to the gross space heating load (92% to the net space heating load) which

gives a 3 to 4 year payback on the cost of the solar measures. Although the occupants experienced some summer overheating in their dwellings, generally the levels of both summer and winter comfort were good.

PLANNING

The three blocks, which vary in length, are built to the north of the site. Two of them face north-east/south-west, and the third block turns a corner with part of it facing due north/south and the other part facing north-east/south-west. Between the blocks there is a communal courtyard/playground area.

DESIGN DETAILS

Each block is a three-storey terrace (9m high), with two apartments on each floor. Access is from a central stairway which is also an axis of symmetry.
The general plan for the flats is very compact. To the south of each flat are the living/dining room and two bedrooms. The bathroom is in the middle, and to the north are the kitchen, a third bedroom and the stairs.

CONSTRUCTION

The flats are highly insulated to minimise heat losses. External walls are a double skin of 120mm brick incorporating 100mm of expanded polystyrene insulation, with an internal plaster finish.
The north wall of the north-facing bedroom in each flat forms part of the convective loop from the air-heating solar panel and so is constructed with an additional 50mm central cavity. The wall to the rear of the sunspace is constructed from 420mm solid brick to provide thermal storage of solar gains.
The ground floor slab is insulated with 100mm of expanded polystyrene. Intermediate floors are constructed from 250mm reinforced concrete covered with ceramic tiles, which provide further thermal storage.
The main roof is pitched and insulated with 150mm of fibreglass in the roof space. Above the stairwell, there is a flat roof.
All windows are timber framed, single glazed units.

View of one of the blocks from the communal play area. The projections on the north side house the staircases and drying rooms.

Design Details

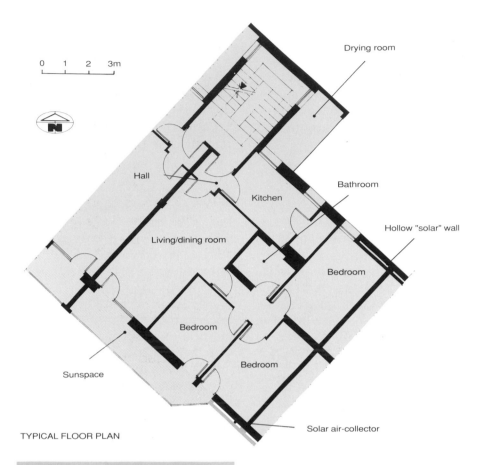

0 1 2 3m

Drying room

Hall

Kitchen

Bathroom

Hollow "solar" wall

Living/dining room

Bedroom

Bedroom

Sunspace

Bedroom

Solar air-collector

TYPICAL FLOOR PLAN

PASSIVE SOLAR DESIGN

The internal planning of the flats ensures that principal rooms are on the south-side with service areas and one bedroom to the north. There are only small windows on the north facade.

In addition, each apartment has three different passive solar elements to enable maximum collection and use of solar gains. A single-glazed sunspace is attached to most of the south facade of each flat. The living/dining room and two bedrooms on this side have glazed doors and windows directly onto the sunspace and receive warmed air from it. Each sunspace has a glazed surface of 7.1m^2, a floor area of 6.5m^2 and a volume of 16.3m^3. The lower part of the external glazing is a wired glass parapet for safety reasons. In the upper part of the glazed surface, some of the windows can be opened to provide ventilation. All the

glazing bars are steel.

Behind the sunspace, there is a 17.8m^2 solid brick wall which acts as a thermal store, and transfers solar gains directly to the adjacent rooms. Although it is a continuation of the brick south facade, its solid construction increases the thermal mass.

To provide solar gains to the north-facing bedroom, an air-heating solar collector is also located on the south-facade of each flat, either to the left or to the right of the sunspace as symmetry dictates. By using a thermostatically-controlled fan, the hot air is transferred through a duct to the hollow wall in the bedroom.

The 4m^2 full-height collector is constructed from 60mm polyisocyanurate foam with a black corrugated surface (to allow maximum solar absorption), a cavity and then fully openable glazing. The duct leading from the top of the panel into the flat is made of fibreglass to reduce heat

losses. It passes through the flat at high level and into the cavity in the north wall of the rear bedroom. The hot air then follows a serpentine pattern down to the bottom of the wall, from where it enters the bedroom through a grille. The cycle is completed by air passing through small grilles in the base of the doors, back to the bottom of the panel. A 35W fan, controlled by a temperature sensor located halfway down the solar panel on the inside, forces the warmed air to follow this path. Reverse circulation is prevented by a non-return valve located behind the fan. Wooden shutters fitted on the inside of the glazed doors and windows on the south-facade, provide night-time insulation and summer shading.

High summer temperatures made it necessary to provide a means of venting the solar panels, and to provide shading for the sunspaces. A vent was introduced into each panel and external awnings were fitted to the sunspaces.

The glass covering the solar air-collectors is fully openable.

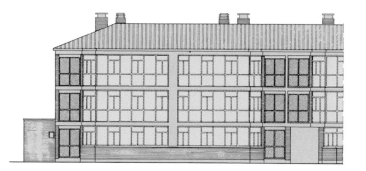

The sunspaces cover most of the south-facade of the building, the remaining area is used for solar air- collectors.

SOUTH WEST ELEVATION

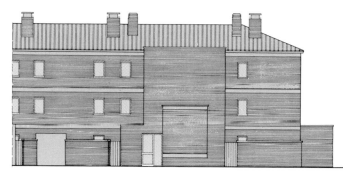

The service areas and staircases are to the north of the dwellings, enabling there to be only few openings on this facade.

NORTH EAST ELEVATION

AUXILIARY HEATING SYSTEM

The auxiliary heating system is a solid fuel boiler which supplies both a wet radiator system and the domestic hot water.

The boiler is fuelled with either wood or fir cones. It is capable of maintaining an internal temperature of 20ºC with a -5ºC external temperature.

OPERATING MODES

In winter, during the day, sun enters the sunspace and the south-facing rooms behind. The wall to the rear of the sunspace collects incident solar radiation and transfers the gains to the adjacent rooms behind. The air in the solar collector heats up until it reaches the thermostat set point, (usually 20ºC - 25ºC) when the fan operates. Air from the adjacent south-facing room is drawn in between the glass and the wall as the hot air passes into the insulated duct and then to the north-facing room. The external vent at the top of the panel remains shut.

At night, heat is radiated to the south-facing rooms from the storage wall behind the sunspace, and to the rear bedroom from the hollow wall which has been warmed up by the hot air from the collector. The non-return valve behind the fan prevents reverse circulation. In addition, wooden shutters may be closed to insulate the south-facing glazing.

In summer, during the day, air is drawn from the north-side of the flat, by the stack effect of the solar collector which has the external vent open to promote ventilation. The thermostat is set to 90ºC so that the air does not reach the set point temperature and therefore none is transferred to the north-facing bedroom.

Shutters are drawn down over the south-facing glazing to reduce solar gains entering the flat. A blind, fitted later, provides shading to the sunspace in summer.

At night, the sunspace windows, those in the south-facade, and the north-facing windows can be opened to allow cross-ventilation.

To avoid condensation problems in these highly insulated flats, positive ventilation is required in winter.

CONTROLS

There are no automatic regulating systems in these buildings, all the controls are manual including those on the auxiliary heating system. The only semi-automatic control operating concerns the fan, which is activated by the temperature sensor inside the air-collector and by a thermostat on the wall of the room behind.

The occupant chooses the thermostat set point between 25ºC and 90ºC.

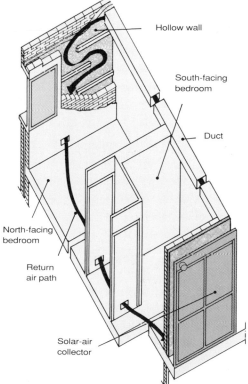

Detail of the forced convective loop which distributes solar heated air to the north-facing bedroom.

Performance Evaluation

MONITORING

The Promotion Department of the Junta de Castilla y León and the Institute of Renewable Energies financed and carried out the monitoring of these blocks.

Two flats in the north/south block were monitored between May 1987 and May 1988. One second floor flat and one ground floor flat were chosen because they represented two extreme cases. A computer program was developed especially to analyse the data. Continuous measurements were taken of: external and internal temperatures; wind speed and direction; internal and external humidities; horizontal global solar radiation; lighting levels; and the heat flux stored in the rear wall of the sunspace. Temperature sensors were located in each of the two south-facing bedrooms, the living room, the sunspace, the kitchen and the corridor, and in the air-heating panel.

In addition, the auxiliary energy used was determined from heat meter readings on the heating circuit and from the standard electricity meter. The results from the second floor flat are presented because the tenants were more typical in their pattern of occupancy.

USER RESPONSE

User surveys were conducted to determine the reaction of the occupants to their homes. On the whole, they are happy with their homes, they often use the sunspaces and some have furnished them. There have been no complaints about the sunspaces being too narrow. In general, how well the occupants have made use of the passive solar features in their homes relates directly to their social and cultural status. Those who both know the whole background to the project and who understand the operation of the manual controls have experienced very good solar performances. Unfortunately, others are not using the solar features 'correctly' to achieve optimal results.

Although improvements could have been made to the systems, they were not done because of the difficulties of explaining procedures to the occupants.

PERFORMANCE OF PASSIVE SOLAR DESIGN

Where controls have been correctly used, both energy and monetary savings have been achieved, together with a good level of comfort.

● The Pedrajas flats used only 32% of the fuel for space heating that would be used by a similar conventionally designed flat including a sunspace.

● Passive solar gains contributed 68% to the gross space heating load.

COMPARISON WITH CONVENTIONAL DESIGN

A similar flat built to a conventional design but also with a sunspace would require 1 313kWh/yr of auxiliary energy for space heating.

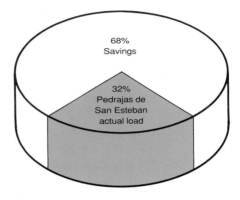

68% Savings

32% Pedrajas de San Esteban actual load

CONTRIBUTION TO ANNUAL SPACE HEATING DEMAND

Solar gains contribute 68% to the annual space heating demand of 6 663kWh per flat.

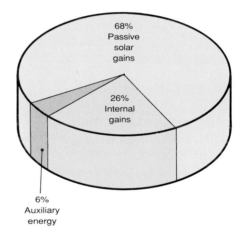

68% Passive solar gains

26% Internal gains

6% Auxiliary energy

● The solar contribution was 208kWh/m² of collector area (sunspace and air collector) hence 92% of the net space heating load was met by the solar gains.

The designers tried to avoid overheating by providing an external vent located in the upper part of the solar collector and by enabling the thermostat governing the fan to be set as high as 90°C. In addition, occupants were advised to attach external vertical blinds to the sunspaces to avoid overheating in summer. Only a few of the occupants did this. No complaints of overheating

COST OF BUILDING AND SOLAR ON-COST

Each flat cost 2.5M Ptas to construct in 1985.

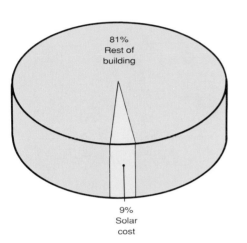

81%
Rest of
building

9%
Solar
cost

NET MONTHLY SPACE HEATING DEMAND AND SUPPLY

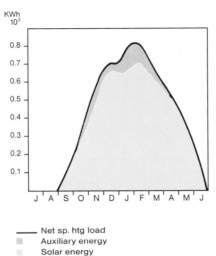

KWh
10³

——— Net sp. htg load
▦ Auxiliary energy
▦ Solar energy

MONTHLY AVERAGE TEMPERATURES

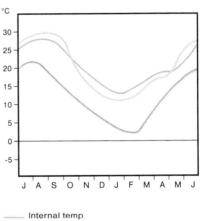

°C

——— Internal temp.
——— Sunspace temp.
——— External temp.

have been received although in the monitored flats temperatures as high as 30°C were recorded in the summer. Subsequently, blinds were fitted to each sunspace.

COST EFFECTIVENESS

The extra costs compared to conventionally designed dwellings are due to:

● increased insulation in the walls, roof and floor slab;

● an increased glazed area for the sunspaces (in a conventional design the sunspaces would have been smaller);

● the addition of wooden shutters to south-facing windows;

● the incorporation of air-heating solar panels.

In 1985, these additional costs amounted to 220 000Ptas per apartment, or an extra 9% on to the total cost.
The additional cost will be repaid within 3 or 4 years by the savings in auxiliary fuel use.

North-facing bedroom showing grille through which solar-heated air enters the room.

PROJECT DATA

Individual flat

Volume	164.5	m³
Floor area	64.2	m²
Roof area	64.2	m²
External Wall area	45	m²
Windows: Total area	21.8	m²
South (inc sunspace)	17.8	m²
Others	4	m²

Thermal Characteristics

U value: Roof	0.17	W/m²K
Floor	0.2	W/m²K
External walls	0.39	W/m²K
Windows	3.74	W/m²K
Global heat loss coefficient	101.5	W/K
Infiltration rate	0.4	ac/h
External design temp	-4	°C
Heated floor area	64.2	m²
Heated volume area	164.5	m³
Net heat load	77	kWh/m²

Site and Climate

Altitude	700	m
Latitude	41.3	°N
Longtitude	4.6	°E
Average ambient temp: Jan	3.3	°C
July	21.3	°C
Degree days (18°Cbase)	2333	days
Global irradiation on horiz	1443	kWh/m²
Sunshine hours	2490	hr/yr

Cost (1985 prices) (Per unit)

Building	2.5 M Ptas	18 000 ECU
Solar features	0.22M Ptas	1 630 ECU
Extra wall insulation	1.3 M Ptas	960 ECU

CHRISTOPHER TAYLOR COURT CREDITS

Client
Bournville Village Trust
Estate Office
Oak Tree Lane
Birmingham B30 1UB

Architect
David Clarke Associates
(incorporating Ralph Lebens Associates)
4 Tottenham Mews
London W1P 9PJ

Solar Energy Consultant
The Franklin Company Consultants Ltd
192 Franklin Road
Birmingham   B30 2HE

Building Contractors
Lovell Construction (Midland) Ltd
Cheshire House
Knowle
Solihull
West Midlands   B93 OLL

Consulting Engineers
Royston Jones Associates
Mews Office
The Drive
Enville
Nr. Stourbridge

Electrical Contractors
MGI Electrical Ltd
Unit 21 Monmer Close
Stringes Lane
Willenhall
W.Midlands WV13 1JR

Mechanical Contractors
E E Horton (Heating) Ltd
8 Stoneleigh House
Selcroft Avenue
Harborne
Birmingham B32

Monitoring Organisation
The Franklin Company Consultants Ltd

Funding Support
Housing Corporation   Bournville Village Trust
West Midlands Office
Norwich Union House
Waterloo Road
Wolverhampton

Directorate General XVII
Commission of the European Communities (CEC)
Wetstraat 200
1049 Brussels
Belgium

Commission of the European Communities

● Sheltered housing scheme for the mobile elderly incorporates passive solar design.

CHRISTOPHER TAYLOR COURT
BOURNVILLE
UNITED KINGDOM

● E-shaped layout maximises solar gain to the flats, allows natural daylighting in all parts of the building and provides two private courtyards.

● Mass wall systems and direct gain windows contribute to a saving of 51% of the auxiliary space heating load when compared to a conventional design.

Project Background

Christopher Taylor Court is a sheltered housing scheme comprising 42 flats and shared facilities for the mobile elderly, situated in Bournville Solar Village, near Birmingham. The land is owned by Bournville Village Trust who have built housing, shopping and leisure facilities in this area for almost 100 years.

Bournville Solar Village is made up of seven sites where all the buildings incorporate low energy and passive solar techniques to a greater or lesser degree. Christopher Taylor Court and the Parklands Estate of simple direct gain houses are both on the same site, and they formed a joint CEC demonstration scheme. The sheltered housing was monitored for two years starting in 1986.

OBJECTIVES

The brief for the sheltered housing scheme required 42 housing units for elderly people, a warden's house, a common room, a guest suite and a small laundry. Six of the flats are especially designed for wheel-chair users with modified kitchens and bathrooms.

The Housing Corporation who funded the project require certain standards for this type of sheltered housing: all flats must be accessible without the use of stairs; the access to all flats must be enclosed and heated to 16°C; and the flats must be constantly heated to 21°C. The challenge of the scheme was to achieve all these requirements whilst at the same time maximising solar gain and the conservation of energy, respecting the character of Bournville through the design of the building, and providing sheltered external courtyards for use by the residents.

Christopher Taylor Court is laid out to orient most of the flats north/south and to produce attractive communal gardens.

ENERGY SAVING FEATURES

● The building is designed so that most of the flats are located in east/west terraces, with the dwellings to the south insulated by corridors to the north.

● All corridors are daylit, reducing electrical energy for lighting.

● Almost every flat has a large single glazed mass wall and windows and a glazed door on the south facade to exploit passive solar gains and natural ventilation.

● The highly insulated structure, with double glazed and draughtstripped windows, reduces heat losses.

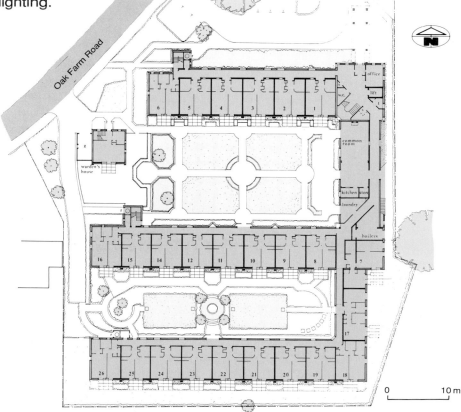

The building takes an E-shape, with flats in three east/west wings and shared facilities in the spine.

Design Details

● Dual purpose internal sliding shutters reduce heat transfer from the mass wall to the room in summer, and insulate the glazing and expose the mass wall in winter.

● An energy management system controls the central heating to ensure maximum use of solar gains.

SITE AND CLIMATE

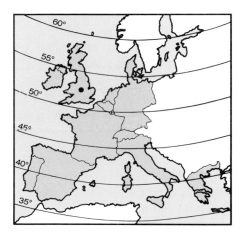

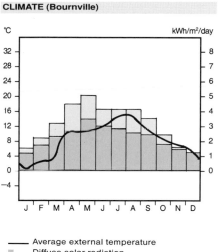

— Average external temperature
■ Diffuse solar radiation
□ Direct solar radiation

The Solar Village at Rowheath is located on the south-east edge of the Bournville Village Trust estates which are themselves situated in the Bournville/Kings Norton area to the south of Birmingham, in the West Midlands. The nearly flat site is in a pleasant area with a park and lake close by.

The windows in the north-facing corridors admit light and provide pleasant views of the courtyard.

Adjacent to Christopher Taylor Court there is a 17th Century timbered barn which has been converted into apartments. To the west, on the same site, is the Parklands development of shared ownership passive solar houses.

The climate experienced here is typical for England and therefore generally damp, with mild winters and cool summers. The average monthly temperature in January is 3.3°C and in July 16°C, July being the sunniest month of the year. The mean windspeed on the site is less than 4m/s.

PLANNING

The building is laid out in two open-ended courtyards on a site that slopes gently down to the north, but which still has a good solar exposure.

Most of the flats are in the three south-facing wings, of which two are two-storey and one is single-storey. The corridors to the north act as buffer spaces to the flats and provide views onto the courtyards or the road at the front. The kitchens are located in the centre but receive daylighting from the corridors, and have views through to the outside.

The wings are linked by a north-south spine which houses the entrance, warden's office, common room, laundry and boiler room on the ground floor, and a guest suite and galleried sitting area on the first floor.

CONSTRUCTION

The south-facing walls are mass walls constructed to have a large thermal capacity. Each one consists of a single sheet of glass, a cavity, a selective surface, 12mm render, 200mm dense concrete blocks and an internal 12mm dense plaster skin.

Other external walls are constructed from 105mm brick, 100mm fibreglass fully filled cavity, 100mm dense concrete block and 12mm dense plaster finish. Party walls are 200mm dense concrete block.

The floors are formed from a 200mm concrete slab with a floating floor on top, and the ground floor is insulated with 50mm of expanded vermiculite insulation beneath the chipboard floor covering. 200mm of fibreglass insulation is laid in the roof space and the roof is finished with concrete tiles.

Design Details

Mass walls increase the use of solar gains, and glazed doors allow the flats to be extended onto the patios and balconies in summer.

All the windows are double-glazed and draughtstripped, and trickle vents have been fitted into the frames to ensure adequate ventilation.

PASSIVE SOLAR DESIGN

The main passive solar features of the building are the layout and internal planning and the mass wall systems. Extensive use of direct gain windows was considered unsuitable in this design because elderly people are sensitive to glare. However, the inclusion of mass walls still necessitated a building where the majority of flats would face south, and hence an E-shaped layout was chosen, with three wings having a north-south orientation. All the old people's flats are on the south-side of the three east-west wings, with enclosed access corridors to the north. The southern-most wing is single storey, reducing the distance required between this block and the next to minimise shading in winter. The courtyard between these two blocks is narrower and is stepped in section to take account of the gentle north-facing slope of the site. Internally, the living room and bedroom are to the south, with the hall, kitchen and bathroom to the north. A glazed door allows the living space to be extended onto the patio or balcony in the summer and allows good ventilation. The simple mass wall is 200mm thick with an internal sliding shutter. Computer simulations of the mass wall predicted energy saving performances very similar to more complex passive systems. The selective surface for the wall was the only innovative component used. A nickel foil with adhesive coating was chosen, which has perforations to allow trapped vapour to escape. The foil is stuck like wallpaper on to a wall coated with sprayed silicone seal. It was necessary to apply cement render to the blockwork to provide a smooth enough surface to which to adhere the foil.

On the first floor, the mass walls are full-height but on the ground floor there is a brick finish over the bottom 500mm of the wall.

The internal sliding shutter behind the mass wall consists

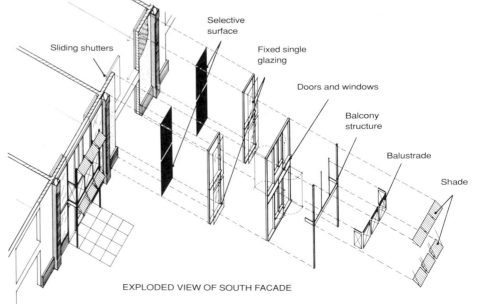

Selective surface

Fixed single glazing

Sliding shutters

Doors and windows

Balcony structure

Balustrade

Shade

EXPLODED VIEW OF SOUTH FACADE

of a wooden panel suspended on free running sliding door gear, and is no more difficult to move than a normal door. Seasonally operated external shading was fitted to reduce solar gains through the glazing in summer and the overhanging roof also shades the first floor windows and doors. Relief vents in the mass walls reduce peak summer temperatures.
The warden's house is a detached house to the west of the site, and it also has mass walls as part of the south facade.

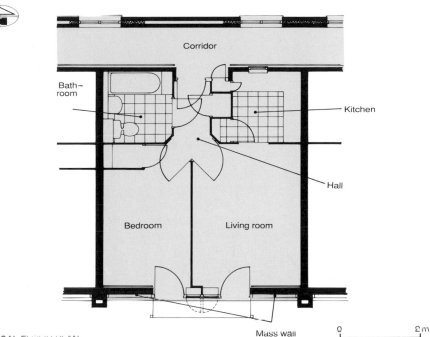

TYPICAL FLOOR PLAN

AUXILIARY HEATING SYSTEMS

Christopher Taylor Court has a hybrid heating system: the gas-fired central heating to all flats, service areas and communal rooms is supplemented by solar heating from the south-facing mass walls in the flats. The centrally located gas-fired boilers have insulated distribution circuits to the flats, branches to each flat being controlled by room thermostats within the flats which operate motorised valves. Low thermal capacity radiators were installed in the flats so that the systems would have a quick response and

could therefore make better use of passive solar and internal gains. Flow temperatures from the boilers are modulated in relation to external air temperatures and to levels of solar radiation. Hot water is not provided centrally because of the inefficiency which would result, especially in summer. The laundry is situated across the corridor from the boiler room, and the hot water supply to it can be heated either by gas or electricity. Other areas and the individual flats make use of off-peak electric water heaters.

OPERATING MODES AND CONTROLS

In autumn and winter, the timber external shades hinge back either under eaves or under the balcony where they are held in place by timber battens. In this position they allow unrestricted solar access to the south facades. Solar gains enter the flats through the glazed doors and windows, and also strike the mass walls, where they are stored. At night, the internal shutters are slid over the glazing providing some insulation to the double glazed units, increasing security and allowing heat to radiate from the mass wall.
In the spring, the external shades are positioned over the glazing, held open on simple metal struts. They then remain open until the autumn. Opening the external doors ensures good ventilation within the flats. Vents in the glazed surface of the mass walls reduce the peak temperatures and leaving the shutters over the internal face of the wall reduces radiation to the room. There are no passive solar controls as such, the

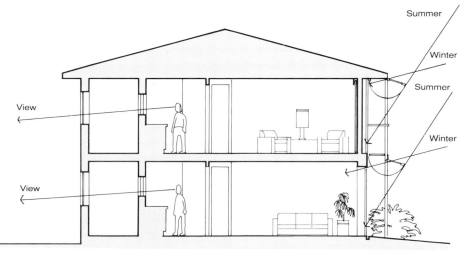

In the winter, the shades are retracted and do not obstruct solar gains, whilst in summer together with the overhanging roof they reduce solar gains to the flats.

Performance Evaluation

The dual purpose internal sliding shutter behind the mass wall is a simple wooden panel on runners.

occupants simply slide the shutter across according to the time of day and the season and maintenance staff adjust the position of the external shades twice a year.

MONITORING

The energy performance of the building was monitored for two years from 1986, as part of a joint CEC scheme involving the Parklands Estate as well. In addition to the monthly reading of electricity and gas meters, individual flats were also selected for more detailed monitoring. Unfortunately, most of the data from individual flats were corrupted because the cables were insufficiently screened. It would have been too costly and far too time-consuming to correct this fault and hence statistical and mathematical methods have been used to extract reasonable information from the data.

USER RESPONSE

Another aspect of the monitoring was a user survey in which the residents were asked about heating in the building, use of the movable insulation, etc.

The general feedback from the occupants was very good: they were very satisfied with the accommodation, which in all cases was warmer and more comfortable than where they had previously lived.

More specifically, on occasions many found their flats too warm, particularly those on the upper floor. 35% of residents did not use the internal sliding shutters at all, again more of these were on the upper floor. Those who already suffered from overheating were naturally disinclined to use them. Few understood the purpose of the sliding shutter as moveable insulation, although the security aspects and the substitution for curtaining it could provide were appreciated by some. Others, however, disliked the feeling of being "boxed in".

Most people liked the layout of the building because of the security it offered. The communal facilities, the individual privacy and the access to the courtyard gardens, were all appreciated.

PERFORMANCE OF PASSIVE SOLAR DESIGN

Compared to the same building built to current Building Regulation standards and with the same heating regime, Christopher Taylor Court saves 51% of the auxiliary space heating demand due to high insulation standards and passive solar design. However, if the building had followed the general pattern for sheltered housing it would have had an east-west orientation, with flats either side of corridors, and would have generally been a more compact shape with a lower energy consumption, thus reducing the above savings. The solar contribution to the gross space heating load is 10.5%. Whilst this would be considered to be very low for family housing, for sheltered housing it is quite acceptable representing 49 600kWh/yr. The average internal temperature within the flats is very high at almost 23°C (the design temperature was 21°C) and 24 hour heating is required by the occupants.

In July and August the solar contributions were 29% and 25% respectively, even though the solar radiation that year

In the spring the external shades are fixed into position with simple metal struts.

was approximately 10% less than the historical average. Whilst the shape of the building was determined primarily to provide a south-facing aspect to all the permanently occupied flats, it has been enormously successful in terms of the security, privacy and communality it provides the occupants.

The occupants did not all use the internal sliding shutters and they certainly did not understand their purpose. This reduced the effectiveness of the mass walls. However, the application of the selective coating to form the mass walls was carried out successfully. The movable external shading blocked out too much light because it was operated on a seasonal basis, and it will now probably remain in the winter position. However, this does not generally lead to serious overheating.

The cost of heating is included in the rent payments and hence occupants are not conscious of the need to be efficient in their energy use. Whilst good control strategies were employed in the flats, the communal areas are not adequately controlled. Hence ventilation is used as a means to achieve comfort conditions rather than thermostatic control.

COST EFFECTIVENESS

The whole building cost £1 003 000 to construct in 1986 including extra costs of £66 690 for the passive solar features, insulation measures, controls etc. The annual energy saving is 353 650kWh, equivalent to £7 780/year, giving a simple payback period of just over 8.5 years. When the solar features are considered in isolation, the payback the payback period is about 12 years.

NET MONTHLY SPACE HEATING DEMAND AND SUPPLY

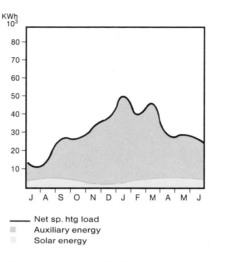

KWh 10³

— Net sp. htg load
▪ Auxiliary energy
▫ Solar energy

COMPARISON WITH CONVENTIONAL DESIGN

If the same building had been built to current Building Regulation standards instead and heated in the same way, the auxiliary space heating load for one year would be 699 730kWh.

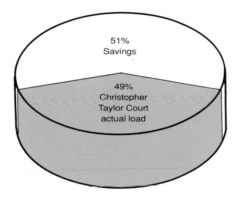

51% Savings

49% Christopher Taylor Court actual load

(However if it were the same shape it would have had a fairly high solar contribution anyway - which has not been taken into account here.)

MONTHLY AVERAGE TEMPERATURES

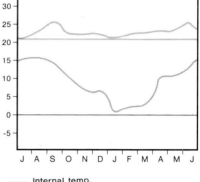

°C

——— Internal temp.
——— External temp.
——— Internal design temp.

CONTRIBUTIONS TO ANNUAL SPACE HEATING DEMAND

The total annual space heating demand for the whole building is 430 640kWh.

80.4% Auxiliary heating

10.5% Useful solar gains

9.1% Internal gains

The solar contribution is low because the average maintained internal temperature was 22.8°C, and the building was heated 24 hours a day.

PROJECT DATA

Building

Volume	5872	m³
Floor area	2447	m²
Roof area	1463	m²
External wall area	1171	m²
Windows: total area	311	m²
south	114	m²
north	111	m²
Mass wall	160	m²

Thermal Characteristics

U value: roof	0.20	W/m²K
floor	0.41	W/m²K
external walls	0.33	W/m²K
mass walls	1.08	W/m²K
windows	2.47	W/m²K
Global heat loss coefficient	3631	W/K
Infiltration rate	1	ach
External design temperature	-1	°C
Heated floor area	2447	m²
Heated volume	5872	m³
Net heat load	160	kWh/m²

Site and Climate

Altitude	163	m
Latitude	52° 20'	N
Longitude	2° 0'	W
Average ambient temp: Jan	3.3	°C} hist fig
July	16.0	°C}
Degree days (base 18°C)	3344	days
		(1961-80)
Global irradiation on horiz.	1081	kWh/m²
Sunshine hours	1295	hr/yr
		hist. figure

Costs (1985)

Buildings	£940 000	1 410 000 ECU
Solar features	£ 13 000	19 500 ECU
Conservation features	£ 50 000	75 000 ECU
Total cost	£1 003 000	1 504 500 ECU